ALL THIS IN
60
MINUTES

NICHOLAS LEE

ALLEN&UNWIN

SYDNEY • MELBOURNE • AUCKLAND • LONDON

References in this book to *60 Minutes* are made solely in the context of describing events in the life and career of Nicholas Lee and not for any other purpose, and there is no connection with or any endorsement of this book by Channel 9, which is the owner of the intellectual property rights relating to the show *60 Minutes*.

First published in 2016

Copyright © Nicholas Lee 2016

Allen & Unwin
83 Alexander Street
Crows Nest NSW 2065
Australia
Phone: (61 2) 8425 0100
Email: info@allenandunwin.com
Web: www.allenandunwin.com

Cataloguing-in-Publication details are available
from the National Library of Australia
www.trove.nla.gov.au

ISBN 978 1 76029 300 0

Set in 13.5/17 pt Bembo by Midland Typesetters, Australia
Printed and bound in Australia by Griffin Press

10 9 8 7 6 5 4 3 2 1

The paper in this book is FSC® certified. FSC® promotes environmentally responsible, socially beneficial and economically viable management of the world's forests.

For my three girls, Sue, Jessie and Kathryn,
with my love and gratitude

Contents

Foreword

Let's be honest. This is a funny book. At this price I strongly urge you to buy it. Do yourself a favour, because Nicholas Frederick Lee—former cinematographer, formerly of Wellington NSW—is a funny fellow.

(I've known him for almost 40 years, yet I can't believe he's actually a . . . 'Frederick'. Now *that's* funny. Nicholas Frederick Lee actually sounds like the sort of Anglo name that Hong Kong Chinese gave their Number-One son before the 1997 handover from Britain.) So, let's do away with the pompous formalities. Let's just call him 'Fred', for the record maybe even 'Freddo'. It's a name that suits his comic bent. Besides, I may have to call in the defo lawyers over some of the stories about me in this book, so I'd prefer not to refer to him as 'Nick', my old and dear friend.

I guess the core question is this—is Freddo's book accurate? Or is it a humorist's work of fiction? Is he really

Wellington's answer to Mark Twain? We'll come to that. At first glance, this literary masterpiece weighs in as almost epic. I managed to cover my full life's journey from birth to epitaph in fewer pages. But let's be blunt. Nicholas does love a chat.

I remember once running into the former prime minister John Howard, who was penning his autobiography at the time. 'How's it going,' I asked, pretending to be keenly interested. 'Ohhh, good. I'm at 700 pages and still have the 1990s to go.'

I suspect Nick Lee's editor has faced much the same dilemma. This creative blockbuster suffers from 'the tyranny of distension',[1] as iconic historian Geoffrey Blainey probably never said. Mind you, I don't want to rush to judgement.

Reading a couple of the earliest, unexpurgated versions of *All this in 60 Minutes*, I found myself laughing aloud. Often. Even on an aeroplane. Much as when I first read Clive James' *Unreliable Memoirs* which, as you'll soon see, might have been a more fitting title for Nicholas Frederick Lee's book.

I must confess, Freddo's stories about George & Ian & Jennifer & Lizzie & the rest of the *60 Minutes*' mob are hilarious, well told, if occasionally piss-takes. For a smart, compassionate bloke, Nick sees the world through a comic, special-effects prism. His 'lens-baby' view of life always seemed to be slightly warped, even if his editorial opinion was sharp and tolerant.

---

[1]   *Macquarie Pocket Dictionary*, 'to make or become stretched; swell'.

Exaggeration? Yeah maybe. To be fair, we all know that a little embellishment in one's autobiography is expected and acceptable. (Like extra butter and a dash of chopped parsley in mashed spuds.) Look, if you want the real story of what happened in Saudi Arabia when Nick and I were offered the sheep's eyeballs to eat (out the back of Mecca), you should read my highly amusing, beautifully written, best-selling autobiography. My version differs considerably from his. How could Freddo get the basic details so wrong—especially the role he played?

Same with my Taiwan tale of how I manoeuvred Nick to eat the bird platter—beaks, wings and every other part of the starling tray—as payback for the goat's eyeballs. Likewise, my version of the Orient Express is a rollicking ride, as is my gripping 'inches from death' yarn about the near plane crash at Sydney's Kingsford Smith Airport. My stories—'the truth' in other words—were all printed years ago in a hardback book, clearly much more reliable.

But I think there are also a number of crucial factors at play here that explain the huge discrepancies between his reporting and mine. There is the undeniable fact that the reason cameramen become . . . ah, cameramen . . . is that they're just not good with words. They tell their best stories with the camera, which—according to legend—never lies. (Wrong!) Now, Nick's unquestionably a really great cameraman—been everywhere, met everyone, done everything. And, around a barby he tells a cracking good yarn, usually with half a dozen laughs and a strong punch line.

I distinctly remember once telling Nick that he should pen his grand story about life on the road with *60 Minutes*. (For his grandkids mostly.) But in actually writing a

300-page book about his peripatetic life, has he gone a bridge too far? Well, you be the judge.

Then, there could be the thorny issue of hallucinogens. This could explain heaps. I mean, in the book there are oblique references (a 'giveaway' really) to the taking of alcohol and drugs—such as the big night in Cairo after the world-exclusive interview with Egypt's President Anwar Sadat. It's no secret that excessive use of social drugs can often lead to memory loss.

(Incidentally, on a couple of occasions in his book, Freddo does suggest that along with my tendency to talk to people excessively I also enjoy a drink or two. Excessively. That's another issue the lawyers will be looking at closely.)

Finally, there is the matter of 'disturbances in the circadian rhythm' of Nicholas Frederick Lee. In other words, massive jet lag, which is the game changer! It is, of course, a scientifically proven fact that jet lag seriously 'affects cognitive skills and can result in acute memory loss',[2] while the resultant sleep deprivation 'punches holes in the human memory bank'.[3]

We all know that NASA officials speak openly about 'the unknown unknowns'.

Sleep deprivation, oxygen starvation, deep vein thrombosis, business class fatigue, etc., all add up to what's called the 'polymorphic risk' of incessant air travel. Almost three decades spent flashing the Qantas platinum card has seen Nick rack up probably the equivalent of flying to the

---

[2]   I certainly read this somewhere.
[3]   Google it yourself !!

moon and back *twice*. Maybe even beyond Inner Space. So, I rest my case.

Again, I should emphasise that the only stories I can categorically deny are the twisted tales about me. Myself. The rest I have only deep suspicions about, although I found them absurdly funny.

So, what category does *All this in 60 Minutes* fit into in the local bookshop?

Fact or fiction? Well, I'll leave that up to the booksellers to decide. The front window is where I suggest it should go. And piles of books, just alongside the cash register. Either way, there's no question it slots easily into the comedy section. Like I said, it's a fun-crazy book. Made me laugh, certainly the stories about George, Ian, Lizzie & the others cracked me up. Well done, Nick. Played a blinder, mate.

And by the way, Freddo, my lawyers will be ringing your lawyers today!

Ray Martin

Prologue

I'm only 32 and about to die in a plane crash. I've survived snipers in Beirut, artillery fire in Israel, an exploding grenade in Rhodesia, and being ripped to shreds by an irate executive producer for having lost not one but two passports in less than six months (though I did wonder if he was overreacting)—and now I'm about to plummet to earth in a fireball. I should have been an accountant.

We've just finished a *60 Minutes* shoot in Lightning Ridge and the four of us are winging our way home to Sydney in a small eight-seater plane. I'm half asleep thanks to the many ice-cold beers supplied by our amicable and capable pilot so I'm not completely tuned in when I hear his announcement. I vaguely register his words 'problem', 'not sure', 'most likely' and 'no wheels'. It's after the 'no need to panic' that I know I'm not dreaming and I get very interested indeed.

'It's sort of possible to land without wheels,' he tells us.

Sort of?! What does that even mean?

Sydney's Kingsford Smith Airport, fifteen minutes away, is alerted to our problem. They tell us to fly over the ocean, jettison all fuel that won't be needed for our fifteen-minute flight to our sort of landing, then head for the airport that's now closed to all traffic except us. A row of fire trucks are on standby.

Our pilot asks if any of us have been in this situation before. The answer, surprisingly, is no. Ray Martin, our reporter, who is handsomely paid to ask questions, asks the pilot if he's ever been in this situation. The pilot's answer is the same as ours. That's a worry. However, a belly landing could be a bit of fun, and a cool tale to tell grandkids. If I survive.

The pilot tells us to take pens or sharp instruments out of our pockets, remove false teeth, and put our heads between our knees. We make feeble jokes about each other's teeth before he tells us he'll leave the radio on speaker so we can all listen to the instructions from air traffic control.

'We have you on radar. Ten minutes to touchdown.'

We continue to crack jokes to ease the tension. I'm not sure if it's working. I'm rather fascinated with how we'll land, and love the idea that the whole of Kingsford Smith Airport is closed to everyone in the world except us. I genuinely have no fear, and am very impressed at how cool I am. I must be made of the right stuff. Then, just as I hear, 'Five minutes to touchdown,' there's a dreadful electrical burning smell and the plane fills with smoke. My heart starts pounding and the fascination with landing deserts me. So does the right stuff. The airport bloody well better be closed to everyone but us.

More and more acrid smoke fills our little plane. My fear is obvious. I'm not running around the plane screaming, but there must be one hell of a scared look on my face because Ray asks if I'm all right.

'Don't worry,' he says, 'I know for a fact I'll never die in a plane crash.'

Nice of you to mention it, Ray, but what about me?

I'm more frightened than I've ever been in my life. My tongue swells up and fills my mouth. I can't talk. Who gets a fat tongue from fear? It seems like such a strange reaction. From the airport we hear, 'Two minutes to touchdown. You're looking good.' He's obviously not talking to me.

The pilot tells us he'll do whatever he can to pull up the plane when we hit the ground. Then we must open the door and run. I'm closest to the door. I make a quick study of how it opens, then put my head down again. A minute later the engines start to slow down. I'm desperate to look up to see how close to the ground we are, but knowing my luck I'll raise my head just as we touchdown and I'll be decapitated, and Mr Know-For-a-Fact Martin will be true to his word and probably a hero. So I keep my head between my knees, easy to do with my anvil-like tongue.

We hit the ground. Seems nice and smooth to me, but that smoothness could be my crossing to the other side. I've read about that. The plane comes to a standstill. I'm not dead. I open the door, hit the ground before the door does and start running Forrest Gump-like. What seems like 100 kilometres later, when I figure I'm far enough away not to be incinerated by a giant fireball, I turn to see our little plane happily resting on all its wheels and Mr Never-Die-in-a-Plane-Crash ambling towards me.

'Do you want this?' says Ray, and hands over the camera I'd left on the seat. A fine gesture, but I'm sure it's a lot easier to think of others when you know for a fact you're not going to die. Truth is, the last thing on my mind is that camera. I know, I'm a cameraman, but under the circumstances I figure it's every camera and every cameraman for himself.

The *Daily Telegraph* and 2GB radio news journos had heard the emergency on their police radios and are already at the terminal as we walk in. Recognising Ray they say, 'Shit, you blokes got here fast, what do you know about what happened?' We say we know nothing. Actually, Ray does. My tongue is still too fat to talk.

Turns out, there was never a wheel problem, we always had wheels, but we did have an electrical problem so the wheels indicator wasn't lighting up.

And the front page the next day: *Ray Martin Says—'I Thought My Sixty Minutes Were Up.'*

Pretty snappy headline, but he didn't say it. Why would he? He knew for a fact he wasn't going to die in a plane crash.

Moments like these were my life for 30 years.

1

Bed of Nails

His Excellency, 'President for Life, Field Marshal Al Hadji, Doctor Idi Amin Dada, VC, DSO, MC, CBE, Conqueror of the British Empire in Africa in General and Uganda in Particular,' aka The Butcher of Africa, had left the building—in fact, the whole bloodied country—in April 1979. Not long after that, we were sent there to see just how much of a basket case Uganda really was.

As usual, there were four of us on this job: producer Allan Hogan, reporter Ian 'Leso' Leslie, soundman Peter Fragar and me. Having no idea how or if the destination country was operating, we stopped off in Nairobi to buy a stack of food and a few dozen bottles of booze. We had been warned that things could be difficult in Uganda, though we weren't too concerned, after all, the Intercontinental Hotel in Kampala had taken our booking.

At Entebbe airport, it appeared as if the famed Israeli raid had only just taken place, though it had occurred three years earlier. Looking at the state of the airport we couldn't help but marvel at the gall and success of the raid by the Israeli army. Three hostages, one Israeli, 45 Ugandan soldiers and all hijackers were killed, while 105 were hostages rescued. All over in 58 minutes.

There were bullet holes in everything, walls smashed in and busted windows. Wires hung dangerously from the crumbling ceiling. Two or three fluorescent lights were struggling to stay lit. What a mess. And amongst it, Ugandan customs officers who couldn't have been more ineffective if they tried. In near darkness they checked our passports and waved us through, with no hint of bribe money, the norm for nearly all African countries at the time.

The Butcher of Africa had been done over beautifully by the Israeli army raid. Furious at what had happened, and suspecting the Kenyan government had been involved, Idi Amin announced that all Kenyans were to be evicted from Uganda. Most left immediately. Unlucky stragglers were murdered. Then, with his paranoia really setting in, The Butcher had anyone suspected of opposing him killed. Not that there were many left. He'd already executed cabinet ministers (live on TV, then kept their severed heads in his fridge), supreme court judges, the chief justice, prominent leaders of the Catholic and Anglican churches, and two-thirds of his 9000-strong army.

And now, in 1979, to divert attention from the country's internal problems, he foolishly invaded Tanzania. His hopelessly prepared army was easily overrun and the

Tanzanians marched into Uganda. When the Tanzanian army reached Kampala, they found the capital littered with dead bodies and His Excellency The Butcher had bolted with four wives, several of his 30 mistresses and twenty of his kids.

A few months later when we hit Kampala, the streets were deserted, apart from Tanzanian soldiers. We wandered into the flashy marble foyer of the Intercontinental Hotel and the only people there were, surprise, surprise, Tanzanian soldiers. And they weren't friendly. The staff at the front desk weren't particularly welcoming, either. When we mentioned our reservation, although not met with fits of laughter, we might as well have been. Despite the semblance of a fully functioning hotel, with beautifully dressed reception personnel, arrival cards, pens, telephones, signs to the restaurants and lifts, the place had no bookings, no available rooms, no nothing. The elegant receptionist stared at us with a look of, 'Have you seen the streets out there? It's war and you're expecting to just prance in here and get a room? What do you think this is? A hotel?'

There was not just the four of us, there was also the small issue of eighteen cases of equipment and four personal suitcases. Oh, and some fine reds and tasty cheeses.

While the others pondered the situation, I went to the gents. If I thought Entebbe airport looked as if it had been done over, this was like nothing I had ever seen, or care to see again. There was shit all over the floor, shit on the walls, and shit clogging every toilet and every sink, and it stunk like shit! What was it about these soldiers? Did their mothers teach them nothing about personal hygiene? Thinking I'd outsmart them, I went to the ladies instead. Obviously, I wasn't the first to have that great idea—it was filthier than the men's with even more shit. This was not going to be a fun trip.

Back in the hotel reception, we decided to worry about getting rooms later—well, thanks to the unhelpful staff, we didn't have much choice. It was 5.30 in the afternoon, time to get shots of this crazy war. We stepped out onto the street and literally bumped into Tony Joyce, the well-known and highly respected ABC journalist. Tony asked where we were going, and we explained that we were off to get some dusk shots of Kampala.

'Curfews don't worry you, then,' said Tony.

Allan, our producer, knew Tony from his own days at the ABC and was well aware of Tony's sense of humour but also his good judgement. Tony was one of the last journalists to leave Saigon just before it fell, and come to think of it, so was Allan. On the other hand, I was new to all this stuff, and planned on being around for many more years. So when Tony explained that there was a curfew at 6 p.m. and anyone caught on the streets was shot, no questions asked, we immediately did a U-turn, me being the quickest, and headed straight back inside the hotel. We thanked Tony profusely as we retreated. We owed him big time.

Not long after that meeting, Tony was shot while on assignment in Zambia. He died in hospital a few months later.

Back inside the hotel we pleaded, threatened and tried to bribe our way into rooms. Nothing was going to work. The entire clientele of this one and only 'operating' hotel consisted of scores of Tanzanian soldiers, and us. But our money couldn't compete with their assault rifles. Now trapped by the curfew, there was nothing else to do but camp in the cold marble foyer of the hotel and see what tomorrow would bring.

And tomorrow couldn't come fast enough. Trying to sleep on marble, surrounded by 22 cases was bad enough, but the relentless sound of rifle fire outside, plus the horrific sight of Tanzanian army thugs dragging girls into their hotel rooms to be raped, made sleep impossible. At about 3 a.m. I got up to stretch and noticed that the contents of both bathrooms had started to ooze into the foyer. 'Great,' I thought, 'if we don't get shot by Tanzanians, we'll all die of some disease that evolved inside the toilets of Kampala's classiest hotel.'

When the early morning sunlight poured into our giant foyer bedroom, none of us could move. A bed of nails would have been more comfortable. We did some stretching, looked around and decided this couldn't go on. We deftly slipped past the front desk and headed upstairs to check out the rooms. Half-naked soldiers, with rifles or machine guns slung over their shoulders, were wandering arrogantly along the corridors. We peeked into a few rooms with open doors. They were all occupied. A few more flights of stairs and—*Eureka!*—two unoccupied rooms. Bugger checking in. We moved in.

Allan and Ian took one room, Peter and I took the other. Our room had two beds, one sheet and one pillow. We'd have to work out later who got what, but for now, we had somewhere to put our stuff and something softer than marble to sleep on. I went to the bathroom, turned on a tap and . . . zilch. There was no water. Nothing at all. I thought, 'Oh well, we can do without shaving, showering and brushing teeth for a week.' After all, we had a bed.

Sitting on my sheetless bed while preparing the camera gear, I spied a hotel worker walking past, grabbed him and asked about the lack of water.

He explained, 'There is water for one hour a day, but we do not know when . . . and some days there is not water, so if there is water, you will fill the bath.'

Just then I heard the distant sound of running water. I raced to the bathroom, plugged the bath and sink, and turned on all the taps. Peter and I now had enough water to last a day or two. It would soon seem like a luxury.

•

Our first task was to record the horrors of Kampala. We hailed a taxi and went for a slow drive. It was raining, but the locals, walking around the streets, seemed oblivious. Not so the scores of dry Tanzanians in their cars. You could bet that's not how they arrived in Uganda. Obviously the locals' cars had been hijacked and they couldn't do a thing about it. To the victor go the spoils and the victors were certainly reluctant to have us film them getting in and out of their spoils, and threatened us with their weapons.

We tried interviewing a couple of old local blokes and they weren't keen to talk. But the young were eager to tell of the atrocities. Their stories sounded so horrific they were hard to believe, but more and more stories came out, each one more frightening than the last, and nearly all were about the State Research Bureau at Nakasero prison, the home of Amin's secret police. We were told of around-the-clock torture and murder to eradicate all enemies and, sometimes, 'just for a bit of fun', the torture was spread over many days. Very few people came out alive.

The State Research Bureau was a three-storey brick building of unimaginative architecture, the type that houses public servants worldwide. There were signs everywhere stating 'no photography', but no sign of people, so Allan and Ian went inside. I was still in the cab, preparing the camera, when the driver quietly whispered, 'I was in there, I was dragged in there.'

I looked up. He was staring straight ahead, as if he hadn't spoken.

'How long were you there for?' I asked.

'Three weeks.'

Hoping he would tell me more, I stayed silent, but so did he. He just kept staring ahead. So then I introduced myself and asked his name.

'Isaac Sowanga.'

'Isaac, you were in this place for three weeks? It must have been terrifying.'

'Yes.'

I think that's why I'm a cameraman. This would be one hell of an interview, but not with me asking the questions. I left him staring as I ran inside to tell the others about him.

Half an hour later we were walking through the State Research Bureau with Ian asking the questions, Isaac answering in his soft, gentle African accent, and me following with a camera on my shoulder. The place had been totally ransacked. Every window was broken, and scattered all over the place were the once well-kept files on all the unfortunate 'political prisoners'. Isaac led us through a narrow door into a four- by three-metre cell. He told us there were 60 men in this room.

'How did you lie down? Presumably you slept?' asked Ian.

'We couldn't lie down,' said Isaac. 'We spent the whole night standing.' He walked to the wall and leant against it with his hands near his ears. 'You put your hands on the wall and you sleep.'

'What are these marks on the wall?'

'Blood. When you are brought here, you are beaten, and the hands are full of the blood, so when you touch the wall to sleep the marks are on the wall.'

We were horrified but it was just the beginning. The next room, larger than the first, was freezing cold and had a horrendously disturbing feel to it. Isaac told us that in this room four or five prisoners were put in a line then ordered to run and knock their heads against the walls.

'They count one, two, three, and run.' Isaac ran to the wall to show us. 'They go back and the one, two, three again.'

'Did men actually do that?'

'Yes. You can kill yourself by doing it. By knocking your head against the wall.'

'Why do it? Why not refuse?'

'If you refuse you are shoot to death.'

'But surely it would be better to be shot to death quickly than to kill yourself like that?'

Isaac explained that the prisoners thought they had a chance if they did what they were told. 'Sometimes you might have the thought of having someone save you from this place, you could fall down and see someone who could help.'

'There was still a hope that you might survive?'

'Yes.'

Isaac then took us into a third room. Nestled in the corner was a large metal bucket with a rag hanging out of it. Ian asked Isaac what it was.

'It is blood.'

'That is human blood, in that bucket?'

'Yes. That is human blood. When they saw you dying, they put a knife on your neck and cut your neck.' Isaac pointed to the bucket. 'Then they put the blood here for some prisoners to drink. If you ask for water they give you human blood.'

Ian leant over to remove the rag from the bucket. I went down on my knees to get the close-up of his hand pulling the rag out. Suddenly he stood up and ran outside. I was still filming and thinking, *What's wrong with him?* It wasn't until I took my eye from the viewfinder that I noticed the stench. It was overwhelming. More than a smell, it was a sudden kick in the head. I felt giddy, the room was spinning and I knew I was about to pass out. I put the camera down, sat on the floor and leant against the wall desperately trying to catch my breath. I felt as if I was totally enveloped in filth, permeating not only my clothes, but my skin as well. Ian was outside throwing up. (Later Gerald Stone, the show's executive producer, would have a go at him for not being able to control his emotions.) Isaac was unmoved. I felt such a wimp. Just the leftover smell knocked me crazy and I'd been whingeing about sleeping on marble. I sat there gasping for breath and as I looked at Isaac I couldn't help but wonder at life's lottery.

With our lungs full of fresh air and the dizziness gone, we went down into the bowels of the building. The final hellhole. Once a prisoner was brought down here, there was no chance of escaping alive. Night after night prisoners were slaughtered with sledgehammers and iron bars, and there was no shortage of volunteers for the guards' nightshift, all of them spaced out on dope, and all coming from Amin's Kakwa tribe. When Amin's apprentice butchers got so exhausted they couldn't carry on, they would line up a dozen men, hand the sledge-hammer to the second man from the front, and order him to bash in the head of the man in front of him. Then he would hand the hammer to the man behind him to have his head pulverised. The slaughter would continue all the way down the line. What sort of human beings are capable of coming up with stuff like that? In total 300,000 Ugandans—or one in 60—were murdered by decree of Amin.

•

We kept Isaac on as our driver, picking his brain for as much information as he was willing to give. He told more horrific stories, all the while remaining seemingly unaffected. His attitude was more like, these things happen, you survive, you get on with life.

Where was his anger? Where was his hatred? It never ceases to amaze me what people can endure.

The longest anyone spent in Nakasero, and survived to tell the tale, was six and a half months. Six and a half months! This extraordinary man was Apollo Lowoko. Isaac arranged for us to meet him. We expected a babbling idiot locked away in a psych hospital, but we found a well-spoken successful lawyer, immaculately dressed, sitting at his desk calmly describing the atrocities he'd experienced and witnessed.

Apollo told us everyone knew that to be taken downstairs at the State Research Bureau meant you would never be seen again. When Ian asked him what he would have done had he been hauled down those stairs to face the hammers, he gently answered, 'Just prayed to die quickly.'

But worse, Apollo told us, many of his cellmates were taken from their cell and told they were to be put on trial or released the next day. There was never a trial or a release. Often the cellmate would never be seen again. But his best friend did return, with a lip removed.

'We knew then that they had decided to kill him by slow system, where they would be dismantling him slowly by slowly, tomorrow another torture, his other lip is removed, and then his nose is removed, his ears are removed, then eyes. And the final day they cut his throat.'

Apollo also told us that Amin himself would often come to Nakasero and more than once he had seen Amin kill people.

Next door to Nakasero, neatly nestled behind rows of manicured bushes, was the French embassy. When asked if the screams of the victims could have been heard at the embassy, Apollo replied, 'The torturers would use engines to drown the sound, they would run engines all night until the killings stopped. But to me, I think the embassy next door knew everything that was going on.'

On our way back to the Intercontinental Hotel after the Apollo interview, we didn't say much to each other, or to Isaac. What could we say? I certainly wasn't going to mention our lack of food and water or bathrooms full of shit, for fear of being full of it myself. What these people had been through was unbelievably difficult to comprehend. Spending time with people who have experienced such horrors is far more confronting than just watching it on television. It's impossible to get across to an audience how we feel, and worse, how victims of these grotesque atrocities really feel. It's certainly not for lack of trying. But it never translates. Hopefully, reporting on the lives of people like Isaac and Apollo helps somehow.

Life is a lottery. It doesn't get any easier than my life. White, male, fully employed, post–World War II Australian who also managed to win the conscription lottery by not being called up for National Service and therefore gaining two years' work experience ahead of friends whose number came out of the hat. It's an unfair world, and the more I saw of it and the more time I spent with the Isaacs and Apollos of this world, the more I was aware of that unfairness.

•

Back at the Intercontinental we cleaned up in our twelve inches of bathwater that now appeared to be real luxury, then questioned the meaning of life and the world. We decided there is no fucking answer and there never will be. So we started drinking.

Over the next few days the hotel began to function. There was still no water, but the restaurant re-opened with big smiles and big menus. We now knew the reason for the smiles. When we opened the menu we were told, 'Tonight there is no choice, tonight there is chicken.' So, chicken it was. We embraced it fully with a few bottles of our Kenyan red, discussing yet again the big question with no answer. So we reduced the question down to how can one true madman, a total buffoon, be capable of causing a whole nation to live in abject misery? I guess if you're a megalomaniacal, totally ruthless President for Life with your own killer squads at your disposal, it's easy. The gentleness and sincerity of the Apollos and Isaacs had no chance.

At night, apart from relentless sounds of gunfire, Peter and I slept reasonably well. Not so Ian and Allan, who had visitors at midnight on one occasion. Two Tanzanian soldiers barged into their room, aimed their rifles at them and demanded they leave the room immediately. Allan told us he thought it prudent to oblige, though deep inside he just wanted to tell them to fuck off. But that was very deep indeed. There was no point complaining to anyone, so Ian and Allan wandered through the hotel looking for another unoccupied room, which they found, and claimed, while wondering why the Tanzanians could not have done the same. It wasn't like Ian and Allan had bagged the presidential suite. But this was war, there was no logic, and to argue the point with men with guns would have been utterly futile, not to mention stupid.

Eventually, we managed to con our way inside one of the madman's many palaces. The highlight of the place was his twelve-seat, 35-mm movie theatre, beautifully appointed with velvet curtains and comfy chairs. We found a pile of 35-mm film cans, all from Europe. *Wow, I thought, maybe even a psycho knows how to appreciate quality cinema.*

The first few cans consisted of European pornography and Tom and Jerry cartoons. The next dozen or so consisted of European pornography and Tom and Jerry cartoons. No wonder Amin found it easy to kill, we knew he had no conscience, but obviously no brain as well in that oversized head.

Next day was Ian's birthday. We headed down to the chicken-only restaurant and asked if they had champagne. We figured we had a better chance of being served pheasant under glass but there was no harm in asking. The friendly waiter said he'd check. Half an hour later he returned with a bottle of Asti Spumante and said, 'This is all we have.'

'We'll take it.'

None of us had had a $6 bottle of Asti Spumante since we were seventeen, but our stash of vino was all gone and, after all, this was a celebration.

'That will be two hundred and fifty American dollars,' said our smiling waiter.

'We'll take it.'

Asti Spumante never tasted so good, I think it was the price. I love expensive wine.

Whether the money went to the hotel or the smiling waiter, we'll never know. I hoped the waiter got it. So many people in the world live in such frightful and frightening circumstances, it's impossible to know how and why some survive. The lucky ones. Then again, maybe they're not so lucky. The dead don't have to fear anything anymore, or live miserable lives. But even today the world's Isaacs and Apollos, with their miseries and memories, remain hopeful that one day their homelands will again be places of peace and freedom.

It struck me that these men were the essence of what *60 Minutes* hoped to show Australia every Sunday night at 7.30 p.m. Gerald Stone, the founding executive producer, often said Noah is a far better story than the Flood. And he was right. *60 Minutes* shone a light on the worst and the best of humanity and that trip to Uganda brought out both. For 30 years I was part of this unique TV show about extraordinary events but mainly extraordinary people.

The world remains hopeful that there will never be another Idi Amin, but as history is full of them, I'm not holding my breath.

2

The Packers and Me (and Phil)

I was a cameraman for 30 years with *60 Minutes,* but I was at Channel 9 for a total of 39 years.

I had started working at Channel 9 way back in 1969 as an assistant cameraman on a 'police drama' called *The Link Men.* After the huge success of the Melbourne cop show *Homicide* on Channel 7, Sir Frank Packer and his son Clyde—owners of Channel 9—decided it would be a good thing to have a similar show made in Sydney.

Here I was, a skinny, raw nineteen-year-old kid from Wellington, a small country town in the central west of NSW, overwhelmed to be working in television and with the star of *The Link Men* Kevin Miles, a great bloke and a great Aussie actor with a big masculine jaw, à la Roger Ramjet. In every scene Kevin oozed machismo charm. It never ceased to amaze me how tough he was when delivering his heavy cop lines. Then, at the shout of 'Cut!' his lips would purse, his voice would soften and he'd fold, oh so elegantly, into the nearest chair.

On day two of the shoot of a particular episode, he was asked to do a bit of an action scene, running from a cop car brandishing a pistol and shouting, 'Stop or I'll shoot!'

On the call of 'Action!' the big tough cop leapt out of the car, arm fully extended, gun raised to fire, his 'Stop or I'll shoot' delivered faster than any bullet. He didn't wait for the 'Cut!' but hurled the weapon through the air, just missing the camera, and with his voice an octave higher he shouted, 'Ooh, I *hate* these things.'

An image of the pistol being fired was still needed for the scene but Kevin refused to do it, so a close-up of the first-assistant director's hand firing the pistol saved the day, and Kevin moved on to his chair to have his jaw powdered for the next scene.

A week later we were shooting a sequence in the city morgue. The smell was overbearing, and we all wanted the shots over and done with as fast as possible. We were told the morgue was full so we must be very discreet. The first scene required Kevin to slide out a drawer containing a body, look down and say, 'Yes, that's him.'

We needed a body. A first-assistant director will offer a hand, but a full body is another thing, this calls for an assistant cameraman, everyone else is far too important. So into the cold drawer I got, terrified in the knowledge that there were real dead bodies in the drawers beside and above me. 'How weird is this?' I thought.

The door closed and claustrophobia immediately set in. It was pitch black and freezing and I started to wonder about wanting a career in 'The Arts'. Finally I heard the director yell 'Action!' and seconds later Kevin pulled open the drawer, looked down at me, lowered his head and . . . kissed me.

The whole crew erupted into howls of laughter. I didn't quite know what to do. I'm pretty sure the heat of my embarrassment started to thaw out the neighbouring corpses.

A few weeks after my onscreen kiss, we were all summoned to the Channel 9 boardroom. Surrounded by mounds of champagne, every other form of alcohol, and some quirky little canapés, we waited for the good news. There was excitement in the air. We all thought the show, only twelve episodes old, was about to be extended by at least another thirteen episodes, along with our substantial pay rises.

Clyde Packer appeared, standing in the doorway. 'The show is finished as of now,' he said. 'You're all fired!'

Some of the women burst into tears. 'We'll just finish this episode,' said the director. 'There's only one day left to shoot.'

'You fucking heard me, the show is finished as of now!' And Packer was no longer in the doorway.

We all stared at each other, too shocked to speak. I looked around at everyone. What did they have to worry about? They were at least 30 years old, or even 40, so their careers were almost over. But I was only twenty. What was I to do? I felt I should also leave the room grumbling about murdering the Packers like everyone else, but there was all this free grog, and it couldn't be drunk in just one night.

Solution? The twenty-year-old assistant editor and I backed our cars up to the rear entrance of the Channel 9 boardroom and loaded them. Cases of champagne, gin, scotch, crates of Coke and soda, all split 50/50. And when the boardroom grog cabinet was completely empty, a quick handshake and we were both on our way to uncertain futures.

•

For me it was straight to Channel 7 as an assistant cameraman in the news department. I knew nothing about news or journalism, but to get myself up to speed I tried to read/understand Marshall McLuhan's *The Medium is the Message*. Needless to say I didn't get the message, but I also saw Haskell Wexler's great film *Medium Cool*, about news cameramen and their ethical responsibilities, i.e. when to shoot and when to help, and whether the story is the be all and end all. I wanted to be as cool but not as detached as John Cassellis, the cameraman in the movie, and when he said, 'Jesus, I love to shoot film,' I couldn't have agreed more.

As an assistant, I was sometimes allowed to shoot minor stories, those which the real cameramen felt were beneath them, and one that was beneath them was Sydney shrouded in early morning fog. So I headed straight for North Sydney for that classic shot of the city skyline, but couldn't find a parking spot. In desperation I finally parked in someone's driveway, hoping they wouldn't call the cops, raced to the footbridge over the expressway, slammed the camera onto the tripod and looked up . . .

The only fog around was coming off my sweaty body. There goes my career again. While contemplating the best way to throw myself into the traffic, I took a look through the viewfinder and, remarkably, there were the tips of the city high-rise buildings piercing a heavy fog. Yet when I stepped back from the camera, there was no fog! Then I realised that I had placed the lens inches from the handrail, which was now beautifully out of focus and covering the bottom 50 per cent of the frame. Best fog I'd ever seen. So I shot it. It did help that it was in the days of black and white.

That night my fog led the news with images of how my dreaded out-of-focus handrail had derailed Sydney's traffic and public transport systems. Nobody ever knew, till now. Had my idea of truth in journalism already taken a hit? Had I become a Cassellis? I figured not, after all, I wasn't a *real* cameraman, just an assistant. But I had a story that led the news. It was a start.

A year later I scored a job back at Channel 9 in the newsroom. I felt I had come home. I was still keen to become a *Medium Cool* Cassellis, but with a heart and conscience. I wasn't keen to go anywhere near the board-room and its wonderfully restocked drinks cabinet.

•

News in those days was a nine-to-five job. The stories were shot on film which took at least 45 minutes to be processed in the lab before editing. The news bulletin appeared at 6.30 p.m., so it was extremely rare for a story to be shot after 5 p.m. At 5.01 p.m. it was straight to the pub.

And it was to the pub that the eccentric and enigmatic cameraman Phil Donoghue and me, his faithful assistant, were headed when we bumped into Ron Casey, boss and presenter of sport. Ron asked if we could shoot a story for him at 7 p.m. World champion swimmer Shane Gould, the hottest thing in the coolest sport in Australia, was racing at the North Sydney pool and word was that she was going to break the world record.

Sure, Ron, no probs.

We loaded the car with the gear and headed straight to the pub, it was only 5.15 p.m., we had ages, Phil said. After a few drinks I started to get a little twitchy, and told Phil it was now 6 p.m.

'Heaps of time,' he said, and ordered another rum and Coke.

'Phil, it's six-thirty, we should go.'

'Don't worry, these things always run late.'

At 7 p.m. we were finally driving out of the pub and I was shitting myself. Phil, cool as, laughed and told me once again not to worry. His air of confidence didn't translate to me, and those few short kilometres from Willoughby to North Sydney were excruciating.

There was not a parking space within a mile of the pool. Phil dropped me off with all the gear then slowly drove away in search of a spot. Half an hour later he arrived back, saying he'd just heard a great song on the radio and first thing tomorrow he must buy it. Wishing I could be cool like him, we walked towards the pool but were confronted by an official asking what we were after.

'We've come to film Shane Gould's race,' said Phil. 'Where would be the best position to shoot from?'

'Shane Gould! You've missed her, mate. Pity, she just smashed the world record,' said the smirking official.

Struggling to speak and hoping I didn't look as pale as I felt, I asked Phil, 'What do we do now?'

'Hang on,' he said. 'I'm thinking.'

A moment later I practically saw the light bulb over his head.

'Got it . . . I'll put the lens cap over the lens, roll some film, and when it comes out totally black, we blame the lab.'

The man's a genius, We rolled film through the camera for about two minutes, packed up and left. A good night's work.

Next morning Ron asked how we went. Phil told him things went well but there could be a problem with the lab. He told Ron he'd been to the lab and checked but the film looked completely black. 'No one seems to know what happened.'

'Well,' said Ron, 'let's lace it up on the projector anyway, we might see something.'

'There's no point, Ron, there's nothing on it, I've checked. It's totally black.'

'Lace it up anyway, boys, there's nothing to lose.'

Still full of confidence in his clever deception, Phil laced up the projector, started it rolling and, sure enough, the film was black . . . But clear as a bell and clean as a whistle was the sound I had unknowingly recorded by accidently leaving all the sound gear turned on. 'And now, here we are, ready for the men's two hundred metres butterfly . . .' revealed the perfectly recorded magnetic stripe attached to the side of the pitch-black film.

A long silence. I wondered, 'How does Phil get himself, and more importantly, us, out of this little number?'

Finally Phil said, 'Ron, aahh, well, Nick and I went to the pub and when we got to the pool we'd missed her race. I didn't know what to do so I put the lens cap over the lens so the film would be all black and then we could blame the lab.'

A longer silence. I was stunned that Phil had actually confessed. What now? Then Ron burst out laughing. 'That's the funniest thing I've ever heard,' he said, shook his head and just walked away. Phil had pulled it off again. Telling the truth—who'd have thought of that?

A few years later a permanent late shift was introduced. The news crew was rostered on until 8.30 p.m. If there was to be a late story, it would make the next night's news rather than be missed altogether. Not a lot appeared to happen after 5 p.m. (thankfully, Shane Gould had retired), so the lucky late crew would just go to the pub and be paid for it. If in the unlikely event a story did appear, the chief of staff would ring Channel 9's local, the Bridgeview Hotel. We'd be called to the phone then finish our beers and stagger off to work.

One night, after being paid to drink at the pub, Phil and I went back to the newsroom to be met at the gate by a foaming-at-the-mouth chief of staff demanding to know where we'd been.

'The pub.'

'I've rung the Bridgeview twenty times and you weren't there.'

'Oh, we forgot to tell you, we went to the Cammeray Rex for a bit of a change. What's the problem?'

'Fucking *problem!*' he shouted. 'Sir Frank Packer rang and said the *Daily Telegraph* building is on fire and to send the news crew *now*! That was three hours ago!'

It was now 9.30 p.m. The other channels—2, 7 and 10—all got great footage of the fire. Sir Frank's own channel had unfortunately missed it. We were in deep shit.

Next day, Phil and I were fired. Maybe we should have told old Frank we shot it but the lab buggered it up.

I'm still not too sure why, but after a few days the news director went in to bat for us with the boss, promising that the newsroom would become far more professional in the future. We were reinstated. Though having to act like a professional was a bit tricky.

•

I stayed at Channel 9 for another 38 years, still nervous whenever I got near the boardroom. But I didn't need to worry. Sir Frank was dead, and Clyde, having sold his share of the station to his little brother Kerry, had moved to California to live amongst the stars in Los Angeles. But Kerry Packer, now the sole owner, was all over Channel 9, much more involved than any proprietor should ever be. Would he be looking for me and the missing grog? I tried to keep a low profile. But it was hard to do when working with Phil.

One Friday morning, Phil and I were returning from the canteen with newsreader Ian Ross when Phil whispered to me, 'When we reach the broom cupboard, open the doors quickly then jump out of the way.' So I did.

Phil grabbed Ian in a bear hug, bundled him into the closet then quickly shoved a broom through the door handles and 'Roscoe' was now trapped. Then Phil got sheets of newspaper (the classy broadsheet type, none of your tabloid rubbish), pushed them under the door and set fire to them, with Roscoe inside shouting, 'Donoghue, you bastard, let me out of here!'

Leaning against the door, busting a gut about how funny it all was and how utterly creative we were, we looked around for passersby to check out our hilarious prank when around the corner came Kerry Packer. Phil and I, enveloped in smoke, could hardly see him, but the anguished cries from the cupboard could clearly be heard.

Kerry gave us a puzzled look, and muttered, 'Everything all right, boys?'

'Yes, Mr Packer.'

And with that he was gone. We then tended to Roscoe's second degree burns.

•

A year later I was a fully fledged cameraman, no longer working as Phil's assistant. I missed Phil, but not the ulcers. In one of my first assignments I was told to meet our new political reporter Malcolm at NSW Parliament House. He looked twelve, seemed like a good bloke and pretty bright. I asked him how long he'd been a journo. He replied, 'Oh, I'm not a journalist, I'm a uni student.' I stared at him in horror and thought, 'Shit, now I have to train some amateur.'

Within a few weeks, the assistant cameraman Jim Chrystal and I were amazed by how professional the uni student was and how quickly he'd picked up this TV gig. We congratulated ourselves: how skilled were we as trainers! And just as we began to really enjoy working with our new reporter, he told us he was leaving because he'd won a Rhodes Scholarship. Jim and I were both disappointed and thought, 'Damn, that's a shame, this Malcolm Turnbull guy might have the ability to go all the way.' We even reckoned that he had it in him to one day become our chief reporter.

With our student reporter off to Oxford, I went back to work with proper journos like Jim Waley. One day we headed off to Kerry Packer's city office to film an interview with Packer about the announcement of World Series Cricket. Packer had just signed up 50 of the world's leading cricket players for his renegade league and was about to stick it up the establishment, the Australian Cricket Board and the ABC. At his office, we were told to wait while he did interviews with channels 2, 7 and 10.

'Cricket is going to get revolutionised whether they [the establishment] like it or not,' he said. 'There is nothing they can do to stop me. Not a goddamn thing.'

We watched our opposition crews leave Packer's office with huge smiles on their faces. They knew they had some great TV. He didn't seem to spend as much time with us as the others, but then again he owned us and could run nothing but stories on World Series Cricket all night if he wanted to. As we were preparing to leave, he was being cordial when he said to Jim, 'I trust this will get a favourable report on tonight's news.'

To which Jim, the consummate journalist, responded, 'Yes, Mr Packer, favourable but objective.'

The room was eerily silent for about point-nought of a second.

'I don't give a *fuck* about your objectivity, son, you give this a favourable report on tonight's news or you're out of a job.'

'Yes, Mr Packer,' said Jim. And the favourable report led the news that night.

Later that year, I found myself shooting a documentary on World Series Cricket. What a bludge. Two months travelling the country with the best cricketers in the world, watching quality matches by day and partying with the players at night. Hangovers both behind the camera and on the field. The cricketers couldn't believe their luck, actually being paid to do what they loved most, playing cricket.

During the series, on a players' day off, Packer asked the West Indies team to give an exhibition and some tutoring to the first eleven at Cranbrook, the exclusive Sydney private boys school. Having just financed the school's new pitch, Packer was keen to put it to the test, and I was there to shoot it for the doco. Packer's ten-year-old son Jamie just happened to be attending the school and just happened to be there that day.

At the time the West Indies had the fiercest, fastest, pace attack in the world and I could see that the eighteen-year-old batsmen of the school's first eleven were shaking as they faced a barrage of balls coming from the arms of these giants. After a while Packer said, 'Now give James a go.'

James said he didn't want to. Packer turned to me and said, 'Put the camera down.' He then dragged the little boy to the crease and told him to be a man. In ran the first of the Windies bowlers, who bowled a straight but gentle ball that James managed to pat away. Packer told the next bowler to bowl faster, so he increased the pace by about 5 per cent. James ducked just in time.

Packer stepped forward. 'I want you to bowl at him full pace,' he said. The bowlers, seeing the little kid in tears, refused. 'You bloody well will!' snarled Packer.

James was now really sobbing as each of the tall, powerful West Indians came running in at full bore and released the ball, obviously not at maximum pace but enough to put the wind up anyone but a top pro. It was a wonder that James could see the ball at all, but he continued to duck just in time. Packer then said, 'Okay, that's enough,' and wandered off.

For the rest of the documentary, I was partying around the country with the cricketers and when things weren't too blurry I sometimes even lifted a camera to my eye. All the interviews had been done early in the season so it was up to me and Tony Curtis the soundman to pick up whatever shots we thought might be interesting for the doco. We were told to capture the 'colour'.

The drinking and partying and the endless parade of beautiful groupies in hotels and dressing rooms would have been the real story, but we dutifully stuck to bat, ball and crowd shots, which actually became unbelievably exciting in Melbourne in one of the many finals.

With no recognised batsmen left, the West Indies had one final ball to face and needed four runs to win. The tail-ender Andy Roberts looked a bit like James Packer at Cranbrook as he faced that final ball. No tears, but real fear in his eyes. But unlike James he took an almighty swing and somehow the ball sailed over the fence for six to win the game. The crowd went crazy.

The director David Hill came running over and told me to get into the West Indies dressing room immediately and get shots of them celebrating. This, plus the final ball, would define the doco. I was as enthusiastic as the unbelievably excited West Indians. Inside the dressing room I went in search of something to climb on, to get some shots that weren't just looking up the noses of these giants, when in walked that other giant, Kerry Packer. He strode straight up to me and said, 'May I ask as to where you are from?'

'Yes, Mr Packer, I'm from Channel 9 Sydney.'

'Then, from that answer, can I assume that I am your boss?'

'Yes,' I mumbled.

'Then fuck off out of here now!'

There was no more dialogue from me. I was outside in a flash where I ran straight into David who said, 'Get back in there now!' For a split-second I wondered what to do. But it wasn't really a difficult decision. One of those two paid my salary and it wasn't David Hill. I gave him the camera and told him to be my guest.

In David's doco there are no images of the victorious West Indies team celebrating that six—the single magical moment that brought World Series Cricket to life.

3

It Could Have Been the End

After six years as a news cameraman, I was invited by executive producer Gerald Stone to join his brand new current affairs show *60 Minutes*. I felt I'd made it. Kerry Packer had given the top job to Gerald, saying, 'I don't give a fuck what it takes. Just do it and get it right.' My brief was to travel the world in search of beautiful pictures. And I did that for 30 years.

So on April Fools' Day in 1979, I was on my first-ever overseas assignment with *60 Minutes,* and under the table I was discreetly but firmly exploring my gonads, hoping the table shielded me from the sight of everyone else in the restaurant. The waiter noticed, but I guessed he'd probably witnessed far worse.

I was feeling for any lumps, the kind that tell the tale of cancer or infertility, though I wasn't exactly sure how those lumps were meant to feel. I couldn't help thinking,

'Will I be able to father children?' I knew I could be overreacting, but what if . . . I wouldn't go so far as to say I'd lose my will to live, but this was heavy. I tried not to let those gloomy thoughts put me off my dinner. I was starving, having not eaten since arriving in Harrisburg, Pennsylvania, early that morning.

Two days earlier in Sydney, just home from the laundromat, I answered the phone, and maybe shouldn't have. It was supposed to be my day off. I was interrogated by the *60 Minutes* chief of staff. Where the hell had I been for the last two hours? Why wasn't I answering the phone? He told me there'd been an accident in a nuclear generating power station on Three Mile Island, Pennsylvania, and that I was to catch a plane to New York in three hours. I'd heard sketchy details on the news throughout the day, each broadcast becoming more and more hysterical. Harrisburg, the nearest town, was being evacuated. The authorities had issued orders that no one should enter the town. So of course the world's press had flooded in.

We hit Honolulu at 2 a.m., cleared US customs then fanged our way to Los Angeles for the next leg to New York. But there was a strike in LA and most airlines were not flying. Along with producer Andrew Haughton and soundman Peter Fragar, I was travelling with journalist Ray Martin on our first *60 Minutes* assignment together. Ray had just spent ten years in New York working for the ABC. He had now crossed to the dark side by joining the enemy—commercial television. He was virtually unknown on the commercial scene but he was about to conquer it.

Ray's ten years in the US had given him plenty of time to do what journalists do best—enjoy lunchtime boozing sessions and build a network of contacts by grovelling, charming and/or threatening. But most of all by shouting drinks. So now, with us stuck in Los Angeles, it was a good time to put those ten years of hard work to good use.

'Don't worry, I'll get us to New York,' he said, and disappeared into the mass of disgruntled travellers filling LA airport.

He was good! Having promised numerous expensive drinks and his first-born to anonymous airline staffers, Ray had the four of us winging our way to New York and on to Harrisburg.

•

In Harrisburg we arrived buggered and badly in need of deodorant, but immediately set off to get radiated. We headed straight to the river where we were told we would get the best view of the Three Mile Island power station and its cooling towers. And that was as close as anyone could get. The security was everywhere.

I shot the cooling towers with a long 300-mm lens from every available angle. Which turned out to be a total of two. I was trying desperately, but not succeeding, in making it look ominous, like the world was about to end. With nothing else to film, we headed back into town to talk to some locals, hoping they'd be running down the street with all their possessions, hysterically shouting that the end is nigh. We finally found a couple of spotty teenagers who told us 'they thought they were a little bit worried'. *A little bit!* The Harrisburg story was perfect for the press, but for television it was a struggle. TV is pictures, pictures, pictures, and we had none, none, none. But before we had time to panic we were told there'd be a press conference in the town hall at 3 p.m.

I had never seen such a vast number of media personnel. Hundreds of press photographers pushing each other out of the way, film crews from all round the world jostling for the perfect position to place their tripods, and a gaggle of journos, pencils at the ready, all there to report on the end of the world, or at least the United States.

All we got was a small bookish man with huge glasses who walked earnestly onto the stage and told us there had been a partial 'core meltdown' in Unit 2 of the Three Mile Island nuclear generating station. 'But,' he announced to the desperate news gatherers, 'all is under control.'

There was a lot of twitching and murmuring and I got the feeling that no one believed him. We knew the place was awash with radiation. He then pretty much confirmed this by adding that women and children should leave Harrisburg immediately.

With jet lag and the fact we hadn't stopped for 36 hours, I didn't feel worried, I felt extremely shat off. Or maybe that's the feeling you get when you're radioactive.

The unconcerned expert went on to say that somehow the emergency water in the cooling tower had been cut off and that had sealed the fate of the reactor. The temperature had reached 4300 degrees Fahrenheit. If or when it hit 5200 degrees, it was called The China Syndrome.

China Syndrome? That rang a bell.

Two weeks before we arrived in Harrisburg, Hollywood had released a movie starring Jane Fonda called *The China Syndrome*, about a core meltdown in a US nuclear reactor. In the movie Fonda speaks to an expert who tells her such a meltdown could make an area the size of Pennsylvania permanently uninhabitable. We were temporarily inhabiting Pennsylvania, but hoping to have permanently departed before life imitated art, or Hollywood at least.

Finally, with heads spinning from lack of sleep, we headed to our hotel to unpack and eat for the first time that day.

As we walked into the hotel restaurant, I pointed out to Ray that legendary reporter Mike Willesee from Channel 7 was sitting over near the wall. Ray, who's blind as a bat, didn't believe me. Willesee, hiding in the darkest corner, slid slowly under his table to hide from his Channel 9 rivals. But Ray finally recognised him and went over for a chat.

'Hi, Ray,' Willesee said, 'I was hoping you wouldn't see me.' And then he explained how he'd been there for eight hours and had no idea where his film crew was. Last seen in Honolulu. The real shame, he said, was that before he left home he'd recorded a stack of first-person promos for his show, speaking of the devastation and how he'd be reporting nightly from the most dangerous place on earth, and what's more, the promos had already gone to air.

After pretending to feel sorry for him, we moved to our table to gloat. There was always a concern with *60 Minutes* being a weekly show that there'd be nothing new to say after the weekday shows had flogged a story to death night after night. With Willesee conveniently out of the picture and no other Aussie competition, we had nothing to worry about.

Well, not nothing, I thought as I slipped my hands under the table for a quick lump check. Who knows with radiation, just one day could be enough.

The next morning while filming women, children and some very smart men getting out of town, we noticed Willesee's crew disembarking from an incoming flight. They were both good blokes I'd known for years and both looked very sheepish. I got a few shots of them for a laugh, then we chatted.

They'd been trapped in Honolulu for two days and finally got on a flight, but their equipment didn't. If Willesee thought he was buggered last night, wait till the boys delivered that little piece of news.

Finding a phone anywhere in Harrisburg was extremely difficult, and often when we did manage to find one the whole system was jammed, mostly due to journalists hogging every phone in town for hours on end as they relayed their copy home. Every call they made sounded more and more like the Fonda movie, beautifully designed to create maximum fear in their readers, listeners and viewers.

With all this radiation around, Ray and I had our own maximum fear. Andrew and Peter both had kids. Ray and I were still hoping we'd be fathers one day. I didn't ask Ray if he, too, was doing daily testicle checks, I just assumed he was. But we did both wonder whether or not we should somehow be investing in lead underpants and trying to gauge our chances of suing Kerry Packer for our infertility.

At the next press conference, we were told the town was too big to be evacuated, and anyone who couldn't get on the single departing flight each day should stay indoors as a precautionary measure. This created a rush on the banks, with many people withdrawing all their money then driving, hitching or walking out of town.

Staying behind were the hundreds of foreign journos, photographers, cameramen . . . and me, still checking my testicles and wondering what the future might hold. Assuming there was going to be a future.

After another three days of fear and lack of pictures, we were told the probable reason for the power station disaster had been a misdiagnosis of the relief valve. It had remained open long enough for major damage to occur. The plant was now seriously contaminated, but nowhere else. The US was safe, Pennsylvania was safe, and even Harrisburg was safe.

So the media relaxed, then the world relaxed. Even Ray and I relaxed. Not only were we safe, we were lump free. Well, I was. Ray didn't say and I didn't ask, but he was smiling more.

•

But what if the bearer of good news was lying and cunningly tricked us all into going home before symptoms appeared? What if I had picked up some of that radiation and it didn't come out in testicular lumps, or any other obvious signs? It would be a great story to tell the grand-kids, providing they were born with ears.

Fact was, despite the dangers to my fertility, I was lucky to have the job at all. It had been only six weeks before the Three Mile Island trip that *60 Minutes* had premiered on Channel 9, with excitement all round. Not only were we the best cameramen, journalists and soundmen in the universe, we were about to change that universe.

For the grand premiere we had all assembled at the house of fellow cameraman, Phil Donoghue, to watch our handiwork.

Tick tick tick tick tick . . . a loudly ticking stopwatch filled the screen, followed by short clips of each of the stories for that night. Then, the convert to commercial television, Ray Martin, pronounced, 'Those stories and more, tonight on *60 Minutes*.' We sat mesmerised, looking forward to patting each other on the back and pissing in each other's pockets.

The first story, which I shot, was an Ian Leslie piece, cutely titled 'Buttleggers', about smuggling cigarettes across the border from Queensland into New South Wales to evade tax. Ho hum. Next came a Ray Martin story on the future of 'two way' cable TV. Yawn. And finally a George Negus yarn about primal therapy, where people eased their troubled minds by going berserk, screaming and bashing anything within arm's reach. Exactly what we all wanted to do as the credits rolled.

The first-ever *60 Minutes* was a shocker. Everyone was stunned. There'd be no pocket-pissing tonight, just lots of piss drinking to ease that unemployment feeling and to help resist the temptation to beat all others to the phone to ring Mike Willesee at Channel 7 and beg for a job.

There was incoming fire as well. That night Kerry Packer rang Gerald Stone, our executive producer. 'You've blown it, son,' he bellowed. 'You better fix it—*fast*.'

And to his credit, Gerald certainly did.

Still today, *60 Minutes* is regarded as *the* place to work in TV current affairs. With generous budgets, and the world as your canvas.

4

Great Pubs

60 Minutes struggled in the ratings for most of that first year, but by August the show was gaining respect and the ratings picked up. We were working our bums off and enjoying every minute of it. We had an open cheque book to go wherever, whenever. Back then there were no Discovery or National Geographic channels. We were it.

The audience was now keen to see where Ray Martin, George Negus and Ian Leslie would be this week. But luckily they couldn't do it on their own, so we cameramen, soundmen and producers tagged along. We were constantly on the lookout for that amazing story. Our brief was to get outstanding pictures and make the reporters look good. It wasn't really hard. They were great journos with a passion for work—and we were all young. Everyone under 35, some of us not yet 30.

A few years later a 24-year-old Jana Wendt joined the reporting team. It was great to have a woman on *60 Minutes* at last, especially one so super smart, feisty and *very* funny. She was a dream to work with. Apart from one memorable story on abortion at a pre-term clinic in Sydney, which helped to cement Jana's reputation as a journalist, I did very few stories with her. She fell in love with, and married Brendan Ward, a fellow cameraman. And from then on they worked almost exclusively together. They were quite a team.

Ray, George, Ian and Jana were all great reporters, and even greater talkers. It was as if words had a use-by date, and that's tomorrow, so all words must be used immediately. Their job was to talk, they were paid handsomely to talk, and practice makes perfect. These perfect talkers were always interesting and fun to travel with, but sometimes 30 seconds silence would have been nice.

Producer Warren McStoker preferred minutes of silence. Which was rare when travelling with George, who was always writing a script then reading it aloud to everyone. One day while we were driving through the beautiful Redwood forests in California, George found himself suddenly lost for words, and a script. Warren had grabbed the script pages, hurled them out the window and shouted, 'George, shut the fuck up!' And, he did, for the 30 seconds we all craved, then away he went again.

Ray was an even better talker. We'd all assume our listening positions, and off he'd go. There was no shutting him up. And he spoke so quickly it was impossible to keep up.

The best restaurants and classiest hotels became our number-one priority. We were on a Kerry Packer expense account, living as if each of us *was* Kerry, just as long as he didn't find out. Gerald Stone, the original and best executive producer, was well aware of this but turned a blind eye to most of the excess, figuring it was worth it for crews who often worked twenty-hour days. So the system worked well, we discovered some outstanding establishments that even Kerry didn't know existed, and no one had cause to complain. Perhaps Kerry would have, but Gerald kept us all well-insulated from above.

Our hotel of choice in Paris was the Hôtel de Crillon. One simply *must* stay there. One can't stay anywhere else. It was extraordinary. Total opulence, built in 1758, filled with Louis XVI furniture and amazingly delicate and colourful seventeenth- and eighteenth-century tapestries. Marie Antoinette regularly had her piano lessons at the Crillon. Woodrow Wilson and the entire US delegation to the Paris Peace Conference of 1919 stayed there. More recent luminaries who frequently dropped into their favourite home away from home were Joe Kennedy, Charlie Chaplin, Orson Welles, Liz Taylor, and of course Skeet, Phil, Fang, Leso, Ralph, Bruce and me.

There was even one occasion in 1980 when all of us plus Ray Martin and a few others checked in. Two *60 Minutes* crews in Paris at the same time! The poor Crillon was aghast, but our credit card was good.

After a good day's work in Paris and a few grogs in the bar, we decided to dine in. Wandering into 'Les Ambassadeurs', the hotel's 18th century rococo-style restaurant, the producer Bruce Stannard, dressed splendidly in coat and tie and a few metres ahead of us, was met by the gushing maitre'd. When Bruce requested a table for eight, the gushing came to an abrupt halt. The problem? He'd set eyes on the rest of us. T-shirts and jeans were de rigueur for *60 Minutes* crews whether it was Paris or The Alice. Eyes firmly back on Bruce, the maitre'd pronounced, 'Oh, non non non.'

After heated words between them, Bruce asked us to flash our room keys, all eight of them. Then we waited patiently while the maitre'd, obviously knowing he couldn't knock back hotel guests, issued hurried orders to assorted flunkies, none of which we understood, then announced that we were to follow him. As quickly as possible, so as not to put fellow diners off their foie gras, we were led to the very back of the huge restaurant and pointed to our table. Through gritted teeth he helped us with our seating then deftly placed a bamboo room divider around our table. Beautifully done, we were no more to be seen, and the well-heeled would no longer be in danger of choking on their canard.

Later in our rooms we donned our stylish white robes, grabbed bottles of champagne and stepped onto our individual balconies. Overlooking the courtyard, we toasted Paris, each other, our unbelievable job, and of course Kerry, for making it all possible. We filmed it all, just to piss off the editors. Someone said, 'This is not a bad pub,' and the word stuck. For the next 30 years, any hotel we slept in, regardless of location or price, was 'the pub'.

Other great 'pubs' we tried in Paris were the George V, the Bristol, the Plaza Athénée, and my favourite the Hotel Le Meurice. Unlike the Crillon's somewhat showbiz clientele, the Pub Meurice was classy, and boasted Queen Victoria, the Sultan of Zanzibar and Tchaikovsky as regular guests. Best of all, our 250 kilos of camera gear was 'never a problem' for the porters at the Meurice; in fact, they were extremely helpful, unusual for porters or Parisians.

•

You see, concierges and porters run the show. If you can get them on side, you've got it made. A great concierge is worth their weight in gold, there is nothing they can't do.

Two of the best I met both worked at the Athenaeum Hotel in London. Alex, a suave debonair Spaniard who managed to put three sons through private schools in London, was the best of the best. Any ticket to anything was right there in Alex's briefcase. You want front row for the Wimbledon men's final? No probs. FA Cup Final? Piece of piss. Latest Picasso exhibition sold out for three months? How many tickets would you like? Sure, you paid for them, but to most of his customers that was the least of their worries.

Then there was Donald. A super-charming gay Irishman who was the favourite of lonely, frustrated, cashed-up wives of philandering millionaires. He had them wrapped around his little finger and inside those little fingers were placed wads of cash as Donald could and would procure anything they wanted. And, boy, did they want. From the Texan housewife who asked him to find two well-endowed black men, to the young couple who requested he rollerskate naked with them around their luxury suite (Donald politely declined), the ever-discreet concierge had heard and seen it all.

And then there are the worst. Such as Joe from The Plaza in New York. This was a hotel I'd seen in movies and had dreamt of staying in since I was eight, so I was pretty excited when I checked in for seven days.

With key in hand, and surrounded by my fourteen cases, I called over the porter and politely asked for help with my luggage.

He looked at me, then the bags and said, 'Nope!'

I was flabbergasted. 'I beg your pardon?'

'I ain't takin' your bags, buddy.'

'You're refusing to take my bags?'

'That's right, buddy.'

'Hang on, are you a porter here?'

'That's right, buddy.'

'And you are refusing to take my bags?'

'That's right, buddy.'

Incensed and jet-lagged from the Sydney to New York flight, I checked his nametag then marched straight to the manager's office. I explained the situation, using every threat and trick I knew. The manager didn't flinch. It was as if I was complimenting him on his wonderful hotel.

'Was it Joe?' he asked.

'Yes, it was Joe.'

'Nothing I can do about Joe, he's head of the union.'

I left the manager's office ready to tear the place apart, and Joe if I saw him. When I got back to the others, I saw two young porters loading everything onto a trolley, only too happy to help. One of them told me he'd over-heard what Joe had said and he'd like to apologise for Joe's attitude. Fifteen minutes later, with all the gear neatly stacked in my room, I handed each of them a $100 note and told them to make sure they told Joe.

That night we went out for a biggy in the Big Apple. Grog, restaurants, taxis, laughter, camaraderie. Back in my room, with bulk food and alcohol swirling round my gut, sleep wasn't going to be easy, but I did feel drunk enough to immerse myself in American TV. Pissed being the only way to watch American television. I grabbed a beer and the remote and made myself comfortable on the chaise longue. Fifteen minutes and a hundred channels later, with a hole right through my pissed TV theory, I got up from the couch and headed for the toilet. Two steps from the couch I heard what sounded like a bowling ball smashing through a cathedral window. Shards of glass went flying past and onto me. I looked back to the chaise longue and saw the remnants of a chandelier all over it. Above that was a giant hole in the ceiling. I couldn't believe my luck. Saved by my bladder! But how would I explain the broken chandelier? I'd heard of lords and rock stars swinging from chandeliers in hotel rooms, but who'd believe that I'd done nothing more than watch crap TV?

The only option was to go on the attack. So back to the manager's office I went. Two hours later, having screamed about their shonky hotel and my near-death by chandelier, and threatened to sue, I had myself a fresh new room, a suite in fact, with *two* chandeliers. And helping me to move were two porters, neither of which was Joe.

•

We were away so often that some hotels became our much-nicer home away from home. One of these was the Draycott, another great pub in London. We stayed so often there were a couple of long-term relationships between *60 Minutes* crews and hotel staff. There was even a marriage.

The Draycott was actually called a club, though I never figured why. Extremely beautiful, small and intimate, the hotel was nestled in the back streets of Sloane Square, a hundred metres from Kings Road, Chelsea, four blocks from Harrods. The heavies from the music and movie worlds loved staying there; the staff didn't treat them as if they were famous and the luminaries loved it. The décor was magnificent. Huge vases of freshly cut flowers everywhere, their beautiful aroma permeating the whole building. Everything was perfect. The service was outstanding for everyone . . . except us. We got none. Instead, we became such great friends with the staff that it was as if we were just bunking down on their floor at home except we—well, Kerry—was being charged three hundred quid a night per room for the privilege.

The bar worked on an honesty system. I don't know how honest it was, nothing was ever written down, but at the end of our stay a gigantic amount of money owed would appear on one of our accounts, preferably someone else's and not mine. Whoever scored the bill was always in shock, but then again we drank nothing but champagne or cognac except when pangs of conscience about the budget hit and we'd have a beer or twelve, but you can bet the Draycott was never out of pocket.

Ludwig (Ludy) the barman was a 5 feet tall Frenchman who spoke at lightning speed. His English was not too bon and nor was his service. In fact, come to think of it, his English was much more bon than his service. We would go behind the bar and help ourselves as Ludy, lying on the chaise longue, would shout, 'Une gin and tonic pour moi while you're there!' I'm sure the G and T ended up on our bill, but it was the mixing with fascinating, eccentric people, both guests and staff, that made the Draycott our abode of choice in London for many years.

•

Another beauty was the Excelsior Hotel on the Via Veneto in Rome. A great pub. All class. With an astute porter who, on seeing Channel 9 logos plastered all over our gear, said, 'Hey, you just missed your boss, that's his car pulling out now.'

'Boss? What boss?'

'That boss, that's Alan Bond.'

We ducked behind our cars in case that boss suddenly remembered he'd forgotten something.

Bond had just bought the network from Kerry Packer for a billion dollars, and obviously realising he'd paid too much, tried to save a few bucks by releasing his 'Nine Manifesto'. It was a ripper. It proclaimed that a few heavies, such as Ray Martin and Jana Wendt, could travel first class. Lesser stars and producers, who were actually working on the flight, could travel business class, and the rest—i.e. film crews—would be at the back of the bus. And hotel rooms? Well, though not proclaimed, he would have assumed we'd be sharing motel rooms or, even better, camping out. If he'd seen us walking into the Excelsior, he would have hit the roof, and probably us. After all, this hotel was for media tycoons and millionaires, which a few years later he wouldn't be. Bond was later bankrupted and convicted of fraud, swapping a suite at the Excelsior for his own room in a West Australian prison for more than three years.

I don't think it was our week at the Excelsior that bankrupted him (though the grog was expensive), I think it was the fact he paid $54 million (which he didn't have) for the van Gogh masterpiece *Irises*. And possibly the fact we *all* continued to travel business class and stay in the most expensive hotels.

•

Establishments such as the Hotel Le Meurice, the Draycott or the Excelsior don't exist in Gaza, most of Africa or places like, say, the Thai border.

On a story about an overcrowded Cambodian refugee camp on the Thai/Cambodian border, we needed accommodation. Easier said than done. There was a small village not far from the camp with not a drop of accommodation to be found, but like every good village, it had a brothel. So we bought it. Girls and all.

Our daily budget was the same as if we were in Paris, so we paid the girls, gave them four days off, and moved in. It was no Meurice but there was a roof over our head, and beds. The beds, normally rented by the hour, weren't super comfortable, obviously planned that way, but they were luxury compared to the toilet and shower, which came in the form of two buckets. The bucket with the ladle was to wash with, the one without a ladle was to shit in. The single 40-watt globe hanging over the uncomfortable rent-a-bed meant not a lot of reading was done, and the deep dent in the bed meant not a lot of sleep. But we kept the place neat and tidy, not wishing to incur the wrath of the girls who had obviously done their best to keep their workplace as comfortable as possible. And we were grateful. At least we had electricity, beds, privacy and a roof.

The camp refugees had none of the above. When tropical storms hit, there was slight relief from the heat, and that's all. Sitting in mud under small pieces of plastic were mum, dad and four or five kids with vacant looks in their eyes, staring, waiting and hoping, hoping that some day they'd be accepted for a new life in the US, or preferably Australia. Some had lived like this for years, grateful to be alive, they told us.

The food drop was heartbreaking. Once a day a truckload of rice was tipped into a great mound on the dirt, and it was every man for himself. The women and children had no chance. There'd be a desperate fight to grab as much rice as possible. It was a horror show, and there was nothing we could do to help these people. Watching felt so wrong. Filming even more so. Some stared down the lens, challenging me. But I did film it all and I did get amongst it, and I did feel guilty. I could only hope that once these images were shown at home they might prick a few consciences and get something done.

Yet there was a sense of hope in parts of the camp. You can't hold back drive and determination. A few entrepreneurial individuals had somehow got hold of sewing machines and set up tailor shops. Others ran small 'stores'. Cardboard boxes piled on top of each other for a counter, selling Coke, ice and sweets. Very few had money to buy any of this but there was no holding down good capitalists. It was truly inspiring, and I found myself trying to imagine just how I would have coped under such circumstances, unfortunately I knew the answer.

Witnessing the refugees' wretched conditions day after day made us appreciate our brothel and two buckets. But in a few days' time, we knew we'd be appreciating a gin and tonic by the pool at the Bangkok Hilton before we'd retire to our air-conditioned suites, all paid for by someone else. We sure were lucky and I never forgot just how lucky we were.

5

Down and Out in Cairo

'You want to buy hashish?' asked the teenager with fewer teeth than a one-year-old.

'How much?'

'Twenty pounds.'

'Okay.'

I took the matchbox-size block of hash and handed over twenty Egyptian pounds, not knowing what an Egyptian pound was worth and not caring either. I was in a foul mood and ready to kill. Surrounded by 22 cases of camera equipment, I was sitting on the footpath outside the Cairo Hilton Hotel waiting for porters.

Five hours earlier we had arrived in Cairo airport for a story on Anwar Sadat, the Egyptian president. Reporter Ian Leslie had been trying for months to get an interview with him. His persistence paid off and Ian was summoned to Cairo. We immediately bought four tickets to Egypt, the rest we'd organise when we got there.

Our first hint that things could get a little difficult was when the customs officers, having taken one look at us and all the gear, told us to 'sit over there and wait'. We flashed our correspondence from the president's office but it made absolutely no difference. So we sat over there and waited. After two hours on rock-hard cement in the very hot and now very empty airport, we once again fronted up to the unshaven, unhappy customs officers to ask what the problem was and why it was taking so long. We were informed our paperwork was not accurate. We needed a special visa to film in Egypt and some of our equipment could not be brought into the country. Why it had taken two hours to tell us seemed a little odd, but we kept our composure, though this was becoming more and more difficult. The stalling continued until the sudden mention, the sighting and the handing over of a few hundred American dollars.

Bribery plays a big part for film crews travelling the world, but every now and then, surprise, surprise, you meet an honest official and he or she takes offence at our assumption that they're on the take, and decides to make life even more difficult. But this time, with huge tooth-less smiles all round, there was no offence taken, only the money. All our troubles were solved. Well, those that involved customs officers.

Half a dozen cabs later, we arrived at the Hilton Hotel. With our rush to get to Egypt we had nothing booked, rare for us, but we figured we'd be fine. We assumed there were hundreds of hotels in Cairo. Probably even more.

Producer Allan Hogan wandered into the Hilton while we waited outside for porters. Five minutes later, Allan was back.

'You'll never believe it, the place is full.'

'Well, we'll try somewhere else,' said Ian.

'I have. There's nothing.'

'What, in the whole of bloody Cairo?'

'Yep, the whole city is booked out.'

'How can that be?'

'Dental convention.'

'Dental convention! Look at 'em, half of them haven't even got *teeth*.'

'I'll go and see the manager, and do the customs trick,' said Allan.

With a one hundred dollar note deftly folded in his hand, he went back inside and asked to see the manager. An impeccably dressed Egyptian with a perfect set of teeth and an outstretched hand walked towards him. Allan responded with his lumpy handshake. The manager looked down at the lump, back to Allan, down at the lump, and with a very pukka British accent said, 'My good man, are you attempting to bribe me?'

'Well, actually I am,' whispered Allan. 'We're desperate.'

'I'm sorry I can't help, we really are fully booked.'

Allan rejoined us on the footpath to consider plan B. And there it was in my hand, the twenty-quid hash purchase from the toothless teen. With nothing else to do, nowhere to go, and no cigarette papers, Allan and I decided we would eat plan B. So we started nibbling.

Ian and soundman Peter Fragar decided not to partake, which was a good thing. Within an hour Allan and

I were completely out of it, and the footpath seemed like an excellent place to spend the night.

Ian went off to find accommodation, any accommodation. For some reason he didn't find the footpath as comfortable as Allan and I. He plunged back into the Hilton and talked them into letting him use their phone. After half an hour, he emerged grinning. Success.

'And it's got a pool, we can do laps every morning,' said Ian triumphantly.

We piled into another six cabs and headed for our new pad, a motel called 'The Kanzy' on the outskirts of Cairo.

Now I know beggars can't be choosers, and if I'd been able to speak I would have said something, but the hash was well and truly doing its job. Which meant that Ian and Peter were doing the thinking for four.

The Kanzy was an extremely small, ugly, dark brick building resembling a pizza oven. There were only two rooms left. We would be sharing. No porters, of course, so the four of us started dragging the gear across the lawn. Then I noticed a ladder and realised that what we thought was the lawn was actually a film of blue-green algae luxuriating across Ian's lap pool. The rooms were tiny, but at least they had bathrooms. We wouldn't be reliving our Thai brothel/bucket experience. There were no phones. Not a good sign for producers who spend their lives on the phone. That is what they do, hundreds of phone calls a day. And the president's office had told Allan they would call when the extremely busy president could spare a few hours for an interview.

Through his hashish haze Allan started to look worried. The one and only phone was in the office, and was not going to be used by guests telling stories about having to ring President Sadat. Luckily Allan found a public phone a kilometre down the road, and advised the presidential office we were in town. After being told to ring back tomorrow, we prepared for dinner. All those dentists couldn't stop us from eating in their salubrious digs, so we headed off to the Hilton for dinner.

I've always subscribed to a 'when in Rome' philosophy, and Cairo was big on chicken livers. The livers were washed down with a couple of fine bottles of red. Perhaps it was the wine on top of the hash. But suddenly I didn't feel too well.

What a time to be sharing a room. Both ends of me opened up like Mount Vesuvius. It was relentless. How could a few small chicken livers produce so much lava? I could manage ten minutes in bed before being hit by more eruptions. The trips to and from the bathroom were wearing me out, so I decided to stay sitting on the toilet and leaning over the sink. I drifted in and out of what I'd like to call sleep, but it wasn't, it was a state of mind I had never experienced before. When I did feel conscious I had strange and confusing thoughts that weren't mine, much more loopy than those the hash had given me. I wanted to die, and I knew Peter, lying on the other side of the paper-thin bathroom wall, was hoping my wish would come true.

Next morning I could hardly move. I was so weak I couldn't lift my head, let alone the camera. Allan made his kilometre walk to the phone booth and was told there would be no interview today. *There is a God!* The others headed off to see the sights. I stayed in. The bathroom that is.

Day Two. I am so happy that Anwar Sadat is busy, but probably not as busy as my bowels.

Day Three. Anwar is still too busy, so are my bowels, and Ian and Allan are getting a bit worried.

Day Four. It's on. The president will see us at 2 p.m.

We were instructed to be at the president's office at twelve noon, allowing two hours for set-up time and security. I wasn't feeling a hundred per cent, but being the true professional, I soldiered on, and hoped my colleagues would lay off the ribbing at my lunacy for having eaten chicken livers in Cairo.

•

We arrived on the dot of twelve. I had never seen such security. Recently we'd been to Israel and I'd thought those security guards were the best. The Israelis even checked the unexposed film using their own dark bag, the type we use to stop light getting to the film and ruining it when we load and unload camera magazines. Sadat's men did that and more. They checked every piece of equipment. Practically pulled it apart. They looked down the lens from both ends, looked through the viewfinder of the camera with the lens on and off, then asked me to roll a few feet of film, to prove that the camera actually worked.

When they seemed satisfied, we were taken into a small, extremely boring room, not the type of room you'd think a president would want to be interviewed in. The minders pointed to a very unpretentious chair centimetres from the wall and told us that was exactly where the president would sit. Diplomatically I asked if it was possible to move the president away from the wall and a little nearer the window. 'Absolutely not,' I was told.

I tried to explain that the background was boring, and with the president being so close to the wall, it not only made the lighting difficult but the picture 'flat'. There was no way to get the president standing out in sharp focus with the background soft and irrelevant. The minder wouldn't budge. I was stunned at how adamant he was. 'What's the big deal?' I thought. 'Why would half a metre from the wall and centimetres closer to the window make any difference to him?' But it did and I had to abide by it.

We set up the lights and microphones around the boring chair in front of the boring wall and were then sent from the boring room and told to wait.

Ten minutes later I asked if I could go back into the room to check if there was any change to the angle or intensity of the light coming through the windows. The minder agreed, reluctantly, and as it turned out, the light had changed. While I was adjusting the curtains, I heard a noise behind me. I turned, and a few metres from me stood the great Anwar Sadat, President of Egypt. He had quietly entered the room from a well-disguised door, and he was alone.

Sadat was handsome, balding and thin, with a small moustache. He looked aristocratic, though he was born in a poor village. He shook my hand and told me how much he loved Australia. With only the two of us in the room, I babbled on about how much I loved Egypt, and what we had been doing. I kept my thoughts of dentists and chicken livers and hash to myself, but I was rapidly running out of conversation and hoping desperately someone else would arrive before I said something I wished I hadn't.

Suddenly in they came. Advisors, secret servicemen, private secretary, press secretaries, and my three colleagues. The room was full. Sadat dismissed all but two of his minders then asked if everything was okay with the room. Ian said he'd like to sit a little closer if possible. Sadat responded with, 'Do anything you please.' So I asked if I could move his chair a little further from the wall.

'Certainly. Do whatever is needed,' he said.

I started moving lights, chairs and curtains. His minders started to choke. There was no way they could stop me in front of their beloved president who had given the go-ahead. I politely helped Sadat move a little closer to the window. I could see one minder's neck veins throbbing and the other clenching his jaw in silent frustration. They looked at each other, out the window, at Sadat, then at me. Did I care? Nope. I was out to get the best possible shot, and I'd won.

It had been made clear to us that the interview was not to exceed twenty minutes, but it lasted an hour and a half. Sadat was enjoying himself, and with the minders not game to put a stop to the president's enjoyment, Ian just kept asking questions.

Speaking in a deep, strong and very loud voice, Anwar told of growing up poor in a small village, as one of thirteen children of a farmer, his school days, his kids, grandkids, the Palestinians, and of course Israel. He was sharp, intelligent, calm, serene, and oozing charisma. He was just back from Washington for the historic meeting with Jimmy Carter and Menachem Begin, which resulted in a peace agreement with Israel. The first since peace was declared between King Solomon and the Egyptian pharaoh three thousand years ago. Begin and Sadat were awarded the Nobel Peace Prize for the treaty, but Sadat—who famously said, 'I am a man of peace'—was now a target for fanatics because most of the Arab world felt sold out.

Towards the end of the interview, Sadat asked us what we were doing the next day, and wondered if we'd like to accompany him to the village where he grew up. We couldn't believe our luck. After telling us he was looking forward to tomorrow, the president left the room through his special door, leaving us with two very irritated minders.

It was then explained to me that I should not have moved the president and he should never be near a window. Not only had there been an assassination attempt on Sadat by someone firing a bullet through a window of his office, but there had been an attempt on his life by a mob posing as a film crew. The cunning 'film crew' had a gun sitting neatly inside the camera lens. Had something happened to Sadat while we were with him, I suspect any guard with a gun would have gladly used it on the pushy naive Aussie cameraman.

The village scenes were great. All the villagers came out to greet Sadat. Kids with huge smiles on their faces walked beside him on the footpath, women wanted to kiss him, old men wanted to shake his hand, and it all felt genuine, not stage-managed as with most politicians, and Sadat was only too keen to help out.

We found the hut he lived in as a kid. It was tiny and made of cow dung and mud. His cousin who still lived there was all smiles as he told us how proud his family and the whole village was of Anwar.

Then Sadat said, 'It's prayer time, would you like to come to the mosque?'

It was a very modest place of worship compared to the gigantic mosques we'd been into in Cairo. We took off our shoes and followed the president in. He spread out his mat, knelt down and started to pray. The shots were amazing. He then asked me if there was anything I would like him to do, and I told him everything we had was fantastic. He finished his prayers, rolled up his mat and headed outside.

Standing near the door of the mosque, Ian asked him whether he ever feared being struck down by an assassin.

'Oh no,' Sadat said. 'This will mean God has said yes, this is your time, this is your hour.'

Eighteen months later, God said yes.

A fatwa approving the assassination had been given the green light from a Moslem cleric. As Sadat stood saluting the troops during an annual military parade, an assassination team ran from a military vehicle, firing weapons and hurling grenades. Sadat and twenty others were murdered. The same cleric was later convicted in the US for his role in the 1993 bombing of the World Trade Center.

•

With a brilliant interview in the can, we decided to do Cairo by night. Fearless, after yet again way too much alcohol, and with what would fall into the category of complete stupidity, we found ourselves more than halfway up Cheops, the last of the Seven Wonders of the World, 146 metres tall, 40 storeys, and largest of the three beautifully lit pyramids. It was almost midnight and we felt as if we could see the whole world from up there.

Suddenly we couldn't see the world, or even each other. Unbeknown to us, the pyramids are plunged into darkness at midnight. Also previously unbeknown to us was Ian's fear of heights and darkness—in fact, this was the moment when Ian himself discovered he had a problem. He was frozen. Couldn't move. For twenty minutes we tried in vain to coax him down, but he wouldn't budge. He finally came to terms with the fact that a night halfway up Cheops would be even worse than the Motel Kanzy, and agreed to try to move. We inched him down each of those two-and-a-half tonne blocks. It took more than an hour, and a bucket load of sweat.

Next morning we were back to get shots of the pyramids. There were signs everywhere saying, 'It is forbidden to climb the pyramids.' A local guide told us that at least two tourists a year fall to their death trying to climb Cheops. They probably weren't pissed enough.

The following afternoon we decided to go for a horse ride across the Sahara Desert. All of us could ride except Peter and he scoffed, 'How hard can it be?'

I knew once I saw the horses.

They were beautiful white Arabian stallions, and huge. Mine was called Spirit, and I started thinking that maybe this was not such a great idea. But it was wonderful, a comfortable gentle canter for about 5 kilometres to an amazing Bedouin-style tent where we sat and drank cold beers as we marvelled at the pyramids in the distance, just like Alexander and Napoleon had done. A quick toast to Kerry Packer for making it all possible and we were back on our steeds.

Now the ponies I rode twenty years ago, Scotty and Taffy, took great delight in getting home as fast as possible. I think it's a horse thing. But Spirit and his mates were twice the size, twice as strong and two hundred times faster than Scotty and Taffy, and once they caught a glimpse of the pyramids and home, that was it. I spent the next ten minutes, all 60 kilos of me, leaning back with the reins pulled as taut as possible and my stirrupped feet braced forward next to Spirit's head. It would have stopped Taffy dead in his tracks, but it had absolutely no effect on my Arabian stallion, so I just hung on as best I could and thankfully stayed in the saddle.

Unlike Peter, rocketing past at a thousand miles an hour, hanging from his horse's neck, feet nowhere near the stirrups, with an 'I'm going to die' look in his eyes. I started to wonder how hard it might be to find a sound recordist in Cairo, though that was just a fleeting thought. My real concern was my own survival.

Only metres from Cheops we were still galloping at full speed and I was about to be slammed head first into one of the Seven Wonders of the World. Thoughts of brain damage and plastic surgery swirled through my mind. Does it exist here? Will my family recognise me? (Though dental work shouldn't be a problem.) Spirit, obviously having the same thoughts, jammed his hooves into the sand. I went rocketing forward but managed to hang on to his head. We were both panting like we hadn't taken a breath for ten minutes, which was about right. Peter had also come to an abrupt halt, his face looking as disturbed as mine at the peak of my chicken liver condition.

And the other two? They loved it.

'How good was *that*!' Ian said. 'Let's do it again tomorrow.' And he did. He went for the longer 20-kilometre ride.

That night there was a knock on my door and in came Ian. I noticed his walk was very strange.

'Mate, can you look at my bum for me?'

Before I could say, 'No, thank you,' he dropped his pants, and aimed his bottom at me. I figured I was up to the challenge, until I saw blisters the size of Cheops. Raw flesh like in a butcher's shop. It was days before he could even sit down, and a week before he stopped walking like Groucho Marx.

On our flight from Egypt there was no Moses, only a lot of dentists that we all hated. And I hated chicken livers even more. Yet we all agreed we loved Anwar Sadat—the most charismatic man I have ever met.

6

I Forgot to Flush

Another glass of very cold, very bubbly champagne appeared in front of me. We'd been bumped up to first class on our trip from Cairo to Berlin. It didn't get much better than this. As thoughts of the Kanzy, chicken livers and bolting Arab stallions dissolved with the champagne, I could already see our Logie Award on the mantlepiece. The interview with Sadat was superb, he had given us so much, was so charming and humble, our audience would love him. I wondered if his Nobel Prize would be as big or classy as our Logie.

From my first class window I looked down on Egypt, thinking of the day of our arrival and immediately my sweat glands went into overdrive. I felt nauseous, and it wasn't the champagne. I looked across at the others with smiles on their faces (probably all having Logie thoughts too) and wondered if it was at all possible to 'deplane' at 30,000 feet.

I'd just realised the remainder of the hash was in my bag, in the cargo of this plane. I hadn't touched the hash since Allan and I got stuck into it on that first morning in Cairo, and since the Sadat story we hadn't given the hash a second thought. It sat in the back of my bag, totally forgotten. Until now. And now I was about to land in Germany.

Shit! What to do? There goes the best job in the world and any chance of seeing my brand new wife Suzie in the near future. I'd only been married six months, and four of those I'd been away.

I was in huge trouble. My sweating escalated. I kept thinking about the movie *Midnight Express* when Billy Hayes, sweating profusely, was in the Turkish airport bus trying desperately to ditch his hash as the cops approached. One of the most chillingly scary scenes I had ever seen.

For possession, Billy got four years and two months in a Turkish prison. 'Maybe I can handle that,' I thought. 'At least I'll be in a German jail, that's got to be heaps better than a Turkish one.'

But possession wasn't enough for Billy's prosecutor, he wanted Billy charged with smuggling as well. And guess what I was doing as I flew at 30,000 feet across Europe?

For possession *and* smuggling, Billy got 30 years. *Thirty years*! That meant I'd be 60 when I was released, and I would have still only experienced two months of marriage. Then again, maybe I wouldn't get the same sentence as Billy; we were both foolish but he was also ambitious. After all, he had two kilos of the stuff. I only had a block the size of half a matchbox. On the smuggling scale that was trivial, but Germans don't tolerate fools.

I looked around the plane for the emergency exit, then changed my mind. I figured I might as well enjoy my last few hours of freedom by getting stuck into the free French bubbly.

We were on our way to do a story on the Berlin Wall, and the giant chasm that existed between the lifestyles of the East and West. I wondered if I would have a view of the wall from my cell, or maybe those smart West Germans used part of the wall for their jail. Knowing my luck I would do a Billy Hayes 'midnight express' (prison jargon for escape) and be the first person to escape *into* East Berlin.

As we landed in Berlin I thought of what I could say to the customs officers. I could tell them that the hash wasn't mine, it was Allan's, after all, he ate half the stuff. Or I could say, 'Yeah, the bag's mine, but I've got no idea how that stuff got into it' (as used by Schapelle Corby 25 years later).

Inside the Berlin immigration hall I wasn't feeling too well, but being a caring bloke I decided not to tell the others of my dilemma, even though it would have been nice to share a cell with someone who spoke English. Allan's English was excellent, but given the possible 30-year sentence he wouldn't be out until he was 65 and that was a bit unfair. So I said nothing, figuring that at the discovery of the contraband my colleagues could look genuinely surprised and hopefully wouldn't be implicated.

I tried to look super-cool (hard to do when sweating like Billy Hayes), as I walked towards the stern faces of the customs officers in uniforms covered in metres of gold braid. But my attempt at coolness wasn't working and I was terrified.

An officer walked casually over and pointed at our 22 cases. I was getting ready to hold out my hands for the cuffs, tell him the others had nothing to do with the hash in my bag, and request my one phone call. He gave me a slow smile and said, 'So many bags.'

I didn't know what to say. If I said, 'Not so many,' he might think I was being a smart-arse. If I said, 'Yeah, you're right,' he might think I was being too honest and trying to hide something. So I just smiled moronically. He asked what all the bags were for. I stepped aside for one of the non-sweating members of the crew to explain what we were doing in Berlin. Placing one hand on the top case, the officer said, 'So, all of this is camera equipment?'

'Well, all except our personal stuff,' said Allan. And I was thinking, 'Allan, do you *need* to bring attention to our personal bags?'

'And whose is this?' said the officer, pointing to my bag containing you-know-what.

That's it, I thought, *forget the 65-year age thing, Allan's coming to jail with me.* But before I could say that he helped me eat it, the officer said, 'Better get that zipper fixed.'

By now I was looking like I'd just stepped out of a pool. But before I needed an excuse for the puddle of water around my shoes, he signed the equipment list, smiled and waved us through. So much for German efficiency. I couldn't believe my luck. I felt like telling him that he just blew a chance for a promotion.

I decided not to tell the others about the hash. Why upset them and give them the opportunity to have a go at me for being stupid. That hash could have wrecked my life completely, so I decided when I got to the hotel I would flush it straight down the toilet.

As usual when I first walk into a hotel room, I went to the window, opened the curtains and checked my view.

'*Mein Gott!* What is that!? It's amazing! I've never seen one of those,' I got straight on the phone and called Allan.

'Have you looked out your window?'

'Yep, how good is that!' he said.

Right in front of us was the biggest, tallest rollercoaster I had ever seen—and it had a *double* loop.

'We've got to give it a go,' said Allan. 'What a ride! Shame we don't have any of that Egyptian hash with us.'

'Allan, there's something I want to tell you . . .'

Forget the flush. We were out of there in a flash to buy cigarette papers. A quick smoke and we were on the ride of our lives. What a buzz. Though it would still have been amazing without our smuggled friend. At the end of the first ride, we were straight back in the queue to do it again. We did it every night until all the hash was gone.

•

The rollercoaster was just the beginning. West Berlin was fascinating, extremely fashion conscious, full of bars and restaurants, and it had the highest standard of living in Europe. That's rubbing it in. One hundred metres away on the other side, the East Germans were struggling to make ends meet while continually being told of the evils and decadence of capitalism. Berlin had always had a reputation for decadence. A few years ago I had read Christopher

Isherwood's *The Berlin Stories* about living in Berlin in the 1930s. *Cabaret*, my favourite movie, is loosely based on his *Goodbye to Berlin*. Now that was decadence. They were the good old days, though the Nazis were a major irritation. I suspected a little less irritating were the communists on the other side of the wall. But for me what was really irritating was the fact that we were there to work.

Isherwood wrote in *Goodbye to Berlin,* 'I'm a camera with its shutter open, quite passive, recording, not thinking.' But, unlike Isherwood, I wasn't a camera. I was lugging one, recording and thinking, thinking of the fun we'd have that night. Then, dizzy after our hash-hazed night flights on the Big Deutsche Dipper, we'd go in search of a cabaret, a Sally Bowles or two, writers and millionaires, trying very hard to relive Isherwood's fun-filled Berlin nights.

Though the nights weren't totally successful, the days were. For the story, that is. Berlin was amazing. If seeing the wall all day was not enough, there were other reminders of the absurdity and barbarity of it all. The Checkpoint Charlie Museum had examples of every successful escape. The best way of escaping was a tunnel, but that was time consuming. It's amazing how ingenious people can be. Some people squeezed into fake petrol tanks, some inside two suitcases in the boot of a car. The guard that day must have been in on it or very stupid.

Trying to cross the wall was suicide and 176 people were killed giving it a go. The difficulty was that it was not just a wall. In some sections there were five walls of 4-metre high concrete, then more barricades, barbed wire, trip wires, attack dogs, machine guns, and the area between East and West was a minefield.

Thirty-year-old Heinz Englehart was just sixteen in 1966 when he escaped from East Germany. He told us they were always being told that everything was bad on the other side, so he decided to see for himself. He walked to the border, it was quiet, no guards. It seemed so easy, so he went for it.

'There were no signs, nothing. I stepped on a mine, which tore off both my legs.' He bent down, lifted up his trousers and tapped on his two plastic legs.

The day after our interview with Heinz we climbed one of the West Berlin viewing platforms to get shots of the East. It was a cold, bleak day, perfect for the images we were after. East Berlin guards watched our every move through binoculars. With us on the viewing platform was a beautiful young blonde woman, waving, blowing kisses and mouthing words to a well-dressed young man on the other side. She told us the man on the other side was her husband. She had been given permission to attend her father's funeral in the West and had never returned, even though it meant leaving her husband behind. They had both decided it was the best thing to do, but through her tears she told us that her life was now utterly miserable.

Every day at this time, at this spot, they waved to each other. We could just see the top of her husband's head over the two or three walls and barbed wire. They kept waving then, finally, he blew her a kiss, turned and walked away. It was heartbreaking. She was sobbing and I'll bet he was, too. We knew we must get over there to get some shots.

To get to East Berlin we had to cross 'Checkpoint Charlie', the main checkpoint used by foreign diplomats and tourists. Pay a few hundred bucks and it buys a trip into East Berlin, the quickest and easiest way the East Germans could get their hands on some hard currency.

We decided we'd roll the camera as we crossed. Highly illegal, of course. And only a few days ago I was worried about spending my life in a *West* German prison. Imagine turning 60 in something run by the Stasi (though I must admit the idea of turning 60 anywhere was a horrific thought in those days).

We drove slowly towards Checkpoint Charlie, rehearsing answers to questions we thought might come our way. Ian Leslie and I were in the back seat, and aimed over Ian's shoulder towards the window I had the already-rolling camera resting nonchalantly on my knee.

At the checkpoint Ian, wearing a radio microphone, asked the sour-looking guard a question, bringing him to the back of the car. The guard leant right into the window and demanded our passports. I was worried he might see Ian's mic and even more worried he'd hear the camera rolling. I wished I'd had it serviced before we left home. It now sounded unbelievably loud. The guard obviously missed the chaff-cutter noise. He checked our passports then, speaking in German, pointed to the camera. We just stared at him. He shouted to the next guard 50 metres down and waved us on.

This next guard was much more friendly and, with a big smile, asked in English how he could help. Ian explained who we were and asked if it was possible to get some shots of East Berlin. The happy guard said it was possible but first we must get permission. 'You must obtain a special paper from our ministry then you can film in the streets, but first you must leave your camera and recorder here. And when you have these papers there will be no problems for you.'

All of this we got on film and sound. And if we did what he wanted that was all we would ever get of East Berlin. If the paperwork did exist, it would take at least six months.

We left the locked car with the guards and went for a walk into East Berlin. Another variation of Christopher Isherwood: I was without a camera, quite passive, not recording, just thinking. The difference between East and West was astonishing. The streets were drab, cars were only grey or black, and the people looked really miserable. Not one smile to be seen.

We wandered into a huge supermarket with 80 per cent of the shelves completely empty. Some shelves had three or four cans of something unrecognisable, and that was it. I felt for all the unlucky people left behind here. They all knew what life was like on the other side.

After the communist takeover in the late 1940s three million people fled East Germany. The communists were not happy. Early in 1961 there were rumours of a tightening up of the borders. Between January and August that year a final lucky 160,000 people escaped. On 12 August 1961 the communists put up the first barriers. Then the walls.

It was way too depressing. We rushed back to wander the streets of West Berlin, soaking it all in, discussing the difference. And we saw one of those differences on a sign right in front of us.

Blue Movie 1
90 minuten Spielfilm
Non–Stop Standigeinlass
9.00–2400
Programmwechsel 4.4

We knew the first two words, if not the rest, so thought we'd take a peek. At the ticket counter the woman asked if we would like our beers in one large crate or separately. We said, 'No beer, thanks,' but were told it was part of the price of the ticket, so it was beers all round. Three large bottles of beer each and all with our own handy little container, not unlike the milkman used to carry. Into the dark cinema we went, deftly carrying our three-packs while fumbling around for seats.

It was probably the images on the screen that startled Allan. Down he went in the aisle, beer and all. The noise of those three shattering bottles drowned out the groans on the screen and an overwhelming stench of beer over-took the room. Giggling, apologising, we plodded further into the darkness through broken glass and rivers of beer in search of a seat. Shushes came from all around the room. True cinema-goers know exactly how important sound is, especially when the plot is so complex. 'Good job they're all wearing raincoats,' Ian said, and our giggling started all over again. More intricate dialogue missed. We decided perhaps it was time to leave, well short of our 90 minuten.

We never did find a Sally Bowles or a millionaire, and with our Egyptian purchase depleted our last night in Berlin was totally boring. We found our way into a couple of nightclubs surprisingly decked out with tacky red velvet curtains and superfriendly women. If that wasn't a dead giveaway, the insipid, salivating clients with their looks of anticipation sure were. We also found a few jazz bars, all playing excruciatingly dull improvisational jazz.

I think Christopher Isherwood's Berlin was probably a bit more exciting, despite the Nazis. He probably even had mind-bending substances, but without the double-loop dipper, his mind was never properly bent.

7

Almost a Murder on the Orient Express

The trips in the first few years were nearly always four to six weeks long, but every now and then an eight-weeker would appear, and it was tough. The producers would leapfrog, so on a trip longer than six weeks there could be three or four different producers. After two weeks and two stories, the first producer would fly home and a fresh, enthusiastic producer (and sometimes even a fresh, enthusiastic reporter) would arrive. The soundman and I would have been on the road for six weeks, with two weeks still to go. Sometimes it was hard for us to stay enthused.

There were three camera crews and three reporters in the early days, but lots of producers, all only too keen to get away from office politics and hit the road and quality restaurants every night. Don't get me wrong, I loved those unbelievable restaurants, but after six weeks I always felt that if I saw another menu and had to make another decision on the pheasant or the salmon, I'd scream. Often on a long trip, I'd skip the restaurant and go to the movies. Sitting alone in the dark, totally absorbed in a film, was amazingly cathartic.

It was my third trip of the year, and an eight-weeker. But with only two producers and two reporters—I could handle that. California, Belize, Amsterdam, Istanbul, then a trip on the Orient Express from Turkey to Lucerne, Switzerland. The first three stories were with George Negus and producer Warren McStoker, a tall, quiet man with a droll sense of humour and an uncanny ability to stun George into silence. A feat very few could pull off.

The morning I was leaving Sydney for the Negus leg of the trip, I raced in to see Ray Martin and producer Bruce Stannard to find out how they planned on doing their Orient Express yarn. They told me they wanted fun, intrigue, a feeling of being with the rich, blah blah blah . . . and we would be intercutting our footage with sequences from a stack of whodunit films shot on the Orient Express, including Agatha Christie and James Bond. Ray, speaking at a million miles an hour, couldn't hold back his excitement. I also thought it was a great idea, but I was finding it hard to concentrate, trying to remember if I'd packed everything.

'And then I'll say to Sean Connery blah blah, and Sydney Greenstreet will say to me blah blah,' Ray was not drawing breath.

With so much going on in my head, I really only picked up on the whodunit bits, so as I headed out the door I told them, 'Make sure you get the angles right, take notes of all the footage you're planning to cut to and be sure you know exactly which direction everybody is looking. See you in Istanbul in six weeks.'

As I fled out the door, Bruce yelled, 'Oh, by the way, on the Orient Express after six every night we have to wear a dinner suit. What size are you?'

'Ring my wife,' I yelled back. Then I got straight into a cab to the airport for the flight to California.

•

After landing in San Francisco, Terry 'Skeet' Kelly the soundman and I headed 250 kilometres north, to the small town of Ukiah. We checked into a beautiful 100-year-old timber hotel with two grand suites, called the Presidential and the Lincoln. We took them both. As always, first in first served. Warren and George weren't arriving for another few days.

We were in Ukiah to do a story on the biggest cash crop in California, sensimilla, the amazing dope that was famous around the world for its size and quality. Sensimilla (Spanish for 'without seeds') is a highly potent form of marijuana, and Skeet and I came early to get a feel for the place, get some postcard shots of the area, and to make some contacts.

The only way to get a good story is with good research, so Skeet and I went looking for the local dealer, found him in seconds flat, and made a small purchase. All in the name of research. It really was amazing stuff and in no time we were off our faces. The things you have to do for a story.

For the next two days as we lay and laughed by a beautiful lake, we marvelled at the fact that we were being paid to do this.

The others arrived and squeezed into their tiny rooms. We continued to laugh, this time from our huge balconies. Warren and George weren't happy, but we sure were.

The rest of the week was a bit of a blur, though I do remember going on a raid with the local police and finding a massive crop deftly hidden amongst tall trees. The plants were huge, way above my head, and each stem was so thick the cops had to use chainsaws to cut them down. The smell was enough to make everyone high. The cops dragged out some unfortunate bloke they found hiding in a shed. Then, making a big deal of it for our camera, brought him over to us before throwing him into their paddy wagon and hauling him off to the clink. I stared in wonder—*Could it be? Surely not!*

With the camera conveniently covering my face, I whispered to Skeet, 'We bought our dope from that guy, didn't we?'

'Yep,' he whispered back.

Luckily the dealer didn't recognise us, so we got on with the job of helping the cops rid the world of nasty drug dealers and their evil weed.

Next day, after shooting a quick interview with our dealer's defence lawyer, we headed off to talk to the sheriff. This guy was the top banana lawman and he was not going to have his town become a mecca for dope heads, though I suspected it was too late.

Somehow Skeet ended up driving to the sheriff's office with the lawyer. Warren, George and I arrived before Skeet, and as I was setting up the lights, in he walked, eyes spinning in his head, with a stupid smile on his face. He slowly began to set up his gear then stopped and stared at his hands. Each hand held a microphone while the look on his face said, 'What the fuck are these?'

Luckily, the sheriff didn't seem to know what a professional soundman should look like. Then five minutes into the interview I glanced across at Skeet and he was out cold, fingers on the faders like a true pro, and like a true pro, he woke up on the final question and no one but me had noticed.

After the interview the sheriff left the room so we could do our reverse questions: this is the showbiz side of what we do, where the reporter asks all the questions again, to nobody, so that it looks like we had two cameras. With Skeet now back in the land of the living, I asked him if he was aware that he had slept through most of the interview.

'I think so,' he said. He then revealed that on the drive over to the sheriff's office, the defence lawyer rolled the biggest joint he'd ever seen. 'Like a fuckin' telegraph pole. And we smoked it in the car.'

When we got back to the hotel, Skeet nervously played back the sound to make sure it was all there. Of course it was, and of course it was perfect. Like I said, a true pro.

•

The next day was my 32nd birthday, so we planned a big night of fine dining in the classiest restaurant in town. We started off with two bottles of champagne then switched to a fine still wine. No classy restaurant can make claim to true fine dining without an obnoxious sommelier, and what a little beauty we had here. Poncing around with his sommelier's cup, or *tasse à vin*, hanging from a ribbon around his neck. Made from silver or nickel silver, each *tasse à vin* has its own individual pattern and this one made our guy very important indeed. He didn't like us one bit. When George ordered the wine, Mr Sommelier made some dig at the quality of what we ordered, then proceeded to question why we'd even bother after having drunk bubbles. And on it went. But we were having a good time, so we ignored him and continued to dine finely.

Being the birthday boy I had probably drunk a little more than the others, and probably a little more than I should, but I swear, it wasn't malicious. Frankly I thought it was funny. Anyway, as I was eating my dessert, Mr Sommelier leant across me (poor form I thought) to dispense some wine, and dangling right there in front of me was his *tasse à vin*, staring me in the eye. Daring me. So I did.

It was only a small dollop of ice cream that ended up in the silver cup, but by his reaction you'd think I'd hit him with hot soup.

Suddenly there was a lot of gesticulating and shouting to and fro, though none of it from me—I'd been pushed into the background by our quick-thinking producer. A large wad of money was produced and Mr Sommelier started to calm down. But judging from the size of the veins in his neck, he would probably never be normal again.

Next day I didn't feel too normal myself. Maybe it was the grog, maybe the ice cream, maybe I was old now. But it sure wasn't remorse.

•

We flew to Central America for the Belize leg of the trip. Weird. I'll tell you about it later.

Then on to Amsterdam. We were there for days, or months, or both. Who knows? I know we had a great time. There's almost as much dope in Amsterdam as in Ukiah. A story went to air so things must have worked out. Skeet and I farewelled McStoker and George, then floated off to Istanbul, for our eagerly awaited Orient Express adventure.

We got to Istanbul three days before Ray and Bruce, giving us plenty of time to forget work and have some fun. What a town. 'Reeks of history,' I overheard an American tourist say.

In Istanbul there was so much happening. So many carpets and so many carpet sellers always looking for their next target, which was us. We then trudged back to the hotel heavily laden with carpets but thousands of dollars lighter, having convinced ourselves such quality is so rare.

With major shopping out of the way, we went for a walk and discovered a sleazy lane chockers with small shops and very much reeking of history. We wandered into a dingy coffee shop full of large Turkish men with even larger moustaches, all sucking on a hubbly bubbly, or water pipe, most with tobacco, some with hash. We ordered a Turkish coffee and our very own pipe with a small amount of hash, and started sucking. It didn't take long for our heads to start spinning like whirling dervishes,

Can't understand why the Israelis thought
I looked Palestinian. *Photo Ray Martin*

My Colombian assistant. He couldn't do enough. *Photo Mark Brewer*

This trip, 24 bags. The trolley gets its own trolley.
Photo Micky Breen

Preparing for a day at the office in the Masai Mara National Reserve Kenya.
Photo Micky Breen

With Micky trying hard to attract a Masai wife. *Photo Stephen Taylor*

IRA soldiers firing over Bobby Sands' coffin.

Mike Munro watches on as the IRA show us the 12 mm machine gun that brought down a British Sphinx helicopter.

Mike Munro in Northern Ireland, illegally, with five IRA members.

Mr Cool— Legishon—presenting me with a perfect birthday cake that he'd baked in an ammo box. *Photo Stephen Taylor*

With Tara Brown in the Masai Mara. *Photo Stephen Taylor*

Bumpy landing of hot air balloon after filming aerials of the wildebeest migration. *Photo Stephen Taylor*

In Africa—looking the wrong way. *Photo Stephen Taylor*

With producer Stephen Rice and Micky waiting for mum and cubs to wake from drug-induced stupor. *Photo Tara Brown*

Trapped in the van. Tara Brown about to become lunch.

The end of the longest day. The poor dead stag being loaded onto the pony. *Photo Mike Munro*

With Mike Munro, Micky, and the one and only Katharine Hepburn.
Photo Ben Hawke

which was obvious to the locals who were smiling and pointing in our direction.

With smiles all round and reeking of more than history, we decided to go outside to clear our heads a bit. And directly opposite was a sign:

Three Hundred Year Old Turkish Bath
Massage
Now Open

'That'll clear our heads,' we agreed, still smiling. So in we went, handed over a wad of money and wandered down the 300-year-old steps into the unknown.

It was steamy. Very steamy. And the whole place was filled with gigantic naked men. Some were luxuriating in the huge marble bath, others wandered aimlessly around, some sat on small wooden stools, Little Miss Muffet-like, scrubbing their oversized bodies.

A huge, fully clothed Turk approached us, told us where to get undressed, then handed each of us a towel the size of a postage stamp. If it was meant to dry us, we had Buckley's or none. If it was to hide our privates, ditto. Most of the other blokes in the place had guts dragging on the floor so their privates were well and truly hidden. Exposed genitals or not, Skeet and I must have been a real sight to them. We each weigh about 60 kilos, probably the size of their five-year-old child, or their lunch.

It was massage first so I looked around for the massage table, hoping the hole for my face would be the right size. I often got a sore neck due to ill-fitting tables elsewhere in the world. A table was nowhere to be seen, obviously it was on its way, so while I politely stood waiting for it to arrive, I had thoughts like, 'Apart from all the ugly men, this is a pretty cool place to be, and a nice massage is just what I need after a hectic six-week trip with two weeks still to go.' I was wondering whether to ask for the remedial massage or just a pleasant relaxing one when an oversized hairy hand pointed to the edge of the pool and someone bellowed, 'You! Lie down there.' Not only was there no table and no hole for my face, the floor was solid marble. But I did what I was told and found myself lying face down, stark naked on unforgiving cold stone.

Immediately I realised that being only 60 kilos was a distinct disadvantage. Already my knees, hips and ribs were hurting from the rock-hard surface, not to mention my genitals, though at least there was a bit of give there. I looked up from my discomfort to see Skeet's face ten centimetres from mine. We were both grimacing, half laughing, half crying, as gorilla hands started pummelling our bodies. I heard a wheeze, and a rush of warm air hit me in the face as his lungs completely deflated. Skeet's masseur was treading on his back. I then heard strange crunching noises. Must have been his ribs and hips. Suddenly, I heard my own body wheezing and crunching. The pain was excruciating. Now we both had 120-kilo Turks parading up and down our backs.

With a lifetime of pain finally over, our 'therapists' handed us our postage-stamp towels, which easily did their job after the cold marble and torture. We then sat on our Miss Muffet stools and were scrubbed all over before staggering across to the 300-year-old bath. We slowly lowered our naked bodies into the warm water, joining the throng of flabby hairy Turks, grinning and watching our every move.

With all bones reconnected and no longer reeking of history and hash but very detectable chlorine, we got dressed, tipped our torturers and headed back onto the street. It's funny how to the Turks and the Thais the word massage can mean two completely different things.

•

Next day Ray and Bruce arrived, along with my rented tuxedo. I packed it carefully then prepared for the Orient Express train ride of a lifetime. Istanbul, Sofia, then Belgrade to Lucerne, where we would finish our trip. The train would then continue on to Paris without us.

We loaded all our gear onto this amazingly beautiful train sitting in Istanbul's beautiful Sirkeci station, the beautiful blue and white engine whispering beautiful steam sounds. Added to all this beauty we had history, intrigue, border crossings and one hell of a crew. This was going to be a ripper of a story.

First, though, we needed an exterior shot of the train leaving the station.

'No way. Once the train starts, that's it,' we were told.

After ten minutes of wheeling and dealing and begging, I was allowed to run 100 metres up the line for the magic shot of the Orient Express departing Sirkeci station. The engine went 20 metres past me then stopped. Not a great shot. I would have liked the whole train to pass, but at least I got the magnificent steam engine sweeping by. I jumped onto the train full of enthusiasm, at least the shots in the next few days would be great, and anyway that was really only an obligatory exterior, it was hardly the shot of the story. Well, that's what I thought.

We wandered through the impressively appointed train looking for friendly faces and ideas, but were confronted with aggressive, well-heeled loudmouths shouting, 'You better not put that thing in my face.' So we went back to our own carriage to shoot everything we needed for our quirky little sequence involving all those great movies. We'd charm the other passengers into appearing in our story tonight, when everyone'd had a few.

As I set up the lights, not so easy on a fast-moving train, Ray told me he'd do reaction shots to Richard Widmark, then Anthony Perkins, then Sydney Greenstreet, and we'd finish off with Sean Connery in *From Russia with Love*. I said to no one in particular, 'Okay then, for Widmark, which way is Ray looking?'

And Bruce said, 'Left to right,' just as Ray said, 'Right to left.'

I couldn't believe they didn't know and reminded them of my parting words in Sydney. They both claimed to have studied the relevant scenes carefully (obviously not together).

It wasn't the end of the world, but it did mean I had to shoot everything twice, covering both angles, which meant lighting twice, and as the filming time increased, so did my impatience. These days with digital filming and editing, they flick a button and reverse the shot, including the part in Ray's hair.

Finally, with two of every shot in the can, we decided it was time to join the mob and enjoy the Orient

Express experience. It was 6 p.m. Dinner suit time. With our sartorial elegance *plus* our Aussie charm, we would easily convince our fellow passengers to appear in our story.

I pulled out my suit. Total disbelief. The pants were big enough for the Turkish boys back at the bathhouse. Being the masochist I am, I tried on the coat. The sleeves dragging on the floor had me looking like the incredible shrinking man.

There was a knock on the door, and in walked Skeet looking every bit the debonair soundman. When he laid eyes on me, he managed to hold back his mirth. Debonair *and* perceptive. The door opened again, Ray walked in, took one look at me and almost busted a gut laughing. Not so perceptive. For a short moment I considered murder on the Orient Express.

Ray still had tears in his eyes as we moved to the soiree carriage, me wearing jeans, my best shirt, a bow tie and an ill-fitting look of embarrassment. The carriage was full of elegant furniture and about 40 overdressed fellow travellers quaffing champagne. Underneath an extremely ornate chandelier sat a well-dressed man playing 'As Time Goes By' on a grand piano. We downed a few champagnes of our own and managed to get some people on side. Unfortunately they were mostly Aussies. We were hoping for a much more international vibe. The mob still refusing to have anything to do with us were all Americans and they remained adamant about just where we could stick our camera. So we ignored them. We were having such a good time we somehow forgot to work, and suddenly it was 2 a.m. 'Oh well,' I thought, 'there's always tomorrow.'

But there was also breakfast, morning tea, a four-course lunch with wine, afternoon tea, pre-dinner drinks with canapés, then dinner. And it's all five star. Who has time to work?

Night time again and with near nought in the can, we decided to shoot a sing-along around the piano. There were too many people to set up lights, so I asked Bruce to hold a portable battery light for me. Thirty seconds into the sequence and I couldn't see a thing through the lens. Bruce had swung the light away as he leant across to pick up another champagne. I grabbed his hand and swung the light back onto the subject. Ten seconds later, same again. It was no good, he was chatting up some beautiful woman. So I gave up and joined the party.

A short time later, out in the dark, the most extra-ordinary scene appeared. We'd stopped in a rundown station just outside Belgrade. A foot from us was another train aiming in the opposite direction, and inside were scores of Yugoslav peasants heading home after a tough day in the factory. Crammed into their carriage, with no room to move, their eyes stared disbelievingly at the wealthy capitalists with pianos, chandeliers and food.

I grabbed the camera and started rolling, and just as I began that one-in-a-million shot, panning from communism to capitalism, one of the Americans started waving into the camera and screaming about being filmed. There went the shot of the story. I put the camera down and decided to enjoy the moment. I gazed across and noticed the look in the eyes of the peasants. So I picked up two crystal glasses full of French bubbles and handed them across. With huge smiles on their faces, the tired peasant workers reached out and gladly accepted. I then handed out two more. Grateful smiles all round. As their train began to move I leant across and shook the hand of the biggest smile, then they and the glasses were gone.

What a story they'd have to tell their kids. And what a story we didn't have. But we soldiered on convincing ourselves we still had a chance. Meanwhile, how good was this champagne.

Next morning Ray decided he wanted to do a piece to camera where he looks down the lens and tells a little of the story in situ. It was an elaborate set up, we were passing through the Swiss Alps and the day was perfect. Ray was over the sink, shaving, rehearsing his lines, 'You wipe the sleep and the slivovitz from your eyes, you open the blind and . . . it's the Swiss Alps.'

The shot was extremely difficult. I had to try and match the light in the cabin with the stark bright light outside. It took a lot of time adjusting the lights, while Ray continued rehearsing. Finally I was ready. We pulled down the blind.

'You wipe the sleep and the slivovitz from your eyes, you open the blind and . . . it's a fucking tunnel!'

Pitch black. Nothing. All we could see were our reflections in the window. We couldn't stop laughing. What more could go wrong? We figured we could just wait until we got out of the tunnel and try again.

Wait we did. And when we finally exited the longest tunnel in Europe, the Alps were gone, replaced by an industrial wasteland, the outskirts of Lucerne where we were to get off.

We had no story, but we had a great time not getting it.

8

He's Dead and the Moon is Blue

Two in the morning, and I was wishing I hadn't drunk so much. I'd taken off my shirt and shoes, unzipped my fly and was stepping uneasily out of my pants when the phone rang. I reached for the phone and went down like a tonne of bricks, caught up in pants and phone lead. *Who could possibly be ringing at this hour*, the pissed and not-so-smart side of me was thinking. I mumbled an incoherent, 'Hello?'

'He's dead. Let's go!'

No! No! No! I can't believe it . . . he's dead. Why? Why tonight? Not tonight, he's had 66 days. Why now?

I lay flat on my back and looked around, hoping none of this was true, that it was all just a bad dream and I had fallen out of bed. I could keep hoping all I liked, but the phone was still in my hand, and I knew well and truly that this wasn't a bad dream. I was in Europe's most bombed hotel, the Europa Hotel in Belfast, and had been there for a week, waiting for Bobby Sands—the 27-year-old IRA hunger striker—to die.

Micky Breen the soundman and I had been so very good since we'd arrived in Belfast, holding back on the booze, retiring early every night and not leaving the hotel—just in case. After a week in the heavily fortified hotel, cabin fever set in, and that night of all nights we hit the piss and had a big one.

I slammed the phone down and desperately tried to get my head together. I went looking for all the gear I'd need: camera, film, lenses, batteries, portable light, tripod . . . *No, bugger it, there won't be time for tripod shots, it can stay right here . . . If only I could . . . I feel like shit. How can I work like this?* This was going to be one hell of a night.

•

Six days ago the *60 Minutes* crew hit town, along with half the world's media, and it struck me as being slightly ghoulish that so many of us from so many different parts of the world had all come to Ireland to cover the death of one seemingly ordinary man. But the circumstances of his death were anything but ordinary. A story is a story, and this was a biggy. After all, it's not every day a member of the British parliament starves himself to death.

Bobby Sands was serving fourteen years jail for possession of a weapon. All IRA inmates were demanding to be treated as political prisoners, and as soldiers, to be treated as prisoners of war, which should mean no jail uniforms, no work, and free association with other prisoners. But all this was refused by the British authorities. Sands was well into his hunger strike when he won a by-election created after a sitting member of parliament died of a sudden heart attack. The seat had a huge Roman Catholic majority and the publicity of his hunger strike had been sufficient to get Sands across the line. Bobby Sands the parliamentarian was now making life very difficult for the Poms, with some foreign governments and the pope pushing for his demands to be met.

Starting two weeks before the other hunger strikers, Sands hoped his death would force the British government to give in to the prisoners' demands, and in turn save the lives of the other strikers. In total, 23 IRA political prisoners joined the hunger strike. But they were up against one hell of an opponent in Prime Minister Margaret Thatcher.

'We are not prepared to consider special category status for certain groups of people serving sentences for crime. Crime is crime is crime. It is not political,' she declared.

After Sands' election the British government immediately introduced the *Representation of the People Act of 1981*, stopping prisoners who were serving more than a year in the UK or the Republic of Ireland from being candidates in UK elections, but the horse had already bolted. So the newly elected Bobby Sands was big news.

Big news means big media frenzy, but I couldn't lose the feeling we were all hoping that Bobby Sands' demise would be sooner rather than later. After all, everyone had deadlines and Bobby obviously didn't realise our budgets weren't limitless. No wonder we're called a pack.

Anticipating the frenzy, a media centre was set up to offer daily updates on the state of the hunger strikers. Belfast was a mess and it was about to get a lot messier. Dangerous, and about to get a lot more so. The world knew Sands couldn't last much longer, and when he died there'd be one hell of a shit fight. We were told we had to carry our passports with us at all times, because we'd be checked often by the RUC (Royal Ulster Constabulary) and the British army.

Each day we'd go out filming to get a feel of the place, and there was no shortage of great footage of balaclava-clad teenagers and men smashing windows and throwing petrol bombs. Wave after wave of them, running from behind a wall to hurl their bombs at local police and anyone or anything connected to the British army. They would then retreat for more ammo. Teenagers said they would not stop until the Brits were out of Northern Ireland. 'The Brits are bastards,' we were told by six-year-olds as they climbed onto smouldering cars to smash any glass still intact.

Early on day three, Micky and I went to investigate a huge cloud of smoke hovering over the edge of town. It turned out to be a pile of burning cars, one of them a British armoured vehicle, and parading around it was a French photographer helping a five-year-old to put on a balaclava. He told the kid to climb onto the vehicle and stand with a clenched fist above his head. I could see the shot appearing on the front page of some big glossy mag in Paris, or worse, on the cover of hundreds of magazines around the world, and probably winning some international photography award for him. As he fired off shot after shot, he was yelling at the kid, 'No, no, don't smile, don't smile.' I filmed the whole thing, and when the photographer finally saw me he was very pissed off, and let me know it. I was just as pissed off, and let him know it. We've all fudged things a little at times but I really thought this was over the top. The Frenchman told me that he'd do what he wanted and I could do what I wanted. So I did. I dobbed him in. Next day the press centre revoked his accreditation and he was on the first plane back to Paris.

Our driver, Jimmy was a very cool customer, indeed. A man of few words, a great accent, an immense hatred of the Brits, and amazing contacts. No problem to get interviews with leaders of Sinn Féin, the political wing of the IRA, or with masked men admitting to be IRA members, every one only too keen to tell us of the chaos they planned following Bobby Sands' death. Whether or not they were genuine IRA members, no one could tell, but to a man they told us they'd get Northern Ireland back in the hands of the Irish, and for that they were willing to die.

Now Bobby Sands has done just that. It was two in the morning and I was drunk and desperately struggling to put on my pants. I thought, 'If it's this difficult to put on pants, how on earth am I going to get out there and do what I'm paid to do?'

I skulled three glasses of water and immediately felt sick so I filled the sink with cold water and shoved in my already pounding head, asking myself how I could have been so stupid. (I decided I'd answer that tomorrow if I was still employed.) I grabbed everything I thought I'd possibly need, plus my all-important passport, and headed downstairs. Micky was not in as bad a condition as me but he was not happy, and also questioning our stupidity. We caught up with our producer and reporter and staggered into the melee.

Shit, it's all happening. There is no quicker way to sober up than having petrol bombs, rocks and bullets flying past your head. It was only 2.45 a.m. and already half of Belfast was burning. Word travels fast in this town.

The first targets were the British-owned banks, and by the time we got to them every one was burning out of control. Great shots for us and easy to film with so much light coming from the flames, but move 50 metres from the flames and the night was pitch black. Even though I had a portable battery light, it was pretty useless; it could light about 2 metres, and that was the extent of it, making it really difficult to show the scope of the devastation.

Suddenly people with masks, scarves and balaclavas started running in all directions shouting, 'Here they come!'

Walking slowly and with intent were twenty British soldiers, guns at the ready. They were lined out across the road from footpath to footpath and heading straight for us. *What a shot!* I turned on my useless light and started rolling . . .

'Turn that fucking thing off! *Now!*'

As feeble as my light was, I guess it didn't help that the soldiers were looking straight into it. I switched it off.

Then as we turned and ran to get out of their way, the soldiers started firing. In all the confusion and darkness we suddenly found ourselves backed up against a wall. I heard a thud an inch from my head and felt something land on my foot. A plastic bullet. I'd read about them but had never seen one. I picked it up, amazed at its size. It was 7 centimetres long, an inch in diameter, and made of rock-hard plastic. These can be lethal if you get hit in the wrong place. I slipped the bullet into my pocket, not knowing there was a jail term if one of these projectiles was found in your possession.

At four in the morning Jimmy the driver took us back to his place for a cup of tea and some R & R. He said he had to make a few phone calls.

I was happy to be out of the action for a while and enjoying my tea when Jimmy's four-year-old boy, in cute little teddy bear pyjamas, toddled up and said in a heavy Irish accent, 'The Brits killed Bobby Sands.' And so on it goes, a new generation to despise the British.

By daylight we could see the full extent of the devastation. Most of the CBD was burnt out. Some buildings were still on fire. There was not a window intact, and if you were unlucky enough to have left your car out on the street, it was now a smouldering wreck.

Jimmy asked if we would like to get some shots of Bobby's body. *Are you kidding?* We now knew exactly how influential our driver was.

We headed off to Bobby's parents' place and Jimmy went inside, telling us to wait in the car. He needed to discuss a few things. Ten minutes later he was back, very apologetic, saying the parents had asked if it would be all right if we didn't film their son. He wasn't really looking very good, they said. *Sixty-six days without food, and he's not looking very good? It's no surprise*, we were thinking, but not saying. We were then told that Bobby's mum and dad had agreed that only the reporter would go inside and view the body. So a tentative Ian Leslie went in.

Ten minutes later he was back in the car, telling us that if he didn't know, it would be impossible to believe what lay inside that casket was a young man. The 27-year-old

Sands looked more like a 72-year-old man. As it turned out, Ian was the only member of the world's media to see the corpse.

•

On the day of the funeral, Belfast was on full alert. There were rumours that the IRA would appear and show their support, but no one knew exactly how or when. I started to pack all the gear for a huge day. The usual lenses, film, batteries, changing bag, passport . . . *Passport! Where's my passport?* I checked everywhere, pockets, suitcase, film-gear cases, under the bed, inside socks. Last time I had any idea where it was, it was in my back pocket during the night of all the action. *Shit. Shit. Shit.* I knew I could be in big trouble here, and not only here, because when we left Belfast we were off to Beirut, then Tokyo, two destinations that required very expensive and very hard to get filming visas. Both of which I had only recently had stamped into my now missing passport.

It was cold and wet outside, but I was sweating as I headed off to the biggest funeral the world had seen for a long time. I decided not to tell the others about my missing passport—there was no point in adding more angst to their day, I thought, and besides, passports have a habit of turning up . . . *Don't they?*

We walked through town. Belfast was full of anger. Funerals have a great way of uniting people. The Brits must have been shitting themselves. There was a crowd of more than 50,000, six deep along the 3-mile route, all pushing forward and hoping to get a glimpse of the coffin on its journey to the cemetery. Hovering above us was a swarm of British helicopters watching everybody's every move, but remarkably, down at our level, there was little evidence of being watched. No local police at all and the British army very conspicuous by its absence.

The rain was getting heavier and the mud thicker. The gear and I were getting wetter and we couldn't be walking any slower if we tried. Then we were forced to detour an extra quarter of a mile so the mourning procession didn't pass through a Protestant enclave. And all the while Jimmy was telling Micky and I to stick with the coffin, because at some time in the next 2 miles, the IRA would appear and fire a round of bullets over the coffin. *Two miles! The gear weighs a tonne. It had better be a great shot.*

As we walked I was thinking *what a weird world we live in*. From Belfast I was off to Beirut, where the Muslims want to see a lot less of Christians and vice versa. I had just got back from Israel, where the Jews or Zionists or Israelis (take your pick) would prefer fewer Palestinians, while the Palestinians wanted to see Israel wiped off the face of the earth. But right now I wanted to see the IRA start shooting over this coffin so I could get out of this rain, and this country, though that could be a little prob-lematical seeing as I didn't have a passport. *What if I'm trapped here? What if I'm caught with my rubber bullet, and no passport? What if . . .*

'Ready! Aim!'

Shit, didn't see them coming. I whacked the camera to my eye, zoomed back to the wide end of the lens and started rolling . . .

'Fire! Fire! Fire!'

Three rifle shots went over the coffin and the balaclava-wearing IRA members, Bobby Sands' brothers in arms, deftly dissolved into the weeping crowd. It was a great image, but it would have been nice to have had a little more warning.

•

Back at the hotel, exhausted and soaking wet, I softened up reporter and producer with raves of the award-winning 'ready, aim, fire' shot over the coffin, then I fired a shot of my own by casually mentioning the missing passport.

I was hit with all the questions a mother would ask: How could I be so stupid? What about the near-impossible-to-get visas? Had I really looked for it? Where did I think I lost it?

I preferred the word 'stolen', but kept that to myself. Still, the loss needed to be reported, so off I went to the cops. Who thought I was hilarious. They couldn't believe anyone could be so dumb as to carry a passport in their back pocket in Belfast. They told me it would already be in the hands of the IRA with my photograph replaced by someone better looking.

There is a God. Even for atheists. I'm not saying a passport fell from the sky, but Northern Ireland being part of the United Kingdom meant I could fly back to London without one. And more luck, a month before we had done a story on Andrew Peacock, then the minister for foreign affairs, so we made a phone call to his home (so as not to be fobbed off by minders) and told him of my dilemma. He must have loved the story because he told me to be at the Australian embassy in London by ten the next morning and there would be a new passport waiting. Same old story, it's not what you know . . .

I immediately flew to London, arrived at Australia House on the dot of ten and headed straight to 'Lost Passports'.

'I've come to pick up a passport.'

'Replacement for lost or stolen?'

'Yes.'

'And when was the passport reported missing?'

'Yesterday.'

'Yesterday!' she sneered. 'I'm *sorry*. *First*, you must fill in this form, return it to me, and we will contact you in two weeks. *That's* the way it's done.'

'But there should be one here for me now. I rang and organised it.'

'As I've *said*,' she sniffed, 'it will take *two weeks* for your passport to be processed.'

'No, I rang Andrew Peacock, the minister for foreign affairs last night. He said I could pick up a new passport here today.'

'One moment . . .'

Minutes later, barging down the stairs, came a really not-so-pleased to see me, immaculately dressed gentleman with a huge plum in his mouth. So huge that coupled with his attempt to be diplomatic, he was struggling to speak. His anger was obvious.

'Mr Lee, there was absolutely *no reason* to ring Mr Peacock, he is far too busy for this kind of thing. That is why we are here. To help people like you.'

Sure, I thought, as I looked down at the two-week form I was holding.

It was then straight to the Lebanese and Japanese embassies where I handed over hundreds of dollars, hung around for eight hours, then after having been berated by officious embassy staff I got two colourful little stamps in my virginal passport. I was told I should count myself extremely lucky. Normally those stamps can't be available in one day. Buggered if I know why, but I thanked them, walked out onto the damp streets of London with not a care in the world and got to live another day.

Not so for Bobby Sands, or the nine hunger strikers who died after him.

Bobby Sands the martyr is now a huge part of history. But the other nine? Their families know who they are, and that's about it. Bernadette Devlin, the outspoken champion of the IRA cause, announced after Sands' death, 'Having paid Mrs Thatcher's blood price, we will not take no for an answer and we call upon all civilised people to isolate Britain for the political leper that she is.'

Thatcher's answer was to send in 600 more troops, bringing the military presence in Northern Ireland to nearly 12,000.

The IRA continued fighting for recognition, survival and a unified Ireland, possibly pushing their luck with a courageous mortar attack on Number 10 Downing Street while Prime Minister John Major and his entire war cabinet were inside. Two mortars overshot the building and failed to detonate, a third exploded in the rear garden of Number 10. The attack was originally intended for Thatcher, but she had unexpectedly resigned. Why waste a good plan? Then the IRA 'accidently' killed two Australian lawyers in Holland who they had mistaken for

British soldiers. Both attacks showed a lack of brains. But they weren't going to give in.

•

After the Bobby Sands story I let the Irish 'Troubles' drift from my thoughts. I did recognise that getting rid of occupying foreign troops was a worthy cause and I should show some solidarity with my great-great-grandfather's people, but I had much grander things occupying my mind, like where to eat in New York, Rome, Paris. So, apart from occasional thoughts of my 'stolen' passport, the IRA was no longer in my mind.

Until ten years after the Bobby Sands story and there I was back in Ireland, sitting in the Shelbourne Hotel, Dublin, about to do the definitive story on 'Inside the IRA'. If we were caught, it was a minimum of five years for being associated with known terrorists.

There was a certain sense of déjà vu because, not unlike the Europa Hotel in Belfast, we'd been sitting stuffing ourselves endlessly with food and grog, waiting for something to happen. Each day consisted of breakfast, morning tea, lunch, afternoon tea, pre-dinner drinks, dinner with mucho vino, supper, and a Drambuie or two before bed.

We had absolutely nothing to film until we knew if and when the story would happen. We were told someone would contact us . . . sometime. Then we would be given a password indicating that the story was on.

Relieving the boredom with me was Micky, reporter Mike Munro and producer Andrea Keir. The story had been painstakingly set up back in Sydney by ace producer Stephen Taylor, who spent months making cryptic midnight phone calls to terrorists, all without ever mentioning the IRA for fear of the phones being bugged, and somehow he managed get them to agree to a story. Then, and it happens to all producers at some stage, the timing of the story didn't fit with Stephen's next trip. As in life, it's all to do with timing, so reluctantly he had to hand over the story to Andrea, who just happened to have a trip to the UK ready to go. It was a good fit. Andrea was a take-no-prisoners producer who was scared of no one, including the IRA. She would stop at nothing to get a story, she was tough and *very* effective, and after four days hanging around our Dublin hotel waiting for something to shoot, she was getting a little edgy.

On the fifth day Andrea scored a meeting with our go-between. She was told to get on and off certain buses until a man would walk behind her and tell her the latest, and at no time could she turn and look at him or talk to him. She did this. And his news was? Nothing. Except that tomorrow he would sit at a nearby coffee shop and update her. *Update her.* He was one hell of a brave man who didn't know who he was dealing with. This was Andrea Keir, not some lightweight like John Major or Margaret Thatcher.

On her next clandestine meeting Andrea was told by our go-between that we were being watched by the British Special Branch, and that the IRA were watching the Brits watching us. As long as they were not watching our bar bill. We were also told we were not to leave the hotel or to make any phone calls to anyone, including family in Sydney. We continued to wait for the 'Moon is Blue' or whatever password the IRA was going to come up with.

I felt like James Bond with all this intrigue, though he was highly trained, drank very dry martinis and had a licence to kill. Hey, I've been trained, love a dry martini, and have a licence to drive in NSW. Close enough. But Bond's not real and I am and if I'm caught I'll end up in jail. Being in Dublin might swing a bit of sympathy our way, but if we were in Northern Ireland there'd be absolutely *none* from the Brits.

And then it was on. At precisely 9.30 the next morning Micky and I must load the car with all the necessary gear, take it a quarter of a mile from the hotel, and wait in the back seat. The contact would walk to the hotel, pick up Mike and Andrea, and all three would walk to our car. There would be no talking, at all, ever, none, nought. Understand?

In the bar, on what might be our last night of freedom, we spent hours discussing the pros and cons of the story, how tomorrow might pan out and what were the chances of us doing five years. At least we'd all be together. Well, Micky, Mike and I would be. Andrea would be on her own. Pity help any female warder who scores her.

I wanted to tell the others that five years is chicken feed, I had faced 30 years in a German cell after accidentally smuggling hash out of Egypt. But then reality set in. I knew there was a much greater chance of being sprung and made an example of with this story. With the laughing and joking increasing as the grog did, deep down we all began to worry, knowing that even Kerry Packer's influence and millions would get us nowhere with John Major, or the Iron Lady who was still in parliament. Neither of them would tolerate any publicity on these murderers, because both had been IRA targets: Thatcher with a bomb in her Brighton hotel in 1984, and Major with the attempt on Number 10 Downing Street.

Next morning, with the moon well and truly blue, Micky and I, both exhausted from lack of sleep and thoughts of sharing a cell with killers and rapists, packed our gear, drove our quarter mile and waited in the car.

Ten-fifteen, and in the rear vision mirror we saw Mike, Andrea and a smallish man in a green sports coat heading towards us. Mike hopped into the driver's seat with Andrea beside him, and joining Micky and I in the back was the mystery man, who sat behind Andrea as a signal to his comrades that all was going according to plan.

He turned out to be very chatty with heaps of small talk, the weather, etc., but at no time did he say to turn right or left, he just pointed in the direction he wanted Mike to drive, or he'd say, 'Follow that truck.' I'm guessing it was in case we were bugged. Every minute or so he turned and looked out the back window.

Half an hour later, we drove slowly into a small village and our passenger said to Mike, 'Move over and let some of our boys go past,' and a small red car overtook us, turning off at the next right. We kept going straight ahead. I really wasn't sure if the red car was part of the charade or not. Maybe he was just having us on, trying to keep us frightened. Which worked. I kept my mouth shut, as did the others. Not long after, we let another car pass then the mystery man said, 'Stop here, I'm going in to buy a paper.'

We waited in silence, still too scared to speak to each other. Finally he came out of the shop. I couldn't see a paper, but I did see him looking in all directions as he approached our car. Another ten minutes' drive, then he said quietly, 'Pull over here, we're going into this pub. Follow me.'

Six blokes sitting at the bar didn't take their eyes off us as we headed for the lounge. We either didn't look Irish enough or we looked like an Aussie film crew. We followed our contact to an obviously pre-arranged spot at the back of the pub and, surprise, surprise, sat and waited. Micky had a hangover so he lay down on a couch. Our mystery man pulled the *Irish Times* from under his coat and started reading. After a short read, he put down his paper and told Mike and Andrea that the two cars we'd let pass had followed us out of Dublin to make sure the Special Branch wasn't watching us.

To relieve the boredom I picked up his paper, started reading and suddenly standing right in front of me was a bloke with jet-black hair and a bright red moustache, wearing a blue parka and a green cap. I recognised him as one of the six men at the bar when we walked in.

He looked at me and said, 'John?'

'Nope,' I said (maybe I did look Irish after all).

'That's me,' said the mystery man.

The way the IRA cell system works, no one ever knows who's who. Later we learned the newspaper was the signal for the guy with the mo and the cap to recognise us. It all seemed so Irish—no offence to my ancestors—but I thought there could have been any number of people in the pub reading the paper. Turned out to be not so. This was a very Republican town, so few around these parts would want to be seen reading the *Irish Times*, still thought of as a Unionist rag.

John and the man in the cap chatted for five minutes until Capman said, 'Let's go.' We shook Micky to wake him up and left the pub with our new contact. John stayed in the pub. Capman told us, 'We'll drive for half an hour then change cars.' Mike asked him where we were going. Fat chance of getting an answer to that, I thought, then heard, 'Armagh.' It didn't mean a lot to me, but in the rear-vision mirror I could see Mike going pale.

'Isn't that in the North?' he said.

'That's right,' said Capman.

All I could think was, *Shit, I haven't got my passport.*

'Then we'll need to go through a checkpoint, won't we?' said Mike.

'Nope. We know how to avoid them.'

The North. This wasn't supposed to happen. Not only were we about to spend a day with a banned terrorist organisation but we'd be on English soil, entered illegally.

Our route took us along unmarked roads that got narrower and narrower until we got to a tiny lane covered in briar bush. The lane was wide enough for a horse but not our car so we scratched our way along until we reached a small partially hidden entrance to a tree-lined driveway. Capman pulled on the handbrake, stepped out of the car and wandered off. When he'd completely disappeared from view, we looked at each other, totally bewildered. We sat and waited, with no idea where we were, or what we were waiting for. But these blokes had been waiting since 1916, so what was another half hour?

Capman reappeared, this time in a very small car, and with him were two men wearing army fatigues and balaclavas. Then, running in from nowhere, two more similarly dressed guys appeared, and very apologetically said they must frisk us. They gave Mike, Micky and I a thorough going-over, but no one touched Andrea. Such gents these boys. They kill and maim women and kids with their bombs, but don't frisk them. Their mums would be proud.

We transferred all the gear into the tiny car, leaving room for only one passenger, so in I got. I then drove off with the two balaclava-wearers, leaving behind my colleagues and my confidence. Half a mile later the car stopped and I watched the two balaclava-wearers looking nervously in every direction.

'It's down here somewhere,' the driver said. 'But I've no idea where. They switched locations on us this morning.'

I thought, 'This is Keystone Cops stuff. How on earth did they manage to get anywhere near the prime minister's residence?'

Then one of them pointed out a British checkpoint a mile down the hill and told me we would have to be very careful. There was a definite atmosphere of confusion and fear in the car. It was cramped and I was getting pissed off. Three British Sphinx helicopters passed noisily over our heads. Now I was frightened as well as pissed off. Then, to my utter amazement, the driver got out a two-way radio, made contact and asked where we were to rendezvous, and how to get there. I was new to all this, but I'd seen enough spy movies to know that the British soldiers at that checkpoint could easily have been listening in. I asked if that was possible.

'Yeah sure,' the driver said. 'But we keep it short and talk fast.'

It felt so Irish. After five days loitering in Dublin, cryptic phone calls, mysterious car trips and three different contacts, we were now on a two-way radio asking for directions because we were lost.

But we drove on, finally pulling up outside a small white derelict cabin where three new balaclava-clad boys yelled at me to get the gear inside as fast as possible. Inside the cabin I looked around and my heart sank. There were cobwebs everywhere, holes in the floor, and one tiny window like a port hole. The room was dark, a cameraman's nightmare. I asked if there was any power. They all glared at me with a 'what a fucking stupid question' look. It wasn't a stupid question. Two months ago from Sydney we had asked about the availability of power. Two weeks ago in London, then two days ago in Dublin, we had confirmed it. No problems, we were told. Not only did we need power for lighting, the IRA had demanded we bring a voice scrambler to be used on location so there would never be a faithful reproduction of their voices. And they'd been told the scrambler only worked off mains power.

My colleagues finally turned up and I delivered the good news. Andrea hit the roof. She got stuck into the balaclava-wearers, telling them how slack they were, how unreliable they were, how arrogant they were, how they'd lied to us, how far we'd come to do this documentary, how she had only *yesterday* got a message through to the executive producer that everything was going according to plan . . . 'And I'm not letting you idiots fuck up my story!'

Silence. These blokes kneecap people for drinking in the wrong pub, but now they all looked desperately at each other through eye-holes in their balaclavas, terrified of this Australian banshee.

Within minutes of Andrea's tirade, I had half a dozen helpers running metres of power cable, borrowed from a nearby farmhouse, and I started setting up lights.

Our first sequence was three men and two women being given instructions on how to dismantle high-powered weapons: AK47s, handguns and rifles, all bought from Eastern Bloc countries. Then from under a table the instructor brought out a 12-mm anti-aircraft gun wrapped in hessian. We were told it was the very gun that, a few days earlier, had brought down a British helicopter worth 10 million pounds. It was big news around the world, and front page of the *Irish Times* that I'd read in the pub lounge.

So we were not only talking to the IRA, which would give us five years in the clink, but if the Brits walked in now, they'd find us surrounded by heavy-duty weapons, including the one which the British army and local police were looking for. That's twenty years right there.

Micky set up the voice scrambler for the interview with 'Patrick' the balaclava-wearer who appeared to be running the show. He was extremely articulate, obviously very intelligent and said he was one of the nine overall commanders of the IRA. With the scrambler up and running, Patrick insisted on hearing how he would sound. Satisfied he was unrecognisable, he was then keen to speak.

Mike began the interview, asking how the IRA could justify their dreadful terror tactics.

Patrick replied, 'If the Irish people were black and not white, I believe the rest of the world would understand more easily how we have been treated like slaves by the English for centuries.'

'But does that mean you have to murder innocent men, women and children?'

'One of the great tragedies of war are civilian casualties,' Patrick growled.

At the end of the interview we were told the helicopters had moved on and asked if we would like to film some target practice. *Would we?* At that point we only had enough shots for a tiny, seven-minute story and that was stretching it.

We raced outside while five of the men set up their targets. Knowing we needed much more footage, I started to film anything and everything that moved. Close-ups of eyes, feet, hands, men walking, Mike watching, a pan down from the sun, views through trees, etc. While I was taxing my artistic brain to the limit, Patrick told us they would fire five bullets and five bullets only, then they were out of there. I wasn't sure if five bullets were all they had or if they were worried about the sound, but I was still worried about lack of pictures. Before they fired any shots, I got close-ups of fingers on triggers, close-ups of eyes inside balaclavas, then shots of trigger-pulling but not really firing. We could put in the sound later.

Mike did a piece to camera with the five men in the background, aiming and ready to shoot. I rushed around filming each rifle and each set of eyes from five different angles, hoping some editor would save my arse. With quick cutting, it might just look like the most wanted terrorists in the world had a lot more than five bullets. I looked around for more filler, any filler, the more balaclavas the better, and just as I was frantically looking for those extra images, our terrorist talent disappeared into the woods and we were left with Patrick.

'Well, how was that?' he asked.

Before we could answer, he shook our hands and he, too, was gone. We were shell-shocked. We did appreciate the access, but didn't they know we had fourteen minutes to fill? We'd come a bloody long way for this and might even have ended up sharing a cell with them. But these terrorists, freedom fighters, patriots, republicans, whatever they were, had done their bit. What do they care or know about television?

What I knew was, we still needed more pictures, so on the way back to the cars, with Mike and Andrea still shaking their heads at the abrupt finish, I filmed everything I could think of, in *and* out of focus. Close-ups of feet, the farmhouse we were told we couldn't shoot, car tyres, tyre tracks and shadows. Maybe now we had enough.

It was far too risky to have the story lying around, so as soon as we got back to Dublin, Mike hopped on a plane to Amsterdam and hid the footage in the ceiling of a friend's house. If we were arrested under the *British Terrorist Act*, we could be held for up to two weeks with no charges laid, but they'd never find any evidence of what we had done.

Safely ensconced in the Shelbourne Hotel, Andrea, Micky and I drank, and laughed, and drank some more, still amazed at the lengths we went to for a story.

When Mike got back from Holland, we did re-enactments of the whole lead-up to the rendezvous in Northern Ireland. Andrea on buses, in the coffee shop, meeting 'John', the *Irish Times* and the pub scene, Capman and car trips. It turned out to be a classic *60 Minutes* story.

9

Frequent Flying

At *60 Minutes* we spent half our lives in planes, from 747s to single-engine jobs to lear jets. On an eight-week trip we could easily do 30 flights, and even home in Australia we'd fly constantly from state to state. *60 Minutes* is based in Sydney but I was amazed at how few stories were actually shot there. If the story was out in the bush, we'd charter a small plane, usually an eight- or ten-seater with three or four seats removed to accommodate all the gear. In the early days we did a lot of single-engine flying, then we started carrying more and more gear, and got a little more plane savvy. We announced there'd be no more single-engine flying. Plane engines do pack up, we read about it often, so why take the risk? Seemed pretty dumb to go flying with one engine if there were planes with two.

Storms in any aircraft were not fun, but in a small twin engine, in complete darkness with lightning all around, it was brown pants territory, and if you'd also been drinking it was paper bag territory. But if you were an unflappable producer with no access to a paper bag, you did as one of my colleagues did. He'd only been with us for a month and was carrying with him the most beautiful Italian leather briefcase I'd ever seen, a present from his workmates at his previous job. A fierce storm had us bouncing all over the place and the producer's sweaty face suddenly turned green. He leant forward, unbuckled the shiny brass clasp of his expensive farewell gift, placed his head inside the briefcase, and deposited lunch and a great number of beers. He then casually closed the briefcase, locked the brass clasp, and said, 'Wow, that was close.' He later carried it regally off the plane as if it contained family heirlooms.

A four- or five-hour flight on a small plane was not uncommon, but a toilet on one of those planes is really uncommon. So uncommon I've never seen one. But we were young and so were our prostates and bladders, so who needs a toilet? Well, Ron Sinclair, our larger than life producer, did.

Ron had been on light aircraft before so you'd think he would've learned, but when he arrived with a slab of beer for our five-hour flight over Western Australia, expecting to be thanked, he was nonplussed when we told him it wasn't such a great idea. We reminded him of the lack of facilities on our very small and very cramped eight-seater aircraft. Not deterred in the least, he reckoned we would be begging him for a beer after a few hours and he just might not be willing to share with blokes who are so boring. Two hours into the flight he'd forgotten his threat and offered beers all round. We all said no thanks.

'Suit yourself,' he said, as he snapped open his first can.

Snap went can number two, and Ronnie was away, the jokes coming thick and fast. He loved his own jokes, and his laugh was really infectious. After cans three and four, hoping not to sound too patronising, I reminded him of the distance we still had to travel and maybe he should take it a bit easy. He reminded me that he was a big man and I presumed he was insinuating that with that comes a big bladder. Sitting at the back of the plane with his slab, Ronnie was having the time of his life, when suddenly he announced he had to have a piss. We replied that he had been warned, there was still two hours to go, we were flying at 20,000 feet, and there wasn't an airport within a million miles.

'I know, but I'm busting, I really have to go.' It was suggested he piss back into the cans.

'Good idea,' he said, and proceeded to deftly empty his bladder.

Minutes later we heard that classic Ronnie chuckle.

'What's going on, Ronnie?' I asked.

'Hey, how come when you drink six cans, you can piss eight?' he said.

We laughed as we pondered his question but not before warning Ronnie that if he spilt one drop of the contents of his cans, he was a dead man.

He spent the rest of the flight delicately holding and balancing those cans as if he was tending to six tiny newborns, and so delicate was he that his babies weren't even aroused by the not-so-smooth landing. That's dedication.

When that plane finally stopped, Ronnie was out of there in a flash, he couldn't wait to rid himself of those six cans, plus the other two.

•

'If you pull the orange cord first, you will certainly lose your testicles. So remember, it's the *green* cord first, because you certainly don't want to make that mistake, though the chances of you actually surviving the 20,000 feet free fall before you can pull any cord are practically zero, so good luck tomorrow.'

After a few blokey pats on the back, our instructor was gone, and if colour blindness set in, so were my testicles.

Back at the hotel pool, Ray Martin and I practised our freefall as we rolled into the water. Was it the green or orange cord to yank first? And if we jumped out of the plane at 50,000 feet, how would we know when we'd dropped to 20,000? What if we pulled the cord at 19,000 or 21,000? And which tag was the one that actually released the chute?

We had been overloaded with information. Orange, green, main chute, emergency chute, oxygen, body position. Way too much to absorb in just one day. Bugger it, we thought, we'd rather die than be castrated. Besides, it could be fun to plummet 50,000 feet. How many people have a chance at that?

So we went back to our beers and tried not to worry about our B-52 flight at dawn the next day. Which wasn't easy. Because it wasn't just a flight, it was nine hours from Guam in the Western Pacific to Queensland. And back.

Nine hours is plenty of time for something to go wrong in a plane that took its first flight in 1952. We might not be in that exact plane, but the last of those monsters was produced in 1962, so I wanted to be in one of the twenty-year-old newer ones.

Before arriving in Guam, Ray and I had to complete a string of physical tests—lung capacity, elevated heart rate, stress, etc.—the same tests that airforce pilots must complete every year to make sure they still have the 'right stuff'. Naturally, Ray and I passed with flying colours. Obviously, we had the right stuff, so next all we had to do was sit inside an airforce recompression chamber then answer a few basic questions to gauge what effects oxygen deprivation would have on us. How hard could that be?

Six pilots going for their annual test joined Ray and me inside a strange cylindrical-shaped room that looked like a submarine. I sat with three pilots on a bench on one side and on a bench directly opposite us were Ray and the other three pilots. Hovering above us were all sorts of wires and cables, and dangling from them were oxygen masks. We were each given a pen and a set of questions—name, age, address, etc., plus some simple mathematical problems. We would be taken to the equivalent of 60,000 feet and told to remove our oxygen masks, then we had to write down the answers to the questions.

Our instructor explained that we were about to experience hypoxia, or lack of oxygen, and that the tell-tale signs will be bluish or purple-coloured fingernails, maybe a sense of panic, but often a sense of euphoria.

'If, at any time you feel giddy, short of breath or notice your nails have changed colour, apply your oxygen mask immediately,' he said. 'Because if the euphoria kicks in when you're flying in a plane, you will die. So be well aware of the signs. Good luck.'

Ray's team, the A team, went first, which suited me fine. They hit 60,000 feet and were told to remove their masks. They all looked full of the right stuff as they confidently stared at us, still with our masks on, then checked their nails and started writing the answers to the questions. But almost immediately one of the pilots—clearly the wrong stuff—grabbed his mask and sucked in the oxygen. Ray was holding up well, regularly checking his nails, then going back to his maths. Then *whack*. Another pilot clamped a mask on his face. Ray, still obviously awash with the right stuff, continued with his maths, turned the page and checked his nails. Suddenly, with an odd look on his face, he slapped on his mask, and I heard rapid breathing. A few seconds later the whole of the A team were re-oxygenated. *A pretty good effort*, I thought.

So then it was the B team's turn, and off came our masks. I was feeling good, I had no sense of panic and my nails were fine. I got straight to the written work. *Name. Age. Address. Employer. How easy is this? Maybe I should be doing it in copperplate.* Another quick check of the nails and I turned to the maths just as a Mr Wrong Stuff next to me wimped out. *How on earth did these guys make it to be pilots?*

The maths was a breeze, first Pythagoras then a quick check of my beautiful nails and onto Fermat's theorem followed by all the prime numbers. Just as the next wimp caved in, I heard through my headphones, 'Number four. Put on your oxygen!' The irritating little man in my head got my best 'not till I've completed this pi to a thousand places' stare. But again I heard, 'Number four, put on your oxygen mask *now*!'

And just as I was thinking how beautiful my nails were, a monster hand swept out of nowhere, whacked the oxygen mask over my face and tightened it around my head. I was indignant: he didn't have to be so rough about it, and I hadn't even finished my maths. I looked across at Ray and he and the others were vigorously laughing. I glared at them.'They won't be laughing so much when they see me triumphantly hold up my proof backing up Stephen Hawking's assertion that black holes emit sub-atomic particles at a steady rate.'

I lifted up my writing pad to show those morons what I'd achieved in such a short time, knowing it would totally impress them.

What I saw on my pad was that some child had written my name, and *misspelt* it. I had never lived at that address with no number and, what's more, 3 plus 3 did not equal 11, 2 multiplied by 4 was not 24, and 7 plus 7 plus 7 would never be zero. *What's going on?*

When we de-subbed, Ray told me that the moment I took off my oxygen mask, my eyes rolled back in my head, I stared and stared at my nails as if I had just had a million-dollar manicure and, while doing my trigonometry and my treatise on the deformation of space time, I kept looking at Ray with a euphoric look, as if I'd just witnessed the birth of my first-born.

So I didn't have the right stuff after all. That test and my humiliation obviously meant nothing; I was allowed to fly anyway and my trip was still a goer. I just hoped the airforce wasn't as lenient on the pilot of our B-52 Stratofortress. I decided to keep a close watch on his fingernails.

•

The morning of the flight I was a bit nervous. But all my concerns about fingernails, parachutes and which cord to pull were forgotten as soon as I cast my eyes and camera over the beast. It was gigantic—48.5 metres long, with eight huge engines, all of which looked far too heavy for the 56.5-metre wingspan. The immense weight of those eight engines caused the wings to droop, creating an injured bird look.

I stared at nothing but the plane as we walked towards it, not because I was mesmerised by the size but because any head movement might have snapped my neck. I was wearing an airforce helmet—that's not unlike wearing two bricks on your head. I was also wearing a parachute that not only made me look like Quasimodo, but made me feel like I was bearing his whole belltower. Plus, I was carrying the camera *and* sound gear. There was no room for soundman Micky. A B-52 can only carry five crew members and 25 tonnes of bombs. Yet somehow they found room for Ray and me.

We squeezed bricks, belltowers, camera, sound gear and ourselves into our designated spot up front, just behind the very small cockpit for five. Behind us was a huge chasm the length of the plane, crying out to be filled with bombs so it could open its wide jaws and spew out its cargo of death.

We rumbled down the runway, the noise was unbearable, and the lift-off felt like a real struggle, yet we were cargo-free. I wondered how the hell these things made it off the ground when they're chockers with bombs.

During the 'American War', the Vietnamese people witnessed on a daily basis hundreds of these take-offs, every plane filled to capacity with what was thought to be maximum killing power . . . until 'Operation Rolling Thunder' was conceived. Then some genius warmonger came up with the idea and means of increasing the bomb capacity, making it possible to squeeze eighty-four 500-pound conventional bombs in the plane *plus* twenty-four 750-pound bombs on each of the underwing pylons.

In December 1972, in 'Operation Linebacker II', otherwise known as 'The Christmas Bombings', over twelve days, the B-52 killing machines dropped 15,237 tonnes of bombs on Hanoi and Haiphong, killing 1600 civilians. All I could think was how terrifying it must have been to look up and see those bombs in confetti-like numbers raining down. The B-52 flying at 60,000 feet couldn't be seen or heard. So the first sign the Vietnamese civilians had of the horror was the sudden sight of bombs falling from nowhere.

When we hit cruising altitude I grabbed the camera and tried to stand up. Impossible. I kept falling backwards, struggling like an upturned turtle to get on my feet. The weight of my parachute was the problem, but then I thought, since I'd decided to die rather than be castrated, why was I bothering to wear it at all? Part of me said I should jettison it completely, and the rest of me saw no reason to disagree. So off it went. I felt practically weightless. And if I did need to deplane at 60,000 feet, my hypoxia experience taught me that I would die with a smile on my face. And beautifully coloured nails.

It was time to work. I slid myself as far into the cockpit as possible to get the obligatory shots of flashing cockpit lights, dials, pilots' eyes and hands, parachutes and masks. Not a hell of a lot more I could do.

Ray decided it was time for a piece to camera, but I could barely see him. There was not nearly enough light. I got him to lean right up against a small window so I could at least see some of his face. He certainly looked the part with the airforce helmet on his head and parachute on his back, but whether the camera would see any of it was another thing.

Earlier, he had told me he was going to mention the altitude, bomb capacity, and whether or not these monsters regularly carried nuclear weapons, the contentious point for Australia. At that time, the Americans wanted to use Darwin as a refuelling stop.

When he started talking, I could see his lips moving but couldn't hear a thing, nor could the Nagra tape recorder. Playing back the sound all I got was a slow, deep rumble, nothing more. The bulbous hand-held microphone was overwhelmed by the monotonous drone of the plane.

After a few more attempts—with Ray holding the mic so close to his teeth he looked like he was devouring a giant ice cream—it was in the can. We then settled down and contemplated the meaning of life . . . *and* death. Plenty of time for it. Another eight hours, in fact.

Time goes so slowly at 60,000 feet. I'd like to say it was because of the thinner air outside pulsating with space time continuum particles defined by quantum chromo-dynamic theory—but unfortunately it was because I was so fucking bored. Just as I was thinking I might as well sleep, the pilot told us we had to refuel. *You beauty, land. A chance to stretch my legs and maybe score a strong double espresso.* Wrong.

We did refuel, but at 30,000 feet. The pilot invited me right up to the pointy end to get some shots. Still without my parachute and helmet, I could just squeeze into my designated spot.

A fuel tanker plane overtook us on the right side, flew hundreds of metres ahead then *backed up*. Of course, it's all to do with the different speeds of the two planes, but the illusion was dramatic, as if he was backing into a parking spot immediately in front of us.

These planes can fly for 13,600 kilometres without refuelling. The first ever mid-air refuel was done between two biplanes in 1923, with a hose and a hand-held fuel tank. Shame I wasn't shooting that one, they might have been able to hand over a double espresso.

This time a giant telescopic boom appeared from the back of the tanker plane and headed towards us. I hoped it wouldn't miss its intended target, penetrate the cockpit and do a Palomares incident on us. In January 1966 a B-52 collided with a tanker right above the fishing village of Palomares, Spain. If the planes get too close, it's the job of the boom operator to call, 'Break away, break away, break away!' but for some reason that day it wasn't called. The tanker was totally destroyed when the fuel ignited, and all onboard were killed. The B-52 broke apart, killing three of the seven crew members.

In case today's boom operator wasn't paying attention, I was all ready to scream, 'Break away, break away!' but I soon realised, having left my audio connection back with my helmet and parachute, no one would hear me. Then I figured if I saw the others rocketing out through the top of the plane still in their seats, it'd be a pretty good hint something had gone wrong. So I went to work shooting the refuelling.

It was surreal. The boom, looking like a giant phallus wavering all over the place, was aiming for a small opening just above us, but finding penetration extremely difficult due to the turbulence created by the proximity of both planes. That wretched turbulence created all sorts of performance anxiety. Palomares made a return thought, then, *bang!* He was in. And when all valves appeared to be closed or locked or whatever valves do, we received our much-needed injection of new life at 1000 gallons per minute.

We had been ordered to fly from Guam to Queensland and back. I thought we would see the whole state from 60,000 feet, but suddenly treetops were coming towards us at 800 kilometres per hour as we'd dropped down to 30 metres. Buggered if I knew why, but what a buzz. Maybe the pilot was as bored as we were and wanted some excitement, but somehow being that close to the ground made our giant airship feel like the *Titanic*. The shots of the trees coming at us were amazing. I hoped we wouldn't run into the helicopter carrying the freelance camera-man who was hopefully scoring equally amazing shots of the plane as we skimmed the trees. We needed those exterior shots.

Later, I thought, *How lucky was he?* His shoot was over in half an hour and he'd be on his way back to a bar in Queensland. I still had five more hours inside the beast.

And on we droned through the hours and finally made it back to Guam, where Ray and I were unable to lift our heads from excessive brick-wearing.

Then we got the news. The freelance cameraman's helicopter had crashed, and the chopper was in pieces. Luckily, he and his pilot survived. Thankfully so had his footage.

•

We all like to 'deplane' (as they say in the US) as fast as possible, especially after a long twelve- or fifteen-hour flight. Even the comfort of a business class seat on a jumbo has lost its allure by then. I once deplaned from a 747 in Tel Aviv almost as fast as I did from my raging inferno at Sydney airport. Mind you, the decision wasn't mine. Minutes after landing in the Israeli capital, our plane came to an abrupt halt in the middle of nowhere, miles from the terminal. I looked out the window and saw six heavily armed soldiers jumping out of jeeps. A large van pulled up alongside them. I couldn't see through the van's darkened windows but somehow I knew this was not a regular catering truck. I was sitting beside Ray Martin, and said to him, 'It's a pity the camera's in the hold. There could be some action on this plane very soon.'

From the comfort of my business class seat I looked over the heads of the mob in front and saw that all six soldiers had boarded our plane and were heading towards us with machine guns at the ready. And they were on a mission. These boys looked mean, and they knew exactly where they were going. I started to feel really sorry for some poor guy back in economy who was about to be dragged off the plane. Whatever he'd done, he was in real trouble.

As they got closer I whispered to Ray, 'Check out these blokes, no wonder Entebbe was a piece of piss for them.' When they were two seats away, they slowed and began staring carefully at all the passengers in our vicinity. I realised they weren't looking for some poor guy in economy, they were after some rich guy in our midst. Everybody stared, terrified of the machine gun carriers and watching where they would end up. And where they ended up was right at my row, glaring straight at me. One of them leant across Ray, pointed menacingly at me and said, 'You! Come with me!' His attitude was hostile but he was also big noting for the crowd.

I was dumbfounded and shit-scared as I climbed over Ray and stood in the aisle. I was too shocked to speak, I couldn't think of a thing to say. Not a word was spoken by anyone as I was marched from the plane and shoved into the van I'd seen from the window.

Inside the darkened van, I was surprised to see a silhouette of someone sitting behind a desk. I was told to take a seat. A lamp was aiming directly at me so I couldn't see the other person.

'Who are you, and what are you doing here?' said the voice behind the lamp. I told him my name and that I was a cameraman with an Australian television show called *60 Minutes* and I was here to do a story.

'What's the story?'

Fucked if I know! I really wanted to say, but instead I babbled on about the war with Lebanon, and how tough life was for the Israelis, and anything else I could think of that might placate him.

'Show me your passport and press pass.'

I took them out of my bag and handed them over.

'Where's the script?' he said.

He obviously didn't know anything about television. I explained that the script hadn't been written yet, but if it had, it wouldn't be with me as I'm the cameraman, the script is written by the reporter. But my answer wasn't good enough, and he started demanding to see the script. I repeated my explanation.

'You are not leaving until we see the script,' he said.

Well, then we're all going to be here for a bloody long time, I thought, but remained silent. I had no idea how I would get out of this.

The situation became perplexing when my interrogator changed the subject and asked how long I planned on staying, who my parents were, where I was born, and who I knew in Israel . . .

Surely not! It can't be as simple as that! But it started to make sense . . . I knew I should have shaved off my moustache before I left home, these idiots thought I looked like a Palestinian.

It was a stalemate. I didn't have a script, and he wasn't letting me go. I wondered if my colleagues felt any twinges of concern as to my wellbeing or whether they were already in some bar telling each other they'd never have guessed I was a terrorist.

In fact, they were concerned, but they were newsmen, after all, and knew this would be great publicity, so they'd made a quick phone call to inform the Channel 9 office of my arrest. The mob in the office then rang other journo mates and away it ran, straight to AAP Reuters, where my brother worked as a journalist. When he saw the story on the wire, he rang my mother, who immediately contacted *60 Minutes*. At the same time, my wife Suzie heard it on the news and she rang the office, too. But the bosses at Channel 9 had nothing to tell them because they knew nothing about the situation. My colleagues in Tel Aviv also had no idea what was happening. And, as it turned out, nor did the soldiers detaining me.

Suddenly someone came into the van. My interrogator stood up and in the half-dark they had a conversation in a language I didn't understand. But it sounded scary. I thought, *This is it, I'm a dead man.* Then my interrogator switched off his light and told me I was free to go. After four hours, no script, and more importantly no explanation or apology, I was driven to the terminal and set loose. It was as if they'd suddenly decided to ignore the problem, if there had ever been one. Or maybe it was just a terrible mistake. Which it was.

I went to Israel at least a dozen times after that, and every time we deplaned I was pulled aside and questioned. Never any of the other crew, which I angrily pointed out to the immigration officials, who always replied that, 'It's just random.' Then when I asked if it was because I had a moustache, they just laughed. 'Of course not,' they'd say. 'It's just random.' And they expected me to believe that?

•

Three in the morning and I was sleeping like a baby when the phone rang. Fumbling in the dark to answer it, I groaned, 'Hello.'

'Mate, can you hang-glide?'

I recognised the voice of John Little, one of our producers, and this made me shitty.

'No, I can't, JL. I'm in London and it's fucking three in the morning.'

'Well, you better learn. You're off to Africa next month to do a story on a bloke who trains and flies with eagles. It has to be you. The other three blokes are all too big. See you when you're back in Oz.'

What the hell was that all about? I lay there wondering if it had really happened or if it was a Drambuie-induced dream. Hang-gliding! It was something I'd never planned on doing in my entire life. Something I thought was extremely stupid, dangerous and about as natural as fairy floss.

A week later I was back home and the bosses told me they thought a great sequence for the story would be me in a hang-glider getting shots of African Eagle Man flying alongside his tame eagles in *his* hang-glider. I pointed out to them that Eagle Man had been doing this for many years and that I would not only be hang-gliding but filming at the same time.

'Yeah, that's right,' I was told. 'And you're booked in for your first lesson tomorrow.' I realised they weren't going to budge. And they were so excited at the prospect of the shots, I couldn't argue.

The next day John and I headed off to Stanwell Park just south of Sydney, supposedly the top spot for hang-gliding. The gliding school was right at the top of a bloody great windy cliff with a dramatic fall to the ocean, and gracefully soaring above us were at least a dozen hang-gliders. The air traffic alone was enough to scare me. I'd brought along a small video camera to see just how difficult it would be to shoot. With my main camera weighing nine kilos I wasn't going to risk it, or my arms.

The instructor told us they were running very late and because there were many people ahead of us in the queue, we probably wouldn't get a run till at least 4.30 p.m. I'd never realised risking death by jumping off a cliff was so popular. It was now noon and I was starving. I'd decided to forgo breakfast, thinking it might not be wise to jump off a cliff on a full stomach.

With so much time on our hands, John and I headed up to the restaurant where I had a double-beef burger with the lot, a caramel malted milkshake and a rock cake not as soft and fluffy as Uluru but about the same size. As I wiped the last few pebbles from my mouth, I mentioned to John that I might have eaten too much, so a siesta was definitely on the agenda. We headed outside to find a nice shady spot, and just as I lay down the boss of the hang-gliding school came running up.

'Quick, you blokes are lucky, there's been a cancellation so you can go now,' he said.

A feeble attempt to offer my spot at the head of the queue to someone more deserving fell on deaf ears. As I waddled past those stupid polite people with their stupid empty stomachs, I looked up and saw three tandem gliders soaring effortlessly above us. And the queue of people with awe in their eyes followed their every move. I couldn't help but think that pretty soon they could have a little more than awe in their eyes.

I signed my life away and was handed a helmet. *A helmet! If I plummet a thousand feet onto rocks, that'll be a great help.*

In no time at all, I had all sorts of harnesses around almost every piece of my anatomy and a condom-like apparatus plastered to my back, making the pilot and me look like we'd just emerged from our pupal stage. My legs, however, were left free so I could run full bore to the cliff edge and leap. Not something you do every day. My heart was pounding and so were the cow, the rock and the milkshake in my gut.

Clinging desperately to the front strut with one hand and the camera with the other, I ran as fast as possible straight to the edge of certain death. Suddenly my legs were running in thin air and, amazingly, the lift-off was as smooth as silk. It was a magnificent feeling. We wriggled into our condom to relieve the pressure of gravity from our legs and sailed into the wind.

But gravity isn't easily conned. Whenever I tried to lift my eye to the camera, good old gravity had other ideas and forced my face earthward, aided by the heavy helmet on my head. Not to mention the swirling mass in my stomach that was my lunch. It was a nightmare. My neck muscles were killing me. Forget shooting pictures, just looking ahead was impossible. The only place to look was straight down.

Suddenly we made a sweeping turn to the left. The horizon, and my lunch, turned right. I knew immediately that I was about to throw up. *Should I tell my pilot, or just let the people below be the first to know?* This was going to be extremely embarrassing and so, like a three-year-old, I closed my eyes so that the pilot wouldn't know I was there.

The closed eyes actually did the trick. With the horizon no longer moving perpendicular to my lunch, my stomach began to calm down. I kept my eyes closed for the rest of the flight but kept telling the pilot how magnificent the view was. It was the least I could do.

We eventually had to succumb to gravity and land. Which we did, with amazing finesse. The glider headed straight for the ground at a speed I figured was way too fast, but at the last second, with our feet inches from the ground, the pilot aimed the glider back towards the sky, we ran a few steps along the ground, and came to a gentle stop. It was a work of art.

I was wondering how I would tell John and the bosses in the office about my dislike, nay, hatred, of hang-gliding. Somehow I *had* to get out of this assignment. But there was no need. I told John it might be a little difficult to shoot, but the next day before I needed to fully confess, the story was mercifully cancelled. I never found out why. But I did let them know of my huge disappointment.

•

The closest thing to feeling like you can actually fly is flying in a Robinson R22 helicopter. If you're not superman, it doesn't get any better than an R22. It's much more fun than a hang-glider, even before lunch. The R22 can go wherever, whenever, it wants. It has glass or perspex all around so it gives you the feeling of being inside a bubble. With all that clear vision in front and above and the doors on both sides retracted, it's the perfect flying machine to shoot from, with a rifle or a camera. Filming a cattle muster from one of these little beauties is amazingly exhilarating. The angles some of the hot-shot young pilots put the chopper into, without plummeting to the ground, says a lot for them and the machine.

Best of all is flying in the Kimberley, heading for beautiful waterfalls through deep, narrow gorges, with steep rock walls zooming past, inches from the chopper blades. Who needs to be superman? I'm doing what he does. And I'm sitting down. Flying doesn't get any better.

In my 30 years as a cameraman, I spent a lot of time in choppers, from snow-covered polar bear territory in the North of Canada through tropical hail storms at night in the New Guinea highlands, to oil rigs all over the world, and I was never scared. I never gave it a thought. But now, thanks to 'Human Resources', I shit myself when I'm anywhere near a helicopter.

Some time in the early 2000s, the HR department in their wisdom decided it was now compulsory for film crews to do a 'helicopter crash landing in water' course. Without it, there would be no more chopper flying. So we all headed off to the local pool for training. It was the first time I was scared inside a helicopter, and it wasn't even a real one.

For an hour we sat and watched videos of helicopter crashes, and there were some doozies. Dramatic shots of rotor blades slamming into the dirt or water while the rest of the helicopter spiralled like a tornado. There were many images of choppers plummeting to earth then exploding into massive fireballs, and in the majority of those cases the passengers were film crews. I knew a few blokes who had survived crashes and some who hadn't, but as usual you just think it will never happen to you. After an hour's worth of crashes, however, I began to think that maybe my time was up and it was definitely going to happen to me. I had no idea that helicopters plunged out of the sky so often.

Our brains overflowing with horrific crash scenes, we moved to the pool, and smack-bang in the middle, floating neatly on the surface, was a mock helicopter. Trying hard to look like the real thing, it boasted two front seats with a joystick between them and room for three people in the back. There was netting around the frame of the chopper with an opening on the right side where a door might be.

Four of us climbed in and took our seats. Sitting waist deep in water, we were told we would be tipped over and we were to find our way out. *Can't be that hard*, I thought, *I know where the door is, this should be fun*.

In the pool were three beefy blokes who chatted and laughed with us while they held on to the frame of our chopper. Then suddenly without warning they tipped us backwards, and down we went. Being upside-down was a bit disconcerting for a millisecond, but with my eyes open I quickly undid the seatbelt and followed a couple of other bodies swimming through the door and up to the surface. No probs.

Next go, we all swapped positions and we now had to jettison our headphones as well as the seatbelt. This time we were tipped sideways, an odd sensation but, with eyes open, easy peasy.

For the third sinking, the cameramen were each handed a 5-litre plastic bottle half filled with water, which we had to place on our shoulder as if it was our camera. Now there was a bit more to think about—put the camera down (if it comes to the real thing, I won't be putting the camera down, I'll be hurling it as far away from my head as possible), take off the headphones, undo the seatbelt. Before our third go, I rehearsed ripping off seatbelt and headphones as speedily as possible so I could be underwater for as little time as I could manage.

This time we were tipped forward. And I was gone. Totally disorientated. In my confusion the headphones and the camera got tangled up and I forgot the seatbelt, but when my head cleared a bit I finally saw I was upside-down, flung off the seatbelt and headed for the door. That was a bit scary, but I'm a good swimmer and with my clear underwater vision I surfaced knowing full well that if ever I crash over water, it'd be a piece of cake.

The next crash was with camera, headphones, seatbelt and *blacked out* goggles. Now I was frightened. The only thing that had got me out before was my ability to see where the door was. Now I was as blind as a bat, sitting in the back seat, and thinking, *Please, please, don't tip us forward.*

Suddenly I felt my face slam into the water. *No, no, no, not forward, I hate that.* Before I had time to take a breath, I was underwater. I'd done a complete somersault—and I had no idea where I was or where the door was. I was upside-down in complete blackness with water running into my nose and ears. I was so confused I forgot everything and tried to swim to where the door had been half a second ago, but the seatbelt and headphones kept me firmly in place. Fumbling around I somehow managed to undo them both, and swam for the door, but hit the netting. Now I started to panic. As I clawed my way round the netting searching for the open doorway, one of my fellow travellers grabbed my collar, pulled me out of the way and swam right over me to the door. *Bastard. Okay, it's every man for himself. I'm in a fucking council swimming pool and I'm going to die.*

I don't know why I didn't just rip off the goggles, swim to the surface and tell all the smarty-pants instructors where they could stick their helicopters. Instead, with aching lungs I kept searching blindly for the door. After what seemed like a hundred metres of netting, I came to an opening and swam for my life. I hit the surface gasping for breath.

One of the instructors was staring down at me. 'How did you do that? he said. 'You didn't come out through the door.'

Amazing what panic can do. I'd ripped the netting apart and created my own door. Obviously, it was never going to work in the real thing, but after that experience I didn't care. I decided I was never going in the real thing again.

And guess what? This 'safety exercise' now has to be completed every two years. Thanks, HR—I used to love helicopters.

•

Aerial shots are tougher with video than with a compact Arri film camera. The video camera is bigger and much heavier, plus it has extra stuff, like microphone, windsock and a large lens hood attached to it. These things are not good for aerial filming. Of course, I should have removed them, but . . . what can I say? A little bit of wind can lift a windsock and lens hood as deftly as a Gypsy pickpocket—I learned that the hard way.

I was filming in an antiquated Soviet army helicopter over Azerbaijan, no harness, of course, and leaning out just that little bit too far. *Whoosh,* my brand new lens hood took off like it had forgotten something back at base. I sat silently, waiting for the crunch and the plummet to earth, all the while thinking I could think of nicer places to die than Azerbaijan. Paris, for example. I took some solace in the fact that the cause of the accident would most likely be attributed to the Soviet Union's sloppy aircraft maintenance. Hopefully the gaffer tape holding bits of the chopper together would be a dead giveaway and no one would notice the shredded bits of lens hood in the rear rotor. But it must have somehow slipped through the rotor, and we made it back to base in one piece.

Years later I was in a small helicopter with no door flying over the New Guinea highlands. This time I had very smartly removed the lens hood, but forgot the windsock. Once again I leant an inch too far beyond the side of the chopper and straight towards the rear rotor the windsock went. Clean as a whistle. Death was inevitable if it hit that rear rotor. How it didn't, I will never know. Just like the pilot never knew how close to death I'd taken him. It stayed my little secret.

Throughout my career, the flying machines we found ourselves in came in all shapes and sizes, as did the film crews. And unfortunately, so did the pilots.

We were in the middle of the outback doing a story on the death of the rivers of Australia. The rivers were slowly dying, thanks to the destruction created by the noxious and obnoxious imported carp, a bottom-feeding fish species that had infiltrated our rivers, causing our native fish numbers to decline rapidly. It was a difficult story to shoot. You've seen one fish, you've seen them all. You've seen one riverbank, ditto. So I opened my big mouth and told Hamish Thomson, the producer, we needed helicopter shots to add a little pizzazz to our boring story. Two hours later he told me the pilot would meet me at 3 p.m.

'Oh, and by the way, he's not in a helicopter, he's in an ultra-lite.'

'How safe is it?' I asked, rhetorically.

'How the fuck would I know? You wanted aerials.'

Thanks to my big mouth, I wasn't in a great position to argue.

In a small town somewhere on the border of South Australia and New South Wales, we went into the pub to wait for the arrival of our pilot. I sat with my back to the door and was about to take a swig of my nerve-calming beer when I noticed that Hamish was suddenly smirking. Staring right over my shoulder while trying to conceal his glee, he said, 'I hope *he's* not your pilot.'

I glanced into the mirror over Hamish's shoulder, and for a moment I hoped desperately that it was one of those distorted mirrors at fun parks that make you feel like you're on acid. Then the acid trip closed in on us and I heard him say, 'Is one of you blokes Nick?'

In horror I turned to face him and immediately wondered, *How can this man fly?* His 150-kilo frame in reality looked way fatter and even more distorted than in the mirror, only reversed, which also meant his eye patch was now over his right eye.

An ultra-lite with an ultra-heavy one-eyed pilot. What have I gotten myself into?

Lucky for me, and him, and more importantly the go-kart with wings, I was half his weight. But it was still a squeeze as I strapped myself into the passenger seat.

It was a struggle for the ultra-lite to take off, hampered by the weight of one of its passengers or the intense outback heat. We managed to just skim the top of the trees with the tiny engine gasping desperately for air, though all that huffing and puffing might well have been coming from you-know-who. I managed a few aerials out to the right. Any shots out the pilot's side looked like a solar eclipse. I love doing aerials, but after a few minutes I lied through my teeth and told him I had enough shots. Mind you, the beautiful shots were there for the taking, but I wasn't going to be the one that took them. I wasn't going to risk one more minute up there than I had to, though we still had the landing to go.

I'd seen footage of the Hindenburg trying to land. I held my breath as we descended. Miraculously, we landed, bouncing a few times, and we didn't burn to death. I told the pilot I thought the landing was perfect, thanked him for a wonderful flight and staggered towards Hamish who immediately asked me if I had enough shots. It was a big day for lying.

Years after my Cyclops adventure I had another brush with death in an ultra-lite. We were in Venezuela doing a story on giant anacondas, the ones that wrap their 60-plus kilos around you and crush you to death, their habitat being the amazingly beautiful wetlands that harbour an abundance of exotic wildlife. And the best way to show all that beauty? Aerials, of course!

Again Hamish was the producer and because in Venezuela helicopters are as rare as some of the wildlife, I had to go up in an ultra-lite. I just hoped I wasn't pushing my luck. But there was a positive side to this flight, the pilot had two eyes and weighed the same as me. Unfortunately, his ego and his not-so-secret desire to be a film director negated those positives.

Cecil B. D'ultra-lite started telling me how to balance the camera and which lens I should use. If only he would stick to the flying and leave the filmmaking to me. I asked him to take me up for a look without the camera to get a feel of it, but his constant yelling in my ear about how I should shoot, plus the noise of that shrieking engine so close to my head, gave me a piercing ringing in my ears.

On the next run with the camera, I made sure I wore a headset. No more engine drone, and no more Cecil B. But I couldn't get the camera close enough to my head to look through the viewfinder because of the great lumps on my ears, so I pulled off the headphones and . . . *whoosh,* straight behind me they went. I made a frantic grab for them as I realised what I'd done, and in doing so let go of the camera, which had slipped down between my knees. I jammed my knees together and held onto the camera with, I'd like to think, a vice-like grip. Immediately my legs began to cramp.

All this was happening as the headphones were flapping in the wind just above and behind my head, which was exactly where the rapidly spinning blades responsible for keeping us aloft happened to be. I fumbled for the camera with my left hand as my right hand tried to reach for the headphones that had somehow missed the killer blades and were now dangling below my seat thanks to gravity and a hell of a lot of luck. Cecil B. must have been aware of my agitation, but hopefully not the dangling headphones, which I gently pulled up by their lead. Somehow the $80,000 camera was still with us, but only just. It was now balancing precariously around my ankles. I had no idea how or why it was still with us. It had nothing to do with me. I had absolutely no control over my badly cramped legs.

Hoping that Cecil B. was too busy flying to be concerned, I slowly managed to gain control of the camera then nonchalantly raised it to my eye, desperately trying to make everything appear normal. The shots were useless because I was shaking like a leaf. The noise of the engine was excruciating and I marvelled at how I had cheated death yet again.

Fifteen years later I still have tinnitus from that engine, but it's a hell of a lot better than death.

10

Food, Glorious Food

Forget pictures. The race was on amongst the *60 Minutes* crews for the best food and food stories. Not for television but for bragging rights. Exotic food. Food deprivation. Food poisoning. Cheap food. And the biggy? The one that made you King. The most expensive. Including wine, of course.

Food played a great part in being on the road. It's not only a gut-filler, it's a time filler, and often there was a lot of time to fill. I've never held back from trying anything on offer, though sometimes my gut would be desperately looking for a place to hide, screaming no, no, no. But the palate was always willing.

I lied in that paragraph. There were a couple of sightings on menus I pretended not to see. Ox phallus (for six), and dog. It's not that I wouldn't have given it a go, it's just that I have a dog, and a phallus, and I love them both.

But there were the sheep's eyes in Saudi Arabia, duck foetus (still in the egg) in the Philippines, snake's blood (taken from a live snake) in Taiwan, and burnt starlings, also in Taiwan. Let me explain . . .

We were somewhere outside Riyadh and our Saudi minder bought us lunch. From inside their Arabic newspaper wrapping, the sheep's eyes were throwing me completely with their constant stare, a stare of 'I dare you'. I took on that sheep's dare plus the one from Ray Martin, grabbed an eye, flung it into my mouth then spat it out. It tasted like newspaper, and I hate newspaper. Of the four of us, only two gave it a go, if you can call a lick a go, but I can't help it if I don't like newsprint. Ray in his autobiography swears and declares he was the only one to actually eat one (he swallowed the lot) and that I declined the offer of that tasty Saudi speciality.

While writing his tome Ray would constantly ring me to check on facts, but the call was mostly to tell me that the facts had already been written. Whenever I disputed his version of events, which was every time he rang, he'd tell me, 'He who holds the pen owns the truth.'

The truth. I now own the truth and suspect he had a loose grip on his pen, and a tighter grip on something else, but he got out there into the publishing world first, and wrote that his reward for swallowing that eye is bragging rights.

Then there was the idyllic flower farm, in the middle of nowhere in Taiwan, and the board of the flower cooperative had put on dinner for us, the honoured guests. With ne'er a common language we signed our way through the evening. During one such riveting conversation, a huge plate of something that resembled nothing I'd ever seen before was put in front of us. On closer inspection the hundreds of whatever they were looked organic and at some stage must have lived. An even closer look into the huge black mass revealed small birds of some kind, complete with eyes, beaks and feet.

Ray pointed to my empty plate then back to our host. Our host, now embarrassed into feeling he had slackened off with his hosting duties, very kindly filled my plate. I quickly whispered to Ray, 'What do I do here?' Stupid question. He was as ill-informed on starling etiquette as I was, but with a 'better you than me' look, he told me not to embarrass our hosts and get on with it. Then he smiled.

Never one to embarrass my hosts, I grabbed one of our small feathered friends and shoved it into my mouth. There was a loud crunching sound, my teeth cracked the beak, rib cage and legs. Then a softer mellow sound as I then did my best to masticate the few tiny feathers that were still embedded. Just as I tried to swallow all of the above, our hosts leaned forward, picked up a starling each, and as one, like finalists in Olympic synchronised swimming, they deftly removed the tiny legs. Then, even more deftly, they removed the miniscule amount of flesh from the drumsticks and rib cage, and threw the rest away. Finally, they each held an atom of bird flesh, gently placed it into their mouths and swallowed. Obviously there was no need to waste energy by using good chewing teeth, the ones that were now very cleanly smiling at me. Still today I'm pulling small bits of feather and beak from my teeth. Thanks Mr Smart-arse Martin.

As for *balut*, a duckling foetus still in the shell, what can I say? After it was explained to me exactly what it was,

I figured, how hard could it be? After all, I love duck, and I love eggs. Piece of piss, really.

The first feeling of squeamishness came as my shaking hands clumsily removed some of the shell from the pointy end of my *balut* to reveal a little duckling looking like a baby taking a nap. With fluid running down my arm, I noticed my lunch had a beak, a few tiny feathers and large eyes, thankfully closed.

Suddenly my love of eggs and duck seemed to have deserted me. I was struggling. My duckling was covered in a freeway of blue veins, with a large area of yellow near its stomach, I presumed it was the yoke, though not being familiar with poultry reproduction I couldn't be sure. I was staring in disbelief when my Filipino host tipped his egg up and sucked out a mouthful of juice, which I was told was the amniotic fluid, and 'so tasty'. Luckily for me I had 'wasted' all my amniotic fluid. Shame. I was then given a freezing cold bottle of San Miguel beer, a pinch of salt, and the order to start eating my well-earned delicacy.

Slowly and extremely gently I bit into the little bugger and surprisingly it was much softer than I'd expected. I could feel the texture of minute feathers but it wasn't gagging material and the whole thing tasted like egg. I took a swig of beer after every mouthful to wash away the foul taste that never seemed to arrive. It wasn't such a bad taste at all. It was the look of this Philippine delicacy that was so off-putting. If it had been handed to me on a plate in a darkened room, I'd probably have asked for more.

•

The *60 Minutes* search for great food became all-consuming, and one fast-talking producer managed to get the okay for a story on, at that time, the best restaurant in the world, La Tour d'Argent (The Silver Tower) in Paris. Best restaurant must mean best food, so I couldn't wait. Overlooking Notre Dame, and the river Seine, the three Michelin Star restaurant had been serving up great meals since 1582. Henri IV often dined in and regularly requested takeaway. The restaurant proudly boasted that the fork had been invented in the establishment, and hanging proudly on one wall was their menu for Christmas Day 1870.

I've seen a few menus in my day but this was unforgettable. La Tour d'Argent had a reputation to uphold, so one small event like the siege of Paris in 1870 was not going to stop its great chefs from creating an extravagant Christmas feast for the aristocrats.

I don't know how the restaurant survived the 1830 and the 1848 revolutions, let alone the biggy of 1789. But when the Prussians arrived in Paris in 1870 there was already a severe food shortage from the killer winter, so the Prussians' hope was that the Parisians would be starved into surrender.

Aristocrats neither surrender, nor starve, they simply must eat, and after all, it was Christmas—so La Tour bought the zoo. Castor and Pollux, the only elephants in France, were delicately squeezed into the restaurant's pots, and were the opening taste sensation on that Christmas menu:

ELEPHANT SOUP followed by
CAMEL, ROASTED ENGLISH STYLE or
KANGAROO IN A FINE RED WINE or
CHOICE OF CAT SURROUNDED BY RATS, or
A TERRINE OF ANTELOPE.

We had one day to create and film our story, and it was nonstop madness. We had it all figured out. There would be sequences with Philippe the barman, the scores of chefs, discreet shots of diners, the cellarmaster in his cellar, plus a major interview with Monsieur Claude Terrail, the owner. And of course, the pièce de résistance on the menu—the duck. *Canard à la presse*, or *Caneton Tour d'Argent*, or *Canard au Sang*, the specialty of the house. Duck was first served about 1890, and every duck since has been given a number, and every well-to-do diner who orders the duck receives a card printed with their duck's number.

King Edward VII had duck number 328, King Alfonso XIII had 40,312, Emperor Hirohito had 53,211 and number 112,151 went to Franklin D. Roosevelt.

The duck is never decapitated, always strangled (of course), and when ordered, word travels rapidly through the restaurant and the other envious diners all stare, point and whisper, fascinated with the ritual that is the cooking and serving of one of the most famous dishes in history.

Our first shots were in the kitchen. It was loud and fast and wherever I stood I was in the way. I didn't get any screams but lots of dirty looks and sometimes a small nudge. Everyone was moving fast. Huge pots bubbled heartily over blue gas jets. Chefs everywhere. A chef each for entrées, soup, fish, desserts, sauces, and one just to decorate the plates.

And of course, the king pin, numero uno chef, Jacques Sénéchal, who slowly wandered around his domain, tasting everything by dipping a large spoon or hairy finger into the pots. And he was scary. I got the feeling it was not a good idea to piss him off.

Philippe the barman was the complete opposite. Friendly, polite and suave as he poured drinks for the lunchtime crowd. The drink of choice was champagne, and it flowed along with his charming personality that dominated the room. With a huge smile on his face he offered me champagne. 'Non, merci,' I replied, pointed to the camera and shook my head. He winked and said, 'Later.' That got the thumbs-up from me. Philippe was only too keen to perform again and again for the camera, greeting the diners, popping the champagne cork with great flair, pouring champagne and creating cocktails while I filmed it all. A great bloke.

Back in the kitchen and getting closer to serving lunch, things were really hectic. The orders came in thick and fast. I was still trying to keep out of everybody's way but not succeeding. The one bloke I did not want to upset was the terrifying Monsieur Sénéchal who was watching me like a hawk. Then he approached me and as he loomed I looked around, wondering what I'd done wrong. Did I sweat into the mousse? Did I accidentally elbow a delicate crêpe?

He stood an inch from me, staring me in the eye. 'You are working too 'ard,' he said. 'You must eat. I will get you some food.'

I thanked him and continued to make it look like I was working too hard. Then, suddenly in front of me was this amazing-looking, steaming hot, Tour d'Argent master-piece. The head chef handed me a knife and fork, and said, 'Bon appétit.'

I was lifting the first forkful to my grateful mouth, thinking how good this would be with one of Philippe's champers, when our producer came barging in, shouting,

'Quick! There's a woman in the dining room smoking, we must get a shot of that.' I grabbed the camera and from behind a pillar got discreet shots of this plebeian woman. *How on earth did she get in here?* Sacrilege.

With the fag shot well and truly covered, I headed back to the kitchen for my taste sensation and . . . it was nowhere to be found. I looked questioningly at my newfound caring chef friend.

'Your lunch is in zee rubbish,' he said. 'If you do not eat my food when eet eez 'ot, you do not eat my food!' More sacrilege.

Before I had time to feel ashamed, the word was out. A couple had ordered the duck, and had agreed to us filming it.

Chefs, and what looked like all the paraphernalia of a surgical ward, surrounded The Couple. They checked out their dead plucked duck and its number, gave their approval, then sat back for the experience of a lifetime. And it was on. Presses (Christofle, of course), crunching, blood, knives, blood, flames, more blood. It was a true work of art, three chefs, all at the table, and nobody getting in anybody's way, except me.

All the other diners were pretending not to look. Very difficult to do when you're fascinated, envious and desperately trying not to look like a tight-arse in the most expensive restaurant in the world. The tight-arses weren't the only ones in the room harbouring envy. I was ravenous. My envy increased in direct proportion to the number of ultra-tight shots I got of duck meat being shovelled into the mouths of Mr and Mrs We're So Rich We're Having the Duck.

Having polished off their *Canard à la presse*, The Couple with orgasmic and superior looks on their faces scanned the room hoping to extract some applause from the rest. But unfortunately the only noise they heard was my rumbling stomach. Watching them peruse the dessert menu, I was thinking, *If I have to do one more shot of you two eating, I might also have to hit you.*

Luckily for them I had enough eating shots. We now needed a sequence filmed in the world famous cellar. I dragged my rumbling stomach down to the bowels of the restaurant. Peering into semi-darkness, I could just make out acres of grog in a maze of rooms. This wasn't a wine cellar, it was a museum.

We were met by the cellarmaster whose name I didn't get. I hadn't heard a word since I set eyes on the nearly 400,000 bottles in the darkness. How on earth was I to film them? I was carrying four lights with me, which at a stretch might show me 400 bottles. To top it off, Ray had decided this was too good to be true, so he wanted to do a piece to camera. When I suggested to the cellarmaster that I might have to set up some lights, he was apoplectic. I, being a wine connoisseur myself, was well aware that it was never good for my bottle of claret to be left on the back seat of the car on a hot day, but come on, a few little lights?

It turned out that the cellar is kept at a constant 12 degrees Celsius to preserve the wines and brandies, worth tens of millions of francs. Each night after dinner, twelve lucky diners, mostly the famous or the rich, or both, are invited down to the cellar for a special tour to inspect and taste a couple of the unbelievably expensive cognacs and ports. That special cellar invitation is limited to a maximum of twelve, because the combined body heat of any more than that will elevate the room temperature to something like the back seat of my car, and could even make the Château Citran 1858 taste not unlike my cheapskate claret.

After much negotiating with the cellarmaster, and lying about the intensity of my lights, he reluctantly agreed to allow us to have them on for three minutes, and three minutes only.

I set up the lights, trying to illuminate as much of the cellar as possible, constantly changing their position, trying to get the museum look by highlighting dust and cracked labels. With the cellarmaster watching my every move, I grabbed a quick reading from my light meter then immediately turned off the lights.

Ray had finally figured out his piece to camera, and it was a doozy. Difficult for both of us. Ray planned to stroll down an aisle of grog, open a metal gate, move through to a large wooden table, walk around the table to a chair, then sit and deliver the punchline. We rehearsed three or four times with the lights off.

Happy with the words and the movement, I turned on the lights and as the lights went on, so did the pressure of having to be quick. Ray buckled. He kept blowing his lines, and each time he did we were told we had to leave the lights off for fifteen minutes to allow the room to cool. The more we laughed and knocked Ray about what an amateur he was, the worse he got.

Forty-five minutes later with the piece to camera in the can we packed up our red hot lights, said 'merci' to the cellarmaster, and got out of there before he found out the Château d'Yquem 1871 had gone off.

Now it was time to meet the boss. Monsieur Claude Terrail, the debonair, supercool owner of this establishment. Oozing French charm with a textbook French accent, he began the interview by telling us that during World War II, his father had said to him, 'Whatever happens, you must save the cellar of La Tour d'Argent.' Months later when Claude heard that the Germans had reached Paris, he went AWOL from his army barracks and raced back to his beloved restaurant. 'It was my duty,' he explained.

So, in the dead of night, Claude and a friend bricked up half the cellar, and when the enemy arrived to claim their booty, the crème de la crème was hidden from them and their philistine Germanic palates. And Claude went back to war.

Still, I suspect the Huns had a great time getting rid of what they found, and I was left thinking had I checked for a fake wall in the Packers' boardroom all those years ago, I might have spent a few years drinking some nice Penfolds Grange 55, or even a 52, instead of my regular flagon of red.

Monsieur Terrail was on a roll, telling of the history of his restaurant, the famous clients, and his nightly visits to La Tour. Every night without fail, he said, he chatted to every guest, and in no time he would have them worshipping him. The women all wanting to bed him, the men wanting to be him. But even though he speaks to every guest every night, sometimes he desists, as, 'If I see zee young man looking into zee young girl's eyes, saying I lerv you, I do not walk up and say, 'ow was zee fish?'

Claude and his charm were the icing on the cake of a great story. After my faux pas with Chef Sénéchal, I had no way of knowing 'ow zee fish was. So to make up for my missed opportunity I pinched an ashtray on my way out. A souvenir, a small reminder of how close I went to experiencing something enjoyed by kings, presidents and rock stars, all of whom have signed the restaurant's hall of fame wall.

Included on that wall at floor level, half an inch above the carpet, was an illegible signature captioned, 'Malcom Freser Australian Prime Minister'. The signatures above waist height, all spelt correctly, included Henry Kissinger and Mick Jagger.

•

That night, having spent an entire day in the world's best restaurant, but still starving, Ray and I went in search of fodder and fun. We started with oysters and beers, then oysters and gin, then oysters and wine, a few more oysters, some substantial food, and substantially more wine.

Then off to Montmartre to check out the nightlife and trace the steps of Monet, Picasso, Dali and of course Vincent. I'm sure there were times when their steps were equally as uneasy as ours, but in the state I was in I felt as if I was trapped in a Picasso or worse, a Dali, and as I looked up, I saw Starry Night clear as a bell. Vincent wasn't insane or on drugs, he'd just had five dozen oysters and copious amounts of alcohol. How good is Paris.

At four in the morning, we cabbed it back to the Left Bank to find more beer, but there was none to be found, so we decided we'd walk across Pont Neuf, the new bridge, built in 1607. Such a beautiful bridge, over such a beautiful river, and we were feeling beautiful. All this beauty naturally called for a swim. We took off all our clothes, left them in a neat pile and climbed up onto the bridge railing. I thought, *How much fun is this going to be!* We were both good swimmers so we planned to allow the current to leisurely carry us 50 metres or so, then, when the fun had worn off we'd swim back, retrieve our clothes and head back to our exorbitantly expensive hotel, refreshed and sober.

Standing side by side on the bridge, the decision as to who would jump first took a bit of time. I said, 'I'll go first, but you're really going to do this aren't you, Ray?'

'Yep, sure,' he said. I hesitated, starting to feel a bit apprehensive, but put it down to the oysters, when suddenly we were surrounded by gendarmes, screaming at us in French. If my French had been a little better, I would have asked if they had towels in their car but they didn't look the swimming type. In fact, they looked like cops the world over: mean and menacing and totally lacking in joie de vivre.

With French coming at us thick and fast, we thought we were being ordered off the bridge, but maybe they were just telling the naked guys to jump. We weren't sure, but as we desperately tried to stifle our laughter our clothes were flung at us, so we figured it was the former.

Not understanding a word that was being said made it all the more funny. We were hoping they were saying we were naughty little boys, we should not be so silly, and we should go home now, but we couldn't tell. Our French stretched to ordering a coffee and a ham and cheese omelette, and oysters of course, but the looks on the policemen's faces led us to believe this was probably not the time to place an order.

As we slowly dressed, I lamented the fact that I'd probably spend the rest of the night in the lock-up and therefore miss out on sleeping in the most amazingly soft bed in Paris, at the Hôtel de Crillon.

Then, just like that, quick as you can order a coffee and an omelette, the gendarmes softened, chuckled and waved us on.

Vincent's starry night was evaporating above our heads and dawn was breaking as we wandered along the Seine back to the hotel. As the morning light grew stronger, we saw just how murky and violent the current was. If we'd actually jumped, our blue, bloated bodies would have been dragged out of the English Channel before we were reported missing. I could see the headlines back in Australia: Ray Martin, Renowned Journalist, star of *60 Minutes*, found drowned off the coast of France . . . and some other body.

•

Six months later, Suzie and I, after travelling around Europe for five weeks, found ourselves in Paris. I knew that La Tour d'Argent was booked out for six months, but remembered the name of the PR heavy, so figured I had nothing to lose by giving him a call. After telling him who I was, I gently asked if there was any way we could get into the restaurant. This week.

'Oh, oui, oui. When would you like to come?'

I was taken aback by his affirmative response and politely said, 'Whenever you can get us in.'

'No, you must choose,' he said.

I whispered cautiously, 'Tomorrow night?'

'Certainly, no problem, and what was your name again?'

I gasped out my name.

'D'accord. See you then.' *Click*, and he was gone.

Suzie and I had spent the last five weeks in jeans and T-shirts, living in cheap pensiones, eating cheese and salami, and now we were about to eat in the most famous, most expensive restaurant in the world.

We tried to figure out a budget, but had absolutely no idea how much this one-off meal would cost. We guessed about three hundred dollars. Maybe four with wine. It was 1980, and I was earning $350 a week. It would be tough. But what the hell. We then had the not-so-minor problem of dress. We looked like hobos. *Quelle horreur.* So now our very expensive meal was to be even more so.

I bought a coat and tie. I hadn't worn either for at least five years. Suzie bought a dress and fur coat. We're not talking mink here, it was rabbit, or *lapin*, as one says when in Paris. But that was difficult to pronounce, so we just referred to it as 'The Mink'.

On the big night I was worried I didn't have enough money, but by now it was too late. We hailed a cab and, backed up by my impressive coat and tie, not to mention The Mink, I triumphantly said to the beret-wearing driver, 'La Tour d'Argent, please.'

He turned to me and stared. 'The restaurant?'

Where else? I thought, but politely gave him a 'Oui'.

'You! You are going to La Tour d'Argent?!'

Glancing at our sartorial elegance, I wondered how he could possibly have seen through us. *How did he pick we were frauds?* Trying desperately to look confident I answered in the affirmative, then asked if he had ever been to La Tour.

'Ooh, non, non, non, I have never been to La Tour d'Argent. My boss has never been to La Tour d'Argent. My boss's boss has never been to La Tour d'Argent.'

Outside the restaurant I hopped out of the cab, leant in to help Suzie and noticed that half her very expensive fur coat was now permanently attached to the velour seat, and the back of the coat now miraculously resembled leather. Amazing. I knew we were trying to save money, but what sort of rabbits do they breed in this country? Although I did think earlier in the night that the orange sheen coming from the fur was not quite organic. Struggling to hold back our laughter, we paid the driver, took one last look at the fur-covered seat, then raced into the restaurant before the driver could abuse us for smuggling vermin into his vehicle.

The meeter-and-greeter on the ground floor, a tall, elegantly dressed woman, gave us a big smile, welcomed us like we really were about to dine in her fine establishment and asked for my name.

'Lee,' I said, then watched her scan down the list of names, across to the next page, over to the next, then back two or three pages, her brow becoming more and more furrowed. I began to panic.

'Your name doesn't seem to be here,' she said. 'When did you book?'

'Yesterday,' I replied.

'Oh, non, non, non! La Tour is booked up *six months* in advance. You do not just ring up and arrive *tomorrow*,' she scolded.

'But I spoke to Monsieur Le Compte,' I said.

At the mention of my PR heavy, she was all elegance again. Two minutes later, it was sorted. Monsieur Le Compte had booked us under 'Mr & Mrs Nicholas'. Madame was all apologies, and we were in.

Trying desperately to reassure myself about the money, I told Suzie that Philippe the barman would look after us. I had filmed so much with him we were practically best friends. As we took our seats, Philippe approached and was met with my biggest sycophantic smile. 'Bonsoir Philippe, how are you?'

'Bonsoir monsieur, would you like a drink?' he replied with the appropriate amount of diplomacy, and nothing more. This was not working out as I'd hoped.

'Oui, merci,' I said less confidently. 'Two champagnes, please.'

Philippe smiled politely, turned, headed for the bar, then stopped dead in his tracks. He slapped his hand against his forehead, swung his body back in our direction, and shouted 'Ooh la la!' before racing back towards us then kissing me on both cheeks. Now we were *really* in.

After two champagnes and plenty of petit talk with Philippe, we were taken to the best table in the house, overlooking the Seine and Notre Dame. This choice spot is kept for the celebrity of the night, so you can bet they would whack up the price. After all, what's an extra few hundred bucks to a Rolling Stone, or even a prime minister, to sit overlooking the best view in Paris. Though of course they wouldn't have sat as I did, nervously checking the nearest exit in case we had to do a runner.

The maître d approached and said how nice it was to see me again. La Tour was an impressively well-oiled PR machine, that's for sure. He then announced, 'You filmed the duck. Now you must *eat* the duck!'

I didn't know what to say, because I didn't know how to say in French, 'Are you fucking kidding, mate?' So I found myself saying how nice that would be.

Unfortunately he couldn't hear a word I said. Someone else was speaking at the time, and she was saying, 'I want to see the menu, I want to see the menu, tell him I want to see a menu.' My request for the menu was politely turned down, and once again I was told I *must* have the duck. But again I heard, 'Can't we see a menu?'

After three more requests, we were handed menus, and I heard, 'I'd like to choose for myself.' I would have loved to have said that.

I gazed out the window to steel myself for the outrageous prices I was about to encounter and right there was Notre Dame, a stunning piece of architecture by day, and truly sublime when floodlit at night. Its beauty and size were overwhelming, as was the glossy silver menu with *no* prices. *What the hell?*

Hang on, I thought, I'd been to classy restaurants before, I'd obviously been handed the ladies' menu. So I grabbed Suzie's to check and there was not a numeral to be seen. Her menu, like mine, only listed the vast number of ways the duck could be served. There was also *Foie gras des trois Empereurs, Cocktail de Langouste serge Burcklé, Oeufs La Rochejacquelein, Quenelles André Terrail*, without going anywhere near the classy stuff.

I was then handed a wine menu and, quelle surprise, it had prices. But I soon wished it hadn't. Who forks out one month's pay for a bottle of grog? Obviously not those who fork out one *year's* pay. With the sommelier stalking over my shoulder I felt pressured into making a decision, difficult to do when the wine list is about a hundred pages with nothing cheaper than the GDP of Liechtenstein, until I discovered the paupers' section, where I noticed it was all in US dollars, and the cheapest bottle was $50. Not wanting to be seen as a tight-wad, I ordered the next cheapest, $60, and was told by the sommelier it was a fine choice.

Back to the menu and the pressure was on, and maitre d would not take no for an answer. I managed to placate Suzie and we agreed to have the duck. So what if we were down and out and had to spend the rest of the night in the kitchen alongside the plongeur. We knew this night would end badly, but we were young and in love and in Paris. So we went for it.

First we ordered the Saumon Fumé, so light, so gentle, so delicious. It was like salmon-flavoured fairy floss. We were speechless, and remained that way as we watched an area next to our table being magically transformed into our own kitchen, hosting a huge press, those same surgical tools, knives, chefs and . . . our duck. Number 586,384.

We then heard loud crunching sounds as we watched the sauce chef place portions of the carcass into the press. With both hands and a huge smile, he slowly turned the beautiful solid silver Christofle handle as if turning on a large tap, and the crimson fluid oozed into the ornate silver tray, the contrast of the two colours was perfect. And so was everything else.

I began to settle in. The 'fine choice' wine was, well, a fine choice, and what I was witnessing was so much nicer from this side of the table: hands, instruments, flames and food all beautifully orchestrated, then voilà, the first of the duck courses was on my plate. Large slices of duck breast sitting handsomely in a blood-enriched sauce. It was a work of art, too good to eat. How do they do it? As we started our taste sensation, the chefs were hard at work again, deftly doing whatever they needed to do to the skin and drumsticks, which were then served confit style. I had no idea what vegetables we were putting into our mouths but somehow they were as light as the salmon. Suzie and I looked at each other and couldn't believe what we were eating, nor could our tastebuds, which had experienced mainly salami and cheese and cheap plonk for the last five weeks.

Then I saw the owner, Monsieur Terrail, enter the restaurant and head straight for our table with an outstretched hand.

'Mr Lee, how wonderful to see you again.'

Did I mention the amazing PR? I stood to shake his hand then introduced him to Suzie, who looked up from her plate of orgasm. In his beautiful accent he said how pleased he was to meet her, then leant over and kissed her hand.

He was even more charming than I remembered, maybe because now I was a paying customer. But I'm being unkind,

Monsieur Terrail was truly delightful and seemed totally genuine when he told us he was so pleased to have us in his restaurant and even more pleased we had ordered the duck.

Though he and his staff are the experts in PR, I wasn't totally lacking in that area. Some may call it crawling, I preferred to think Claude and I spoke the same language, metaphorically speaking. Casually from beneath my chair I whipped out a videotape copy of the story I had filmed six months earlier and presented it to him, adding that it was such a hit in Australia, Air France now showed it on its Sydney to Paris route. Touché!

Monsieur Terrail was not totally lost for words, but he went close. Thanking me profusely he took the tape, telling me he would watch it that night. I considered that this could be an opportune time to tell him I didn't have sufficient funds for the duck I had been pressured into ordering by his maitre d, so perhaps I could give him an IOU. But why ruin a beautiful moment, so I let the opportunity pass. We said our au revoirs and he headed off to another table, leaving my wife salivating and staring at the back of her hand like a schoolgirl.

After dessert of Flambées de Pêches and feeling totally ducked, I leant back in my chair, marvelling at the whole experience. It couldn't get any better. Then it did. The maitre d told us we'd been invited down to the cellar. Presuming this to be the quid pro quo for ordering the duck, we accepted his invitation.

I was looking forward to wandering around and having a really good look at the acres of grog without the pressure of work and an unhelpful cellarmaster. So off we strolled with our ten rich new friends, past those less fortunate, to enter the hallowed cellar, and who was there to meet us? My old friend the cellarmaster, who came straight up and told me how happy he was to see me again. He then proceeded to tell my new friends how six months ago I had nearly ruined his entire cellar. Everyone had a good laugh, and once again I was overwhelmed by the charm of the place.

The cellarmaster was jovial and the perfect host. He offered us our choice of a 1937 port or an 1890 cognac. Neither of us like cognac, so we opted for the port, and watched as he pulled out an unopened bottle covered in dust. He poured two glasses then handed us the 1937 bottle to inspect. He then told Suzie how worried he had been for his wine when he had watched me setting up the lights six months ago.

He didn't know the meaning of the word worry. I couldn't stop thinking of my impending financial doom as we wandered through his astounding liquor labyrinth. We finished off our second glass of million-dollar port, thanked him for his hospitality and headed back up to our table.

The moment of truth had arrived. I hailed the maitre d and with my final effort to look the part of a man with his wallet flush with francs, I said in my best French, 'L'addition, s'il vous plaît.'

'Oh, non non non, Monsieur Lee, theez eez on zee 'ouse!'

Total shock. We were unbelievably grateful, of course, and I put up a token argument, saying I *insisted* on paying, and we were extremely embarrassed. That lasted about as long as a mouthful of the salmon fairy floss, then I shut up.

If we'd been aware of this vital piece of information much earlier in the evening, I would have enjoyed the meal a hell of a lot more and I wouldn't have lost bucket loads of sweat and heart beats I could ill afford.

With handshakes and merci's all round, we exited the most expensive restaurant in the world, having spent not one centime, our reputation intact. Which was more than we could say for the mink.

11

A Few Good Men

Even bigger than food in a *60 Minutes* life, was the amount of time spent travelling. Sometimes we just wished the stories would come to us.

Earlier I said concierges and porters run the show, but life was also made a hell of lot easier by a great driver. We spent a lot of time in vehicles. Sometimes it felt like we lived in a van. If we were hiding out trying to get sneaky shots of some crim, we actually *did* live in the van. Though I shouldn't complain about vans, they were a luxury if we managed to find one. Often in the back of nowhere in Africa or Asia, the transport was a ute, with us in the back sitting on top of all the gear.

Most of the time we drove ourselves, but in major cities where parking is a nightmare, a driver is a must. I found that out the hard way. We once hired a car in New York. Not smart. Half the day was spent looking for parking spots.

At the end of that week in the Big Apple, with only four hours to go before our plane was to leave for Sydney, we rushed from our interview in the World Trade Center, to find our car had been clamped, something I'd never seen before. The clamp was as big as the car and that car was going nowhere. We'd been away for a month and were all very keen to get home. So we hopped in a cab, fanged back to the hotel for the rest of our gear then straight to JFK airport. I still don't know what happened to the car, but three months later I got a letter from Hertz saying I was banned for life from hiring their vehicles.

So we started nurturing drivers round the world, and surprise, surprise, they vary as much as cameramen. Some were shockers, some were just plain stupid, some invariably got us lost, some were always late. With a few drivers we knew it would only be a matter of time before we were killed or maimed. There were even a few who couldn't drive, so we'd shove them in the back seat and do the driving ourselves.

Our driver of choice in New York for a few years was a great bloke who unfortunately suffered from verbal diarrhoea. He was very bright, hated George W. Bush (which proved his brightness), and all politics and politicians right of Lenin. But his conspiracy theories surrounding JFK, 9/11, tobacco, cancer treatment and food shortages were a worry. Very interesting the first hundred times, but after that we all feigned sleep. It made absolutely no difference. He babbled on.

The maestro of drivers was a super-smart and very intuitive Cockney in London by the name of Steve Edwards. I'm doing him a major disservice calling him a driver. He was actually co-owner of a company consisting of dozens of cars and even more drivers. But the CEO enjoyed driving us and we loved being driven by him, so every time we hit London, Steve was part of the team for the duration of our stay. His other clients included CNN, Canadian Broadcasting and many more media types, so over the years, by osmosis, Steve picked up the knack of putting a TV story together. His input was invaluable, not to mention his knowledge of all the equipment we used. I would ring Steve from some far-off place to tell him the light/lens/camera/whatever had packed up and I'd need one or all of the above when I hit the UK in X days' time. Then, knowing Steve was onto it, I could relax.

The first time I met Steve he had driven us to the Thames to shoot the annual Oxford versus Cambridge boat race. As we got out of the car the producer said to me, 'By the way, we're shooting the Annual Ball tonight. We might have to go straight there from here.'

This was not okay with me and I let the producer know it. I was furious that I hadn't been given more warning. I didn't have a portable battery light with me and it was impossible to get decent shots without it. I raved on about slack producers and headed down to the river, fuming.

Three hours later, we'd filmed the boat race and I was still fuming. As I trudged back towards Steve and his van, he held out a box and said, 'Here's your battery light.' He explained that he'd overheard the conversation, noticed my anger (hard not to), got on his mobile, which in those days was the size of his van, booked the light, charged it to his account and had it delivered to the river.

There is not one *60 Minutes* crew member that doesn't love Steve. Richard Carleton was fascinated by him and marvelled at his vast knowledge of world events. The acid test came in 1992, when our guest reporter was none other than ex–prime minister Bob Hawke. Bob was a great bloke, easy to work with and fun (even though he was now a teetotaller). He caught on very quickly with the way we did things, which is surprising as what we did was rocket science and very tricky and all he'd done was get himself to Oxford on a Rhodes Scholarship and run a country for eight years. Oh, and create a new world speed record for drinking beer from a yard glass. Two and a half pints of beer in eleven seconds.

Three months earlier Bob was prime minister of Australia, now he was sitting in Steve's van with us, about to do a story on the 1992 British election. The election was too close to call and it looked as if the UK might even end up with a hung parliament. The main contenders were John Major, the incumbent PM, and Neil Kinnock, the Labour leader, who appeared to be narrowly in front, with Paddy Ashdown of the Liberal Democrats giving them both a little scare.

Producer Andrew Haughton had lined up interviews with all three, made easier by the fact that our reporter was Bob Hawke, who knew them all personally. The first interview was with Paddy Ashdown and, as always, Steve helped carry the gear inside then waited in the shadows in case we needed something more from the car. He also knew that sometimes it was more prudent to stay in the van. His radar to know when to leave, or not, was uncanny.

This was Bob's first interview for *60 Minutes* and although his voice didn't show it, I could tell he was nervous by the way he threw himself around in the chair during the chat. But he did a good job and on the way home he mentioned to Andrew he thought it all went pretty well and he might even end up liking being a reporter. Then Steve who had been quiet for the first ten minutes of the trip home said in his diplomatic way, 'It was pretty good, but I think you should have asked him about his affair and the *Sun* newspaper headline.'

I was flabbergasted. Normally we discussed everything with Steve but this was Bob Hawke, who none of us really knew and had been a force to be reckoned with in Australia for decades. Micky the soundman and I looked at each other in shock, wondering how Bob would react to the driver giving him advice.

'You really think so, do you?' said Bob. 'And why do you think that?'

Away went Steve with Bob hanging on to every word.

Back at the hotel, Bob invited us up to his suite to discuss the next day's shoot with Kinnock. He told Steve to park the car and come up, too. Bob spent the next hour picking Steve's brain about English politics and what he thought of Kinnock.

After the Kinnock interview, Bob, ignoring our producer, asked Steve how he thought it went. Steve said it was okay but he forgot to ask Kinnock why he had dropped his commitment to unilateral nuclear disarmament. That night back at Bob's suite, Bob asked Steve what he should ask Prime Minister Major the next day. Steve didn't hesitate to offer sage advice to an ex–prime minister on what questions he should ask a present prime minister.

The interview was set for 11 a.m. at Number 10 Downing Street and Steve, determined to show respect, turned up resplendently dressed in coat and tie. He was aghast at Micky's and my attire, the regular jeans and T-shirt. He told us we couldn't possibly meet the prime minister dressed like that. We told him it's how we dress for our PM and we weren't going to change for his. He was horrified at our disrespect, ignoring us completely on the drive to Number 10, choosing only to chat with his new friend Bob.

Inside the PM's residence Bob introduced us all, including Steve, to John Major. And again Steve sat in on the interview, and afterwards Bob was very happy to get Steve's seal of approval.

The next day we had a meeting with Ted Heath, the ex-PM who was still bitter at having been rolled by Margaret Thatcher as leader of the party. He had an air of aristocratic arrogance about him. After shaking Bob's hand, he asked Bob who we all were. 'This is Nick, the cameraman, blah blah blah . . . And Steve, our driver.'

'I don't allow drivers in my house,' Heath sniffed.

'I do,' said Bob.

'It's my house,' said Heath.

'He's with me, and he stays,' said Bob.

Micky and I just stared silently at our feet. The two ex-PMs, both used to having their own way, kept arguing while Steve quietly left the room—out of respect for Bob. Heath probably thought it was the English class system working just as it should.

The interview went ahead. This guy was no Kinnock or Major. He was full of bombast before the interview, but on the election and the political situation, monosyllabic. Until the discussion returned to being about him, then he droned on relentlessly.

Outside after the interview, Bob apologised to Steve for Heath's rudeness. Steve, way too smart to be upset by it, thanked Bob for sticking up for him then asked how the interview went.

'He just fuckin' waffled on. Steered round the fuckin' questions, just like Ashdown the other day. Fuckin' politicians,' Bob said, 'they'll never answer the bloody question.'

•

Maybe sometimes you can't blame them. In 1983 Richard Carleton asked Bob Hawke, who had only a few hours earlier rolled Bill Hayden to become Federal Labor Party leader, 'Mr Hawke, could I ask you whether you feel a little embarrassed tonight at the blood that's on your hands.'

A startled Hawke responded curtly, 'It's a ridiculous question. You know it's ridiculous.' Then attacked Carleton for his, 'Damned impertinence.'

Carleton was completely unmoved.

Richard George Carleton, legendary reporter, journalist and iconoclast, was the most enigmatic person I ever met. This was the guy, only inches from Gough Whitlam on the steps of Old Parliament House on 11 November 1975, who famously rolled his eyes as Whitlam described Malcolm Fraser as 'Kerr's cur'. He ate politicians for breakfast, his unique interview style set him apart from the pack, and nothing ever seemed to faze him. When he arrived at *60 Minutes* after about a million years working for the ABC and the BBC, his reputation had us all terrified.

Richard was totally incapable of small talk until he knew you, then he'd let his guard down. I'd been working with him for six months and he still didn't know my name. Maybe he just couldn't be bothered. I just didn't know how to crack this bloke. The other reporters were all easy-going, as I thought I was. Richard's replacement for small talk was performing magic tricks, which he practised endlessly. He performed a disappearing red handkerchief trick for interviewees from Margaret Thatcher to Untouchables in Nepal. The Nepalese loved it. Thatcher was Thatcher. 'I'd prefer it to be blue,' she sniffed.

When Richard wasn't performing magic, he'd mangle someone in an interview. It was always a contest. He'd take them apart then wander off as if he'd just joined them for afternoon tea. I've never seen anything like it. He once told me his job was more as an entertainer than a journalist. This he proved on his famous 'dole bludger' story.

Randy Savage weighed 50 kilos, had six kids from two wives and had been on the dole for ten years. Richard's opening line on the story: 'Here we have one Randy Savage.' From then on the savaging was all Richard's. I shot the interview with Randy standing against a brick wall. Richard's gigantic frame towered over him.

Richard: No work in ten years. You haven't even tried.

Randy: I've tried very hard.

Richard: Rubbish! Where?

Randy: I'll work anywhere, anytime.

Richard: But can you see how illogical your position is? Ten years have gone by and you haven't done a day's work.

Randy: Yeah, it sounds bad, but it's not as bad as it sounds.

Richard: You agree it does sound bad?

Randy: Yes, I agree it does sound terrible.

Richard: Shocking.

Randy: Uhuh.

Richard: Disgusting.

Randy: Mmmm.

Richard: Disgraceful.

Randy: Yes.

Richard: You're really not much of a human being, are you?

'Not much of a human being'—I couldn't believe what I was hearing. I felt genuinely sorry for Randy. Their intellectual difference was far greater than their size difference, and probably a good thing. Randy should have been incensed but instead he hung around for Richard to do it all over again from another angle. Randy didn't seem to mind, but the viewers sure did. Channel 9 was inundated with calls about Richard's rudeness.

He could be a contrary bastard, who sometimes didn't do his homework just to piss off the producers. In 1997 in Murmansk, Russia, the story was on the Russian nuclear fleet. The Soviet Union was broke and the navy couldn't afford to pay its electricity bills to make sure the nuclear reactors powering the mothballed subs remained stable. They were also dumping waste from the reactors with criminal neglect. Producer Allan Hogan had gone to extraordinary lengths to line up a secret interview with a Russian whistleblower, Alexander Nikitin, a former submarine captain who'd been charged with treason. Allan had given Richard folders of his copious research notes. It was an amazing scoop. But on the day of the interview, Richard was in a bad mood and as they got out of the car he said to Allan, 'So what exactly do you want this chap to tell us?' Allan was furious, it was as if Richard had no idea what the story was. But Richard, the smooth professional, sat Nikitin down and produced yet another amazing interview.

In some interview situations, Richard could be so insufferably rude that his *60 Minutes* crew would fear for their safety. In an Allan-produced interview with Radovan Karadzic, leader of the Bosnian Serbs (now in jail for war crimes), at 1 a.m. in the Serb's war HQ, surrounded by heavily armed men wearing black uniforms and balaclavas, Richard asked Karadzic, 'How does it feel to be a mass murderer?'

Karadzic was not happy, but his goons were furious. They swung on Allan. 'I was pretty sure we wouldn't make it out of there alive,' our producer said later.

Richard blithely kept up his interrogation, but he'd noticed the sudden chill in the air. He could also flatter with the best of 'em, so he changed tack just in time. Five minutes after the interview, Richard and Allan were drinking slivovitz, laughing and joking with the mass murderer.

•

We were in the West Bank and Richard, who at least now knew my name, was interviewing the mayor of

Hebron. Once again I felt he was inexcusably rude and I was embarrassed. It had been a long day and we were all buggered. I couldn't help myself. Walking to the car after the interview, I said, 'Richard, without doubt you are the rudest man I have ever met.'

Richard replied, 'You really think so, do you?'

'Yes I do.'

Richard turned, walked back into the house and dragged out the mayor.

'Mr Mayor,' he said, 'I would really like to thank you for what is one of the best interviews I have ever been involved in. How's that, Nick? And I'd like to compliment you on the way you run your town. Is that all right, Nick? And please thank your wife for the beautiful coffee. Is that enough for you, Nick?'

What could I say? It was so absurd I laughed. Something had cracked in both of us and from then on we were firm friends. For years, at the end of the day, he'd say, 'Was I rude today, Nick? Tell me if you think I was rude.' I always looked forward to working with him, knowing I'd have a great time. I now know he was never deliberately rude. He'd just spent far too long covering politics in Canberra.

Actually, come to think of it, he could be deliberately rude if he decided the interviewee was a charlatan. He absolutely hated hypocrisy. The Maharishi Mahesh Yogi, otherwise known as the Giggling Guru, was in Holland when Richard arrived to ruin his day.

The Giggling Guru, the guy who increased his fame substantially as spiritual advisor to the Beatles, was living in an amazing wooden palace in the grounds of a former

Franciscan monastery just outside the town of Vlodrop in The Netherlands. The yogi had built his palace from the vast fortune he'd collected from adoring worshippers. It housed him, a few top banana followers, and a TV studio so he could communicate with his devotees via video and the internet. There was also a subscription-based satellite TV channel called Veda Vision, broadcast in 22 languages, and it had all the latest technology, making Channel 9 look like a provincial 1940s wireless station.

For years the Giggling Guru had been teaching transcendental meditation and yoga. 'For good health, it is necessary for everyone to do something with the body so that it remains flexible and normal,' he advised. I couldn't agree more and I'm a great fan of yoga. But somewhere along the line, megalomania set in and the guru, who claimed to have a degree in physics, told everyone he could fly, and for a price his followers could also gain flying skills that would culminate in world peace. Again I'm all for world peace and obviously so were all his apprentice pilots, but maybe being so gullible they deserved to be parted from their money.

It's alleged that John Lennon, having realised the Maharishi wasn't all he was cracked up to be, wrote a song called *Maharishi*, with the lines, 'What have you done? You've made a fool of everyone.' Some of the other Beatles, still undecided over their guru, made John change the name of the song to *Sexy Sadie*.

So the Beatles were now off-limits and Richard had been told there were to be absolutely *no* questions about them.

Before we hit The Netherlands we went to Iowa in the United States for shots of the guru's Maharishi University of Management. It was like Fort Knox. Security around the campus was heavy. Except for fee-paying followers, no one, especially film crews, was allowed anywhere near the place. And this was just one of the many Maharishi universities round the world. You could get degrees in business, law and science. How, I had no idea. Most of the academic day was spent in the huge halls for the learning of yogic flying. And when you gained master's status, you could make yourself invisible, know everything, and, wait for it, walk through walls. As well as universities, the Giggling Guru had a global empire that owned hotels, shops, schools and factories. He was raising hard cash as well as consciousness.

While in the States we interviewed John, an ex-insider, who told us the Giggling Guru was now laughing all the way to the bank. John told us he'd personally spent 23 years and $250,000 searching for the promised nirvana, and he wasn't alone. Another ex-disciple named Dianne suffered a nervous breakdown from what she called brainwashing.

'It's sad,' she told us, 'I am one of thousands of bright young people who were scammed by one of the greatest con artists of our generation.'

So Richard had plenty of ammo for his interview with the Maharishi Yogi.

When we arrived at Guru Central in The Netherlands, we were met by a softly spoken, overweight Australian in a whiter-than-white suit. The whiter your suit, the closer you are to the Giggling Guru, and having been a follower for 30 years, the Aussie was now a major player in the sect. I suspected the ultra-white suit meant ultra-sycophantic; for the rest of the mob in their beige suits, not only the art of flying but the art of working the system had also eluded them.

The Aussie told us that he, too, was learning to fly, all in the name of world peace, and that they had recently proposed to the Australian prime minister John Howard, 'That it would be good to take two or three per cent of the military and have them practise transcendental meditation and yogic flying to act as a prevention wing. When one practises yogic flying, one stimulates and enlivens that basic universal field and that is what neutralises the cause of war.'

Richard then asked him, 'How *far* can the Maharishi fly?'

'I would imagine he can fly any distance, he's not in the mode of demonstrating such things to the world.'

'Have you seen him fly?'

'No.'

'Has anyone seen *anyone* fly?'

'I don't know in this generation but throughout the history of the world it's been recorded again and again.'

Then a beige-suited man took us to a large room filled with white mattresses, and bouncing on their behinds on those mattresses were eight Maharishi devotees all convinced that the look on their faces conveyed enlightened euphoria. Unfortunately they all just looked like morons. With legs crossed they hopped on their bums from one end of the room to the other. They were certainly gaining more height than I ever could, but it wasn't flying. And let's not forget, they were doing it all for world peace.

In one of our conversations with the white-suited Aussie we let slip we had filmed the yogi's university in Iowa. Lead balloon territory. He responded unhappily, telling us we'd deceived them and the interview with the Maharishi might now not happen. Richard and producer Hamish Thomson went into damage control, apologising and saying there was *no way* we were trying to deceive them.

Well, we had tried to deceive them, of course, but we needed the interview with the yogi so we told them whatever they wanted to hear.

The interview was set for 9 p.m., then 5 p.m., then finally settled for 8.30 p.m. And we weren't to be in the same room. The Maharishi would be upstairs in his TV studio and we would be downstairs. Richard would be interviewing the yogi on a TV monitor.

Our claim that it would be more beneficial for everybody if Richard actually got to personally meet the great man was ignored. It was the TV monitor or nothing.

After setting up lights around the monitor, I decided to light Richard as well, then gave a small video camera to Micky to aim at Richard. The quality of the two cameras didn't match, but we knew we'd never be able to get the buzz of what was going to be an explosive interview by doing reverse questions later. Richard was going to get stuck into the Giggling Guru. He'd had enough of this charlatan. Hamish, knowing what Richard was like, pleaded with him to go easy. 'Richard, *please,* no questions about the Beatles,' Hamish begged, knowing that if they were mentioned it would be all over.

Seated a metre or so from us, monitoring everything, were our white-suited Aussie, a white-suited woman we hadn't met, and a guy in a beige suit, all taking notes.

Meanwhile, Richard stared at a blank monitor for ten minutes while his agitation grew. I could tell he was not happy. Then the Guru miraculously appeared on the screen. He was a small man with droopy eyes, bald, with the long hair from his temples joining his long white beard, whiter than the corpulent Aussie's suit. The Maharishi was in a white shirt, though we only saw him from the chest up. Around his neck were three leis of white flowers.

Richard asked him why they couldn't meet in person.

'It's very difficult, I don't meet new people these days.'

'Why?'

'Because new people waste my time! I don't have time to waste anymore, now I'm busy, very busy, creating a perfect man.'

'What's your favourite Beatles song and can you hum us a few bars?'

I looked over at Hamish, who had dropped his face into his hands, while the three devotees appeared to be having serious blood pressure problems.

Before the poor Maharishi had time to react, Richard said, 'Come on. The Beatles established you in the world.'

'No, no, forget about it, forget about it. The Beatles made me popular in the world? Forget about it.'

'How many followers do you have?' Richard kindly asked.

'Countless (laugh). I've stopped counting.'

The next question was about the Health Education Centre which the yogi was planning to set up on 53 acres, almost 20 hectares, on Sydney's beautiful Pittwater, courtesy of the New South Wales Labor Council who owned the land.

'How much money are you prepared to pay for the land?' Richard asked.

'I don't have any money. I don't *think* of any money. The Australians spend all the money and do all the money matters.

Don't waste my time, if you have no other proper questions for enlightenment, we stop *here*.'

'But it is important to Australia who gets hold of that piece of land.'

'Piece of land is not important for Australia. My *teaching* is important, to which Australia can become an invincible country. Just now Australia is a slave of Britain, my tran-scendental meditation can make Australia invincible. Take this message and stop here.' He slammed his hands down onto his knees.

Richard smiled.

'Okay,' he said. 'Tell me, are you able to fly yourself?'

'I don't want to talk to you!'

'Why's that?' said Richard.

And as the flunky in the beige suit jumped up and switched off the monitor, the ashen-faced Aussie leapt to his feet screaming, 'Your questions are really stupid! Your questions' superficiality and crassness are beyond belief! You should go now. Now you have to leave. All of you! It's a ridiculous interview!'

'Can't I ask him if he can fly?' said Richard, still sitting calmly in his chair.

Then, like the voice of God, we heard the Maharishi's high-pitched voice screaming from who-knows-where: 'Send these people out of the house!'

Micky and I were still rolling but the devotees, finally noticing this, went off their brains. I told them we weren't filming. They might have been gullible but they weren't stupid. Now the shit really hit the fan. The plump Aussie lunged at the camera. Richard leapt out of his chair and shouted, 'Get your hands off the equipment, fatso! You're all mad. He's mad. You've ruined lives and you all think you can fly!'

'You must leave the premises this instant and give us the videotape,' said the Aussie.

Richard and Hamish were escorted out of the room while Micky and I stayed to pack up the lights. The three devotees stood there glaring. We were going nowhere until they had that tape. I took a new tape out of my bag, ejected the used cassette from the camera, carefully labelled it, then placed it on a chair very close to me. I put the other tape into the camera, and clicked it closed. Behind me the beige-suited man dashed to the chair, grabbed the tape and took off shouting, 'I've got the tape! I've got the tape!'

How could I have been so stupid? I was devastated.

'Now you may leave,' we were told.

We had to get out of there—fast. I knew they'd be checking that tape within minutes. Micky and I grabbed the gear, dashed outside, jumped into the car with Richard and Hamish, and we took off. I sat in the car, grinning, knowing the enlightened ones were up in their video suite staring at a blank screen. I had switched tapes. An old sleight-of-hand trick that cameramen keep up their sleeves for such occasions.

•

Richard had an insatiable appetite for knowledge. Well, knowledge he thought was important. He only ever read fact, never fiction. There were no shades of grey in his thinking. Everything was black or white, right or wrong, yes or no . . . perhaps because he studied higher mathematics at university, not the norm for a journalistic career. He was at uni in the 1960s, but somehow missed the sex, drugs and rock'n'roll part. Consequently he'd never smoked dope, his music knowledge hadn't gone beyond Doris Day and Johnny Ray, and he stopped watching movies at *Ben Hur*. When he interviewed Michelle Pfeiffer, the hottest film star around at the time—you couldn't pick up a magazine or paper without that glorious face staring out at you—he'd never heard of her. Luckily he had producers to fill him in.

Michelle Pfeiffer was amazingly beautiful. She was bubbly and happy, yet Richard ignored her until I told him I was ready. Pfeiffer was totally bewildered, she was used to being flattered by journalists and just about everyone else. Richard tried hard in the interview but he was the wrong man for the job. He once told producer John Little, 'I'm uncomfortable [with celebrities], uncomfortable because I'm out of my depth. I don't know anything about it. I just simply don't. And also I don't find terribly appealing the entourages that go with these people. All the bullshit and the crap.'

But his lack of knowledge of popular culture sometimes made good TV. He'd ask questions the stars had never heard before. Some got it, some didn't.

After the encounter with Michelle Pfeiffer, Richard decided maybe it was time to catch up on popular culture. He asked for help and Micky gave him a list of music from 1964 to the early 1990s, and I gave him a list of movies I thought worth seeing. He immediately watched every one of them. Seventy per cent he liked. He especially loved *Cinema Paradiso* and asked if there were more like it. The man was mellowing.

On a story about eighteen-year old Abbey Meyer, I saw Richard cry. Abbey suffered from brittle bone disease and had broken bones at least 200 times. She was permanently in a wheelchair, and due to all those broken bones she was about three feet tall. Her attitude to life was extraordinary, which is why she became an exchange student in America where we did the story. She was always happy, bright, and loved a joke, but if she laughed too loudly her hearing aid would be set off into a loud squark. It got to be a running joke with Abbey and Micky because he'd have to re-do the sound which the hearing aid had wrecked. The more it happened, the more she'd laugh and the more we had to reshoot. But I had a problem, too. Richard did a lot of his interviewing while pushing Abbey around in her chair. Richard's height and her lack of height meant that when I went for a tight shot of her happy face answering a question, all I saw was Richard's crotch. Not a great shot. When I told Abbey my dilemma, the hearing aid nearly exploded with her laughter. We did the in-depth interviews with Richard sitting down.

At the end of day three, Richard and I were sitting together in a bar.

'How does she continue?' he said. 'How can she stay so happy? Why isn't she angry?' Then he wept.

His evolvement continued. During that story he bought his very first pair of blue jeans. But he needed help, so he asked Micky and me to shop with him, to make sure he bought the right ones.

•

Not long after the Abbey interviews, Richard did what Richard does best. A confrontational story that most TV reporters would shy away from. A story on ultra right-wing extremists in South Africa, the Afrikaner Resistance Movement (AWB). With a membership of 70,000 they couldn't be ignored. Eugène Terre'Blanche (translates as 'white land' or 'white earth'), the founder and leader, was a South African ex-policeman who told us when we first met him that he loved apartheid and hated blacks and journalists.

I know I said Richard didn't do small talk, but somehow with a few of his magic tricks and telling Terre'Blanche what he wanted to hear, he got the ex-cop bigot totally on side. It was beautiful to watch. Terre'Blanche genuinely thought he had a new friend, and the new friend was given permission to film the AWB rally being held that night in a local hall.

It was like stepping into a Hollywood WWII movie. The AWB flag looked so much like a swastika it was hard to see the difference. And it was everywhere. All over the hall and all over the rabid Boers wearing brown uniforms and pistols. They were an angry, ugly mob, and the planned late arrival of their hero gave them the opportunity to get even uglier. This lot made the KKK look like a bunch of schoolkids playing dress up.

To get inside the hall we first had to walk through a corridor of brown-shirted guards and a pack of foaming-at-the-mouth dobermans, ready to rip someone/anyone to shreds. I filmed the whole spectacle with a moronic smile on my face, hoping the excited troops would think I was one of them and not some kind of spy.

I went looking for more material. I couldn't lose. Every shot a gem. More flags, more manic faces, more dogs and monstrous bodyguards with batons and guns. It was as if Steven Spielberg's set dresser had spent weeks creating it just for me.

Terre'Blanche walked on stage and the adoring mob went berserk. When they finally calmed down, I was allowed on stage to get close-ups of the hero of the night as he delivered his tirade against blacks and the rest of the non-Afrikaaner world.

Then just as I came off the stage, Richard grabbed me.

'I want to do a piece to camera now, while he's still on stage,' he said. 'How close can we get to Terre'Blanche and still hear me if I whisper?'

With Terre'Blanch ranting nearby, Richard leant into the camera and whispered, 'I wasn't around in the 1930s when Hitler's Brown Shirts started rampaging across Germany. If I was, I probably would have been as frightened as I was coming into this meeting tonight. These fascists are truly terrifying even to be alongside. They believe they've got God on their side and they sure as one thing have got guns in their belts. These are white racists at their worst. Listen to them.'

Still to this day, it is the best impromptu piece to camera I've ever heard, and if any of the rabid mob had heard it, we'd have been dead. It was tough for Micky with the ranting in the background, but we weren't going to do it again. We got out of there fast.

•

Another fascination for Richard was the Israeli–Palestinian conflict. He went to Israel and Gaza at least twenty times, though I don't think the conflict was the only thing that drew him back. I suspect a lot had to do with where we stayed.

The American Colony was one of the great hotels of the world, and having stayed there so often, Richard was treated like royalty. Nestled in mainly Arab east Jerusalem, the Colony, with its flower-filled courtyard, wonderful food and very cold beer, was a mecca for all journalists, left, right, Arab, Israeli. In summer the courtyard was the place for breakfast, lunch, dinner and heated arguments well into the night. There was a small fountain that bubbled away 24 hours a day, so if you were unlucky enough to score a room adjoining the courtyard, the fountain and the arguing would keep you awake until dawn when the mosque next door took over. Then the unbelievably loud call to prayer, an alarm clock for the faithful, felt like it was inside your head. Really unfair for we unfaithfuls who'd set the alarm for 8 a.m. Guess who organised that room for me on my first trip to the Colony? While he had a suite as far away from the mosque as possible where he could practise his magic.

Richard wasn't a chef but he could make wonderful food magically appear. There was a huge food shortage in Iraq so Richard, on his way via London, dropped into Harrods to stock up, also picking up the most exotic food hamper they had. Knowing about the lack of food in Baghdad, the rest of us had already stocked up in Amman on staples such as crates of beer and soft drink, wines and a few good malt whiskies.

After two days of blazing heat in Amman in Jordan then seven hours into the fifteen-hour desert drive to Baghdad, it was time to start eating. Richard declared, 'Lunch on me,' opened his exclusively packed hamper, pulled out a soggy parcel and announced, 'I always thought these could be a problem.' The rotting four-day-old prawns were immediately hurled into the sand. But the quince paste, the pickled quail eggs, the foie gras d'oie, the truffle, the tinned Beluga and the caramelised onion relish, along with a vast assortment of foreign cheeses, got us through the harrowing week.

In Baghdad we had so much food it needed its own hotel room, so we checked it in under the name 'Fahoud'. From then on, after a long day it was always, 'Drinks in ten minutes in Fahoud's room.' Throughout our stay we gave a lot of Fahoud's supplies to the disbelieving maids, but even after a week of nonstop eating, when Fahoud checked out there was still heaps of food left, so we distributed it all to the maids to take home for their families.

•

The longer Richard spent at *60 Minutes*, the more relaxed and sociable he got and the funnier he became. Something the audience never got to see. Overwhelmingly they hated him. When people found out I worked for *60 Minutes,* the first thing I was told was what an arrogant arsehole Richard Carleton was and they refused to watch any of his stories. But they could tell me in great detail what he'd said and done on screen. I spent a lot of time telling people what a great bloke he was.

They never believed me. Richard couldn't care less what other people thought.

He once said 'I know people say I'm opinionated, I know people say I'm arrogant. Well, I've got to whatever position I'm in now over thirty years of doing this job and I'm not going to change. I'm not going to change for you, for the general manager, for Kerry Packer, for anyone else. I mean, that's what I am, and you can like it or lump it.'

In May 2006 Richard was in Beaconsfield in northern Tasmania for a story on a mine collapse that had killed one miner and trapped two others for twelve days. At an afternoon press conference just outside the mine, all the reporters' questions were about the health and wellbeing of the miners. Then Richard stepped up. Controversial as always he hinted that the mine collapse was manmade.

'Why is it,' he asked, 'is it the strength of the seam or the wealth of the seam, that you continue to send men into work in such a dangerous environment?'

He then walked from the press pack, leant on the shoulder of producer Howard Sacre, and collapsed. Minutes later he was dead from a heart attack.

I miss him.

12

Rembrandt Had it Easy

'Every frame a Rembrandt.'

What every cameraman loves to hear. Mind you, it's not said all that often, so hearing it is extremely rare. Mostly all you hear is, 'What is this shit?' And mostly it's from film editors. A powerful bunch. They're the ones who physically place all our Rembrandts into the story according to the script written by the reporter and producer. A bad editor can ruin your stuff, but a great editor can work wonders, and if they somehow score some Rembrandts it's astonishing what they can do. They can make a cameraman look like a genius. I'm now wishing I'd bought them more duty-free stuff.

The fact is, editors are the only ones that can be, and are, totally objective with the story. They're given a script and miles of footage, and away they go. They don't want to hear how you worked a twenty-hour day with jet lag, how you were up at 4 a.m. to get that sunrise shot, or that you were being chased down the street by criminals and that's why the footage looks a bit shaky. Editors' ears are closed to producers telling them it took a year to get this story up, or a reporter saying, 'Please don't use that shot, I was tired that day, so I don't look too flash.' In fact, making reporters look flash was my job, but often I was just as tired, mostly from a big night out with same reporter. After a big night I could barely see through the viewfinder let alone detect hair and makeup.

Editors, by the nature of their job, are loners. They sit in a dark room all day, doing things over and over again. An executive producer will change an 'and' to a 'but,' or demand that a shot be removed because Jana's hair looks terrible, or Richard's stubble makes him look like a hobo. Then it can all be changed again because the story suddenly needs to be made shorter due to some timing problem. So the poor bloody editor in his or her little dark room does all of the above, knowing it will probably be changed again tomorrow.

Meanwhile, tomorrow I'm off to Paris, Rome and Nicaragua, so they can keep their objectivity and their creativity, and I can keep the best job on earth.

But there's a downside to the best job on earth. Leaving home. It was never easy for any of us, and Mike Munro, intrepid reporter, was no exception. He hated being away from his family. Didn't we all, but Mike drove us all mad trying to get us to work faster to shorten the story and the trip.

Two weeks into a trip to Nicaragua there was a 2.30 a.m. knock on my door and in walked Mike, in tears. He told me he could no longer cope with being away from home so often. He sat on my bed, sobbing. He couldn't stop. It was a struggle not to start blubbering with him. His father had only recently died, which wouldn't have helped. We both had kids around the same age, and he asked me how I coped. I didn't have an answer. I didn't want to think about it in case I stopped coping. Six months later, in London, more tears in my room from Mike, so I told him he should leave the show before he tore himself apart. He had already been discussing it with his wife, Lea. Eventually he made the big decision to go. You've got to admire him for that.

At home I had my calm Suzie and my two beautiful girls, Jessica and Kathryn. There were often tears as I walked out the door—not mine, though, I saved them for inside the taxi, knowing if the kids saw me sobbing they'd be even more upset. When they were very young with no concept of time, it was a little easier, though when Kathryn was two she refused to look at me or allow me to kiss her for three days after I got back from a trip. Seven was the killer age, and the kids would ask how long I'd be away. I couldn't lie and never did, but many times I was lied to by the office. Often, near the end of a trip while my three girls and I were counting down the days, I'd be told that another two stories had been found, adding a week or more to the trip. Those phone calls home were the worst.

In 30 years I was home for three of Suzie's birthdays. I missed practically every swimming carnival, parent–teacher meeting and concert the kids had. I know I'm not the only father to do this. I think of the poor blokes like my father who went away to war. But it doesn't make it any easier . . . and there must be some connection with an absent parent and their kids' immune system. Kids *only ever* get sick when you are away, and that's verified by every travelling parent at *60 Minutes*.

Balancing family and career was difficult, but I really did get a buzz out of having a camera on my shoulder and trying to capture Rembrandts. But they're hard to come by, and there are a million reasons why. A beautiful scene can be spoilt by overhead powerlines. The angelic face of a child in a crowd should be a breeze, but get too close and the kid pokes out his tongue or runs screaming to mum. But the main reason is that we were always running late. Trying to get four people to leave the hotel at the same time was impossible. With lack of time comes, 'Fuck art, just get the shots done. We're late for the next appointment.' Where there's a jackhammer next door, a bribe is needed. Soundmen carry loads of cash to buy a slice of silence, but often they're told to fuck off and the cacophony continues. Then we find the location has stark white walls, a nightmare for cameramen. With the soundman sweating over jackhammers, and me sweating over a flat, lifeless background, it's no good protesting: it's taken the producer three months and thousands of phone calls to get this reluctant piece of talent to talk, and so the interview must go ahead. *And now.* No Rembrandts today.

Some great Rembrandts only occurred after a stash of local currency had changed hands. Did money change hands in Cerro Muriano in September 1936, when Robert Capa took his famous shot, the 'Falling Soldier'? In some quarters it's deemed to be a fake. I hope not. Because Capa is one of the all-time great photographers, and shot many fearless Rembrandts, specifically during the Spanish Civil War and World War II. Those shots are revered around the world.

Capa almost single-handedly invented the character of the photojournalist. In horror situations—war zones, urban riots, military takeovers—guys like him helped define the 20th century. But they were alone with their cameras. I was always with a team of friends.

One of the great things about working in a team of four is there are four sets of eyes. Extremely helpful in a dangerous situation. We were in the ancient city of Hebron, one of the most confusing places on earth. The Palestinians, the Jordanians, the Israelis, all claim some sort of ownership. There were 120,000 Arabs and 500 Jewish settlers permanently living in Hebron. The tension was frightening. Nobody wanted us there, especially the settlers. I was filming a group of Jewish settlers when some loopy who hated Palestinians, the world, and us, went for me with a knife. Richard Carleton dashed in, wrestled the guy to the ground and snatched the knife from him. I hadn't seen it coming. Richard then pocketed the knife, and as I filmed the guy bolting away I was extremely grateful for that extra set of eyes.

Real teamwork is what happens with a cameraman and a soundman, and I worked with the best. Micky Breen—a great soundman, and an even greater bloke. His sound was always perfect, even with jackhammers nearby. I could do a 360-degree shot and not see him. He'd watch me like a hawk, anticipating the shot and ducking just in time. Sounds simple, but with some others I've tried the same shot and seen a stunned soundman staring down the lens with a moronic look, saying, 'I didn't know you were coming round this way.' If Micky suggested a shot, I'd do it immediately, knowing full well it'd be a beauty. The general misconception was, 'What do soundmen do but aim a microphone at peoples' faces? How hard can that be?' So, whether we liked it or not, they were always at the bottom of the crew pecking order. Reporter, Producer, Cameraman, Soundman. Some soundmen were treated appallingly. But soundmen tend to be tough guys, and I've seen a few producers with bloody noses, or chairs hurled at them, and they deserved it.

In 25 years I spent more time with Micky than I did with Suzie. Probably not healthy for all concerned but we were away from home more than seven months of the year. I can honestly say Micky and I have never had an argument; maybe a few disagreements on minor things but nothing serious.

That wasn't the case for everyone. Every trip was a lottery. You never knew which reporter and producer you might score. You did try to stick with the ones you liked, but that couldn't always be achieved. These other crew members got Micky and me as a unit, and some of them travelled with the unit better than others. We were all different, some more so, and living with each other 24 hours a day for six to eight weeks, often in very difficult circumstances, sure stressed those differences.

I've seen separate flights and separate hotels, screaming matches, chairs and punches thrown, tears, walk outs, calls to executive producers demanding a sacking, and even a producer and reporter who were not on speaking terms.

That was a beauty. They were both claiming ownership over the story and neither would budge an inch, so a second producer was flown in to 'translate'. The feuding couple even sat at the same dinner table and the reporter asked the number-two producer to ask the number-one producer to pass the salt!

Micky and I dubbed ourselves the A team, not just because we couldn't spell B, but because we came up with it first. The A team survived six executive producers, sixteen reporters and five million producers. Producers are a dime a dozen, their attrition rate huge. Executive producers thought it kept producers on their toes if they chopped a few at the end of each year. Seems counter-productive to me to control through fear, but what would I know about office politics.

Absolutely nothing, and I'm glad. Because once my eye was up against the viewfinder of a camera, the size, shape, colour and length of the shot was all mine, nobody else's, though the subject was not always my choice. Over time cameramen somehow develop a way to become totally detached from the subject, and under most circumstances it's a marvellous thing. Just as I hadn't smelt the blood in the bucket in the prison cell in Uganda until I'd taken my eye from the viewfinder, while filming I was always removed from any horrors coming at me through the lens. Having filmed natural childbirth at home and in hospital, caesareans, heart surgery, mastectomies, brain surgery, a sex change, a circumcision, implants of all kinds, penis straightening, prostate surgery, knee reconstruction, burn victims, tortured animals, poverty, wars, bombings, crimi-nals, politicians, priests, paedophiles, paedophile priests, film stars, rock stars, dead children (that's tough), grieving parents of dead children (even tougher), my camera protected me not only physically but emotionally from everything I shot.

Some will argue I don't *have* to shoot any of the above and they're right, of course, but I did and I know that without a camera a lot of it would have turned me into a blithering wreck. How the others coped, I have no idea. I loved my camera . . . most times.

I developed an interesting relationship with my cameras. All the *60 Minutes* cameras were the same, but not unlike your car they somehow develop a personality with eccentric traits you must learn to live with, and just like that irritating younger brother, you end up loving them or wanting to kill them. Or both.

Cameras hate water, sand, extreme heat and cold (mine hated early mornings), and they go into total shutdown mode when dropped. They hate that. Sometimes they just need a rest and act like a spoilt child refusing to do what they're told, and just like the child, their timing is impeccable. Just as the reporter asks that confrontational question the talent was dreading, or you're inside the helicopter that's been waiting an hour for the weather to clear, the camera decides it's allergic to work. Then it revels in the cameraman's embarrassment. If all this seems a little weird, not a lot of people have a bloody great lump attached to their body for up to fourteen hours a day, unless it's a child or brand new lover, and as with the child or lover all the camera wants is a little love and respect.

The first twenty years of *60 Minutes* everything was shot on 16-mm film using an Arriflex (Arri) SR. Shooting film meant there was a break every ten minutes to whack on a new magazine of film. That could be done in ten seconds if need be, but after three magazines a longer break was needed for all three to be reloaded again. I did this with my hands inside a black light-proof 'changing bag', unloading the already-exposed film and replacing it with a new 400-foot roll. Sometimes monumental hangovers meant the changing bag was forgotten and I'd have to climb into the boot of a car to change the film. Very black in there when it's slammed shut. Tough if it was summer. I did it only twice in the tropics, but I might as well have been in a swimming pool, sweat gushing out of every pore and making my hands extremely slippery. And it's never a good look seeing 'water marks' all over a reporter's face.

On a long trip, some of the finished stories (hopefully full of Rembrandts) would need to be shipped back to Sydney. But often there was no shipping company, or there were dodgy governments with heavy censorship, so we had to sneak the footage out. I'd head to the airport in search of a courier, who often turned out to be a pilot with a friendly face, then hand over our hard work to him and just hope to hell it'd make it to Sydney. Try doing that today.

With film I had no idea what the footage looked like and, more to the point, neither did the reporter or producer. Nobody got to see a shot until the footage finally made it to Sydney, was developed in the lab and put into synch with the sound. Often the script was written on the road without anyone having seen a single shot. All the reporter and producer had to go by was their notes and what I could tell them about what I may or may not have filmed. This was always fraught with danger. Not only would they have in their minds scenes that never existed, but also shots that Steven Spielberg would have had difficulty conjuring up. They'd get most upset when told those shots didn't exist. It was as if somehow I'd lost the shots they had so beautifully described in their script. Plus we'd often shoot up to 30 ten-minute rolls—that's 300 minutes or *five hours* of film—for a fifteen-minute story. The amount of Rembrandts that ended up on the cutting room floor was soul-destroying.

•

But if a shot absolutely has to be used, it's used. Even if that footage for some reason is soft, scratched, the wrong colour, edge fogged, underexposed or overexposed, there are only so many times you can blame the lab. Which works for the first few hundred times. After that, producers, and more importantly executive producers, having dismissed a few lab technicians, begin to suspect others. Namely me.

Then there's the lens. Which must be treated with utter respect. If it gets a bump, and it does regularly, it can create all sorts of problems with focus. Soft (out of focus) pictures are not acceptable, but if you're in the middle of Africa for three weeks and the lens has had a knock, there's not a lot you can do. On such a trip my lens was suffering from a six-hour ride in the back of a ute over rough, rocky terrain. When I started shooting, I found the lens was a bit soft on the wide end, completely out of focus in the middle range, but sharp as a tack on the telephoto end . . . So telephoto shots, millions of them, dominated the story.

The only people to notice were the editor and a very cool producer who looked at the shots over and over. When the producer asked why so many shots were on the long end of the zoom, I leapt in with, 'Stephen, please, with the long end of the lens, the less difference is observed between close and distant subjects, making it appear as if they are closer regardless of the distance between them. It's called "compressed perspective", and by doing this I feel I've made the audience think they are more a part of what they are seeing rather than just being an observer. What do you think?'

I was expecting, 'Impressive. Yes, I agree.' But what I got was, 'Piss off. Go and get your lens fixed.'

The 'hair in the gate' is a beauty. In old movies you might see a little hairy thing wriggling all over Katharine Hepburn's face for five seconds. Then it miraculously disappears because the projectionist, having looked into the 'gate' of his projector and seen the culprit and with no lab man to blame, quickly blows some air from a compressed air canister, or more likely his mouth, into the gate and Kate is blemish-free once more.

But in the camera that hair in the gate is not noticed until it's too late. At the end of the scene, the magazine of film is taken off for a gate check and sometimes, lying across it, is what looks like a piece of driftwood. Has it been there the entire 400 feet? Or did it drop in halfway through. However long it has been there, the shadow of that hair is now permanently, for as long as that piece of film exists, plastered right across the scene.

Even though the term is 'a hair in the gate', I should explain that 99 per cent of the time it's not a hair. It's a thin slither of film that could have been shaved off by a wonky magazine, but most often it occurs because the manufacturer hasn't cut the film cleanly and has left little dags hanging off the film edge. Try telling that to the bosses. I've had a moustache all my life, well obviously not all my life, only since I was three, and every time there was a hair in the gate I was told, 'Shave off that fucking moustache.'

Scratched film is a killer. A scratch can come from slack handling of the film when it's loaded, from dirt, or even a grain of sand. Once that tiny grain gets into the magazine, it sits there waiting to ambush that beautiful brand new roll of film. Scratches really upset executive producers, reporters even more so. For some reason they are not too keen on giant scratches across their beautiful faces.

Then there are filters. Depending on the type of film being used, different filters are needed . . . and somehow (mostly due to a hangover) wrong coloured filters end up on the lens, and the pictures can be red or blue. All attempts to explain that this was 'my Picasso-like *blue* period showing a marvellous expression of poetic subtlety and personal melancholy' fall on deaf ears and I get reminded that only recently, while going through my *rose* period, I had told them I felt, 'My subjects now had a melancholy feel and I was evolving as an artiste.'

As for the under/over exposure thing, of course being a professional it should never happen, but in haste it can, resulting in a call from Sydney asking why Richard Carleton suddenly looked like an African, or how come the scene in the nightclub looked like virgin snow at midday.

But there's not a cameraman in the world that hasn't done some or all of the above.

•

Digital cameras brought on a whole new set of bigger and more irritating problems. Give me hairs and scratches any day. At least they were simple. But digital cameras have a mind of their own. They pixelate, dictate, hesitate, deliberate, decide your fate and, I suspect, masturbate. Pixelation is a ripper. With pixelation all the colours go wonky, the picture is out of whack and bits of the shot appear where they shouldn't. An electronic nightmare.

The look of digital pictures is, I think, fake. Film mimics our eye much better. Film has an organic calmness to it, softness, an overall smoothness. The digital pics have unbelievable clarity, so bloody clear the shots look magnified. Sweat looks like Niagara Falls, wrinkles the Grand Canyon, and an unfortunate little cold sore looks like Vesuvius on the morning of 23 August AD 79.

Talk about spoilt child, the digital video camera is the sickly spoilt child that is somehow capable of ruining everyone's day. Everyone else catches a cold. He gets pneumonia. He has to travel on the plane with you. The Arri went in the hold. He hates to come out of his air-conditioned hotel room in the tropics, so throws a tantrum and can't be used for half an hour while he sulks about the humidity. The sudden change of temperature sends all the electronics loopy and shuts down the recording part of the camera. We know this because the spoilt brat has the digital world's equivalent of tears. A flashing red light that cries until it feels acclimatised. But even worse, at that time the viewfinder was not in colour. Everything I shot with a digital camera, I saw only in black and white. I never, ever, got used to it. I'd be utterly amazed when later I saw the day's footage in exquisite colour.

But I came to love my petulant child of a camera, as all parents do. We were a good team. Rembrandts were few and far between, but not for lack of trying on both our parts. The camera and I both knew how hard it was, even on the best show in town, to make *every* frame a Rembrandt.

13

Shit Happens

In all jobs things go wrong. Shit happens. For a pilot or a doctor one tiny mistake can result in death, and how bad would that feel. But a pilot can blame Boeing, if he's still around, and a doctor can always blame the hospital system or even Hippocrates for not teaching him exactly how not to fall into the twin traps of overtreatment and therapeutic nihilism. But for a cameraman working for a top-rating TV program, that tiny mistake is seen by millions of people. The doc and the pilot don't have to put up with *that* humiliation.

On *60 Minutes* the shit that happened wasn't always cameras, schedules, sound, airlines, etc. They couldn't compete with, for example, an idiot producer wearing riding boots. It happened in Oklahoma. Having arrived late as per usual, we had to set up in a big hurry with all of us offering an endless amount of apologies to the already reluctant interviewee. With tension in the room, I leant away from the camera towards the reluctant TV star for a quick light meter reading. At the same time the manic producer came racing across the room with arms flapping, yelling, 'Let's go! Let's go!' In all his eagerness his bloody great clodhoppers clipped one leg of the tripod and down it all came. I lunged at the falling camera a millisecond too late.

We all stared in total disbelief. I had no idea a camera was made of so many different parts. How could a fall of only one and a half metres onto thick carpet cause so much damage? The lens had snapped in two. The viewfinder was bent, the magazine had severed all ties with the camera body, the light-proof door of the magazine triumphantly set itself free, and emerging from the rubble was 400 feet of film beautifully unwinding itself across the carpet, not stopping until it hit the door. It'd be impossible to duplicate that perfect unwinding.

Standing frozen, the producer looked around and said, 'What do we do now?'

'Well, I know what we won't be doing,' I said, 'and that's an interview.'

We must have looked like a bunch of amateurs as I crawled round the room picking up small pieces of my precious Arriflex camera. What I really needed was a vacuum cleaner. My diary entry of that day, 24 July 1986: 'It was a perfectly shithouse ending to a perfectly shithouse story at the end of a perfectly shithouse day in a perfectly shithouse trip.' Sometimes the perfect job can be too perfect.

I have never left a camera on a tripod again, not even to go half a metre away. But the floor is another thing.

Twenty years after Oklahoma, the floor where I left my brand new $80,000 Sony 700 Digital Betacam was the one at carousel five in Melbourne airport. I'd placed the camera carefully on the floor, surrounded by all my other hand luggage, stepped half a metre to the conveyer belt to collect one of my twelve bags, turned back and . . . it was gone. No camera. And only a millisecond had passed. I knew I had to see someone walking or running to the exit with a professional digital Betacam over his shoulder, so I raced for the door.

Not a glimpse of the bastard Betacam bandit. I searched the whole airport inside and out. Shit, he was quick. And I was sick.

Above carousel five was a security camera. *You beauty.* I went straight to airport security and told them the story.

'What carousel was it?'

'Five.'

'Sorry, that camera is turned off.'

I tried to stay calm as I asked why.

'Oh, we do that every now and then.'

Livid, I went to the airport police station. Doing his best to look concerned but holding back a smirk, the cop told me it was the fifth professional camera to go this month and it's probably winging its way to a studio in Asia as we speak. I made the dreaded phone call to the bosses and was told, hey, these things happen, don't worry about it. Huge relief. I had a reputation for looking after gear. But then I was told it better not happen again because if I lost another very expensive camera, my job would be gone with it.

Sometimes shit happens and it's oh so funny. For everyone else. I copped it in Los Angeles due to my packing habits. Packing was always a drag. I would try not to unpack at all when it was just a one-nighter, not wanting to disturb the perfect layers. I'd deftly lift out the essentials and on a good day if I was lucky I would replace all with ne'er a ripple when it was time to go. But if I had the luxury of spending five or six nights in the one room, I'd spread out. Spread out is an understatement. The room was a mess, with gear and clothes covering every inch of the floor, a real sense of real freedom. Until it was time to re-pack. Then I cursed my slovenliness. I only ever had one bag and always tried to squeeze too much into it. Micky travelled with two, Richard Carleton with four. After all, he had to have somewhere for his stereo, tennis gear, Vegemite, mustard and pepper grinder.

We had stayed for six nights at the Beverly Wilshire Hotel on Rodeo Drive, Beverly Hills, where a Polo T-shirt costs $US350 and a pair of men's shoes, $US1200. Twelve hundred bucks for shoes! I pay that for a car. As for shoes, I have two pairs, one for walking and one in case my walking shoes go missing. I think they cost me 30 bucks, but the shoes are so old I can't remember.

The hotel, situated right at the end of Rodeo Drive, is U-shaped, built in the style of Italian renaissance architecture and made of Tuscan stone and Carrara marble, the same marble Michelangelo used to create his David. Not having to leave the hotel until eight in the morning, I decided my last night in the City of Angels shouldn't be wasted on packing. That's what mornings are for. If you're a morning person. And I'm not.

So I had a huge night out on the town, slept through the alarm but luckily was woken by the arrival of my room service breakfast, which I had cleverly ordered at 2 a.m. when I'd staggered back to the hotel.

Now I was running very late and hadn't started any packing. I rang for a porter, knowing from vast experience that porters always take aeons. I then started packing. Five minutes later there was a knock on the door, and I was totally rattled when I saw a porter standing there. *Why? Why today for the first time in my life has a porter decided to be efficient?* In a mad rush I feverishly squeezed everything I could find into my bag, slammed the lid, zipped it up and handed it over to the finger-tapping porter along with twelve cases of equipment. *Phew, what a scramble.* I quickly demolished my spinach and fetta omelette and double espresso, picked up the camera and hand luggage, and headed for the door, then realised I'd yet to put on my shoes and socks. I leant over the bed to where I'd placed them an hour ago and they weren't there. I looked around frantically. I knew exactly where I'd put them but didn't want to believe it. I now had to go down to the foyer of the Beverly Wilshire to check out. This was one classy pub. All I'd seen all week was money, money, money. I know that doesn't necessarily equate with class, but the Beverly Wilshire was happy to think otherwise. This hotel gladly put up with poodles in the foyer. But bare feet? I probably should have gone down and wandered across the marble floor with all the aplomb of an avant-garde artist. But in a fit of panic I grabbed the white fluffy slippers all good hotels supply, put them on and headed sheepishly down to the foyer. I took the stairs to avoid the stares, and decided to bypass checkout and head straight outside, hoping to grab my bag before it took off to the airport in the pre-arranged van.

Between the stairs and the front door were acres of foyer and hundreds of well-heeled customers. None of them knew anything about avant-garde artists and rudely showed that lack of knowledge by staring at my fluffy slippers. Trying to present my avant-garde look as *au naturel* but looking like Tuffy the Little White Bear, I shuffled outside to Micky and asked him where my bag was. He told me he'd selflessly done all the work on his own, packed up the van and sent it on its way.

'It's gone,' he said. 'Everything.'

My bag and shoes had departed along with my dignity. Then Micky noticed Tuffy's paws and said, 'What the *fuck* are you wearing?' Laughing uncontrollably and pointing, he then invited all the porters, doormen and assorted guests to 'Take a look at *those*.'

Which everyone did. Of course.

•

As a cameraman, and in life generally, I never thought much about what I stuck on my feet. But I learnt that lesson, too, thanks to a bunch of Scottish deer hunters.

In true *60 Minutes* fashion we were doing a story on the barbarity of deer hunting and hoping to prove what cruel and heartless killers these hunters were. Mike Munro, Micky and I arrived at the foot of Ben Nevis, the highest mountain in the UK, in the highlands of Scotland, on a beautiful summer's day, met our hunters and their gillie and headed up the mountain. They seemed like good blokes but were already complaining that there were too many people, but we told them to leave the TV to us. This is how we worked.

Three hours later with ne'er a wee deer to be seen, we returned to the carpark to be told that the deer can see, smell and sense anything unusual on the mountain. If we really wanted to see a deer being shot, the hunters would have to come back tomorrow with just the cameraman. Micky and Mike argued that they were needed, but were told it's one or none. Regardless, there was no mention of footwear.

Next beautiful sunny morning I returned wearing a light T-shirt and the same smooth-soled zip-up leather shoes as I'd worn the previous day (and every day). I waved farewell to my colleagues as they sat in the sun, sipping coffee and reading.

We immediately took a different route to yesterday and headed into much thicker heather. The heather perfectly disguised the potholes that had a magnetic attraction to me—I must have tripped into every hole. 'Keep up with us. I hope you're fit,' the leader said. I was fit at the time and also 40, round about the same age as he was. But I was carrying two magazines loaded with film, an extra roll of film, a zoom lens, a tripod and a camera with a heavy, very expensive lens hanging off it. He was carrying a rifle. His gillie carried everything else.

The four of us stopped, and way in the distance I saw a huge stag amongst a mob of deer. 'That's the one we'll go for, but we have to get a lot closer,' said the chief hunter. Trying hard to be quiet, we scrambled down rocks, with me desperately struggling to protect the lens that wanted to hit everything. We inched our way in the direction of the stag that still looked a hundred miles away. It was way too far for my 300-mm lens, but I did have a doubler to whack onto the lens to create a 600-mm effect. As I fumbled to get out the doubler, I heard, 'Shit, the wind has changed,' and looked up to see our target disappearing at full speed.

'The bastard got our scent, he'll now go all the way round to the other side of the fucking mountain.'

Thank God, I thought. I'd had enough. Maybe we could try again tomorrow. No such luck.

'Let's go, it should only take three hours to get round there.'

Three hours! Are you fucking kidding? We'd already been going for two hours and my feet were killing me.

An hour later we all sat down and the gillie revealed what he'd been carrying in his backpack. Lunch.

About time, I'm famished. The gillie got out three beautifully wrapped sandwiches, handed one to each of the hunters then started eating the third. My feet, legs and shoulders were aching while I watched the three of them hoe in. One of them looked up, and through a mouthful of sandwich, said, 'Did you bring lunch?'

'Ah, no,' I said.

'That's a shame,' he said. The other two were totally unmoved.

No one had briefed me on footwear or the proper apparel for deer-killing. And no one had mentioned this could take five hours. I thought we'd find a stag, shoot him and be back in time for morning tea. Pissed off at their attitude and my naivety, I said, 'I work for the richest man in Australia, I'll give you one hundred quid for a sandwich.'

To which I got, 'Bad luck, laddy, if you go stag hunting without food, that's your problem.'

I thought I'd see if the gillie, the one who wasn't born with a silver spoon in his mouth, was a little more caring. I looked down at his lunch box and saw a Mars Bar.

'I'll give you fifty quid for your Mars Bar,' I said.

He looked at me, then the Mars Bar. He'd already demolished a fine sandwich. 'Okay,' he said.

I then had to explain to him that I didn't have the money on me but he had my guarantee he would be paid as soon as we hit sea level. I'm not sure if his look was one of disbelief at the IOU or whether he couldn't believe someone was dumb enough to pay 50 quid for a chocolate bar. Either way, his quizzical look was a little eerie and I began to wonder if his agreement to give me his Mars Bar was his idea of a really funny joke and they'd all have another good laugh at my expense. I was ready to explode, but thought better of it. We were at least four hours from the nearest town, which could have been in any direction. And three of the four of us knew the way back.

Without a word the gillie reached into his lunch box and handed over his Mars Bar. I savoured every bit of it and was even lucky enough to wash it down with a cup of tea. And for no extra cost!

The day was endless. We walked and walked and walked. Up 2000 vertical feet and down 2000 vertical feet. After a while the gillie even offered to carry the tripod. A fine gesture, but I think he just wanted to make sure I wasn't going to die and leave him short 50 quid.

Then the hunters even helped me with some of the gear. All this effort for a shot of some poor stag being murdered. I was beginning to think he wouldn't be the only one to die that day. I was so buggered I could hardly move, but I couldn't let my hosts be aware of it. Probably just what they were waiting for.

So on we went, and *eight hours* after we started, we saw our stag. Well, they did. There were so many deer that I couldn't tell which one they'd spotted. We quietly scrambled over loose rocks, hoping not to dislodge any and frighten our target. I finally stopped and asked them to wait until I found a firm spot to place the tripod. They couldn't give a shit and were getting ready to aim. I still didn't know which stag they were aiming at.

I could now see four stags in amongst the mob. I quickly found what I hoped was a secure spot for the tripod, slammed the camera into its slot then asked one more time which was the stag they were after.

'Left hand side of the tree on the far right.'

Shit, there's two of them and they're both magnificent.

'Is it the one in the group of three or is it the bigger mob?' I said.

'The bigger group,' he said as he lifted the rifle to his eye.

I put my eye to the camera, hoping he was having as much difficulty finding the target through his tele-photo sights as I was. I took a guess at the exposure for the late afternoon sun, adjusted accordingly for the long lens, found a stag in the middle of my shot, hoped to hell it was the right one and started rolling. *Bang!* My ears were ringing, and through the lens, dead centre, I saw the stag go down. A great shot, his and mine. Though I knew if I hadn't been ready he wouldn't have waited. As they congratulated each other, someone said, 'I hope you got that.'

I got it all right. Yet I couldn't help but feel sorry for the hapless stag. I just hoped he was dead.

I've never understood hunting, or the yearning to have a huge set of antlers hanging on the wall as proof to your mates what a man you are. It's not like it was a battle and the best man won.

It was then an hour's walk down the steep rocky cliffs to get to the dead stag and wait for a bloke with a pony to come and drag it for another hour to a waiting truck, and my deeply relaxed *60 Minutes* colleagues.

Back at base I was so buggered I could hardly move. I paid the gillie for my sumptuous lunch, resisting the temptation to ask for a receipt, then raced back to my hotel room in Fort William to bathe my aching body.

My room was on the third floor in an old hotel with no lift. Just as I took the first step my legs cramped, and I could not, under any circumstances, walk up those stairs. My legs would not and could not move. I dragged myself up by my arms. This is true. Never in my entire life had I felt so exhausted. I made a cup of tea, poured in eight sugars and fell into the bath. Sitting in the bath, happy that I'd scored such a great shot and looking forward to a beer, I started to cry. I couldn't believe it. And I couldn't stop. This must be how exhaustion felt.

The next day it snowed all day. Had I been in the Highlands in my T-shirt and thin leather shoes, I'd have been as stiff as the stag.

I was sore for a week, and extremely shat off that we'd been so under-researched and ill-prepared. I swore I'd never let myself get into a similar situation.

•

Fatigue can do many things, and one of them is to make you unaware of your surroundings. Not good for a cameraman. I'd just arrived in Denmark for a story on pornography. Someone had come up with a great story title, 'Danish Blue'. Not wanting to waste such a gem, we went in search of a story. At the time pornography was taboo almost everywhere in the world, but the Danes had just lifted their ban on porn, so it was now sold, and eagerly bought, in most convenience stores. With no fear of prosecution it wasn't hard to get people to appear on camera whether they were selling it or participating in it.

After a few days of research we tracked down a film studio and porn stars who were only too willing to appear in our story. When we met the female star, we were all instantly smitten. She was extremely beautiful, charming, intelligent and so very nice, a university student who figured it couldn't be too difficult to be in porn movies. Plus she could do with the extra cash. It was easy money, she said, but she tried not to think of the devastating consequences. She had contracted every STD in existence. Luckily for her, these were pre-HIV days, but as a result of all her diseases she was now infertile. She said her only fear was that one day her father might see one of her movies and she wouldn't know what to say to him. We promised her our story would never be shown in Denmark.

After her interview we went to the studio to shoot the making of one of her films. We were introduced to the other female star while she had her makeup done. Makeup? I admit I hadn't thought of that. There she was in front of a mirror with a thousand light bulbs, taking great care to get her hair and face just right. I didn't have the heart to tell her nobody'd be looking at her face. But I guess deep down she already knew that.

What really blew me away was that these girls hadn't yet met their male co-stars, who were just coming out of the shower with towels wrapped modestly around their waists. The director introduced everyone, the two female stars, also modestly covered up, shook their co-stars hands and said how nice it was to meet them. They then all discussed the weather. The two guys didn't quite know what to do or say, and sat there checking their nails, agreeing with everything the girls said. Wrapped in towels they all looked like they were about to change back into their school uniforms after gym, but in ten minutes, in front of a couple of film crews, they'd be doing unbelievable things to each other and pretending they were enjoying it.

Time to go to work. We followed them into a large cold studio where a cheap double bed was surrounded by half a dozen lights, a small 16-mm film camera on a tripod and half a dozen men all looking like a bunch of account-ants who couldn't wait to get through another boring day at the office.

The stars, with towels still diplomatically wrapped around them, sat on the bed. The director told them their motivation, and the men removed their towels. We knew what our motivation was. Leave. We didn't want to hang around long enough to embarrass anybody, namely us. Plus, not only could we not show any of the action in our 7.30 p.m. timeslot, we couldn't have shown any of it, ever, anywhere in Australia.

We left the studio for our many interviews with pro-porn politicians and anti-porn advocates and finished the night interviewing the owner of a porn shop. It was midnight, it had been a very long day and we were all exhausted. We did the interview inside the porn shop, then went back to the hotel for a well-earned rest.

With the story finished and packed off to Sydney, we moved on to our next assignment during which I got an irate phone call from the studio. 'What the fuck is going on!?' yelled the executive producer. 'The interview with the porn shop owner's got a TV screen right behind his head showing hard-core porn, clear as a bell. Is this some kind of joke?'

It was no joke, I just hadn't noticed. Today it'd all be instantly pixellated at the touch of a button, but as it was the editors spent weeks trying to blur out the background image. Shame. It might have increased the ratings.

•

Sometimes the shit happening is of my own creation. We were staying in Brighton, England, doing a profile on the Pommie cricketer Ian Botham, who was about to tear the Aussies apart, so he said. There was no love lost between Botham and the Aussies, particularly him and Ian Chappell. There'd been rumours that the two had a pub brawl at some stage and that Botham had gone at Chappell with a glass. When we mentioned this, he told us he wouldn't need a glass to take care of Chappell. All great stuff for our story, and we knew it'd be even better when we got Chappell's response.

Our hotel in Brighton was *not* five star. It was more like Fawlty Towers, but sometimes that can be fun, depending on your mood.

Before we left on the trip, Geoff Cameron, the unit manager, told us all, 'Please be careful and lock away all your valuables.' There'd been a few thefts on trips and a few blokes, me being one of them, had been done over. Normally I would have let Geoff's plea go in one ear and out the other, except it hadn't been long since I'd had my room done over beautifully. They got away with $5000 in travellers cheques, a still camera and my passport, which didn't go down well with the bosses, because after Belfast I'd given them my word it'd never happen again. Two passports lost. I was obviously a risk.

Some classy hotels have small safes with a combination lock in the room, but I was scared I'd forget the combination or I'd forget I'd even put the stuff inside. I'd taken to putting all my valuables inside my over-packed suitcase and locking it with my own combination lock. Any light-fingered burglar would have a difficult time lifting my stuff. Though even my own locks can be tricky for me. If you don't check the combination as you lock the thing, it might have accidently spun around a notch or two and cunningly changed the combination right before your eyes.

Which happened to me in New York in a five-star pub that had safes in the room, so it was a little embarrassing when I had to ring the concierge to bring up a hacksaw to cut off the lock on my suitcase to get to the credit card I needed to pay my hotel bill. It was such a classy joint that the concierge very kindly did the sawing for me. He probably thought I was so dumb I wouldn't be capable because he did enquire as to why I hadn't used the safe they provided.

Back in Brighton's Fawlty Towers, still a bit nervous from all of the above, I'd decided to hand over all my stuff to the front desk. They had a huge safe where they kept everyone's valuables, and now I wouldn't have to memorise a string of numbers. And safely it was kept for five days, and each of those days the place got more and more like Fawlty Towers. I was getting madder and madder. When you live in hotels for seven months a year, you expect certain things to be done, poncy as that might sound. And this place was crap. Nothing worked and the service was terrible. So when we checked out, I gave them an earful. I told the front desk what I thought, and seeing as I was on a roll, I demanded to see the manager, then told him exactly what I thought of him, his staff and his hotel. I told him I was a seasoned traveller who lived in hotels for half the year and this was one of the worst I had *ever* seen, and if I was as bad at my job as he was at his, I'd have been sacked years ago. I turned and stormed out, happy with the thought that I would never need to see him or his dreadful hotel again.

By the end of the drive back to London, my blood pressure had returned to normal and when I saw the front desk of our extremely classy five-star London hotel, I just knew all my stuff would be extremely safe and sound here, until I realised it was already safe and sound . . . back in Brighton. When I mentioned my dilemma to my colleagues who had witnessed my tirade back at Fawlty Towers, it goes without saying I was on my own. I pleaded with them to drive back with me and for one of them to *please* go inside to get my stuff and save my embarrassment. They were, of course, all loving this and they all declined.

I started thinking of ways I could tell the bosses how I'd been mugged, and even though I'd managed to put up a good fight, I still had all my stuff taken. But sooner or later Mr Fawlty would clean out his safe and find Mr Perfect World Traveller's travelling documents. There was no mention of Channel 9 on them so I considered ringing my wife and telling her to sell the house so we could move to another country, but that wouldn't work because the house was in both our names. Plus I couldn't get home to sign anything because I didn't have a passport. All these thoughts swirled round my head as I sat alone on the train back to Brighton.

When I arrived at the hotel I was hesitant to go in. Should I say it was all a misunderstanding? I really love the hotel and I was being ironic? Or . . . 'Oh you thought I was talking about *your* hotel?' No, no, no.

It was now 6 p.m., maybe there'd been a change of shift and I'd be in and out without anyone recognising me. I took a quick glance from behind a pot plant and who should be behind the front desk but my old mate the manager. There was no way round it. I raised myself up to my full 5 feet 7 inches and sauntered in. He knew exactly who I was and why I was there. With a gigantically self-righteous look on his face, far bigger than the one on my face earlier in the day, he said, 'Can I help you, Sir?'

I really wanted to say, 'Sir demands his documents immediately before Sir sues for theft.' But unfortunately Sir was now shrinking fast. I told him, ahem, it appeared I may have inadvertently left some personal items in the hotel safe and may I retrieve them, please.

'Certainly, Sir. And will that be all?' His smile grew in direct proportion to my shrinkage.

'No. That is all, thank you.'

'If there's any more I can do for you, *please* don't hesitate to call, it's been a *pleasure* having you, Sir.'

All 4 feet 6 inches of me felt the daggers as I traipsed out clutching passport, money, credit cards but no dignity.

•

Sometimes shit happens to other people too. Mind you, I get a bit embarrassed for them and try to do the diplomatic thing and hold back any laughter. We've all felt that sense of relief that 'this time at least it's not me'.

We were shooting a profile on Rex Pilbeam, Mayor of Rockhampton. Rex was a great story for us, outspoken, out of date, a true dinosaur. Most of his ideas belonged in the 19th century, but he must have been doing something right, he'd been mayor for 30 years, an independent in a very Labor town. He'd been a chartered accountant, a fight promoter and rodeo organiser. He was a very large 73-year-old with a thin grey moustache, a million chins and a laugh for each chin. His dog, a female border collie called Nicky, was with him every minute of the day.

And he was tough as nails. He told us his biggest problem was married women in the workforce. He blamed them for divorce, delinquency and the dole queue.

'The finest role a woman can have in this world is as wife and mother.'

Any woman working in his office had to leave within twelve months of being married. Surprisingly, the women in his office agreed. 'I don't believe in married women working. If you can't afford to get married, you don't get married,' one of them told us.

Maybe the whole town was 19th century, and Rex was the perfect man for the top job. He had a huge painting of a reclining naked woman above his desk. The view was from behind to give it taste. The type of painting that was everywhere in the 1960s before people (women) began to object to these images in the workplace.

Ray Martin was the reporter. 'Modern women would call you a male chauvinist pig,' he said.

To which Rex responded, 'I think it's a wonderful epitaph, cos I think a pig is a long way preference to a cold-hearted indifferent bitch. If women were meant to grow certain organs, God would have put them on 'em.'

That might have been what the married Mayor Pilbeam said to his mistress back during his first year in office, because something had obviously upset her, right before she shot him. He almost died. Next election he romped in.

Rex made no attempt to be tactful even while we were filming him. When a Japanese delegation was a few minutes late to discuss investing in his town, he joked, 'They weren't bloody late for Pearl Harbor, eh?'

For all his faults he was fun to be with, and only too willing to do whatever we wanted. We needed a few more shots to end the story, so we decided we'd get some footage of him in his car as if he was driving to work. With Nicky his faithful border collie in the passenger seat, I sat in the back seat and filmed Rex driving. I commented on what a nice car he had. 'Is it new?' I asked.

'No, this beautiful Volvo is seven years old. I get it washed every day and polished once a week. I love this car. I always keep it looking like new,' he said.

We pulled up at the Town Hall and I told him we only needed one more shot and we'd be out of his hair. I asked if he would mind driving into the driveway, stopping the Volvo a few metres in front of me, walking between me and the car, and then up the Town Hall's ornate stairs and through the front doors. Of course he obliged.

'And Rex, put a little oomph into your walk. This'll be our final shot for the story.'

I set up the tripod in the middle of the driveway and waved him on. When he pulled up, Nicky jumped out the passenger window. Great shot. Rex then got out of the car and headed for the steps, oomph and all. Just as he reached the bottom step, I noticed his car slowly heading towards me, and I could hear the motor still running. I grabbed the camera and tripod and yelled to Rex that his car was moving. The 73-year-old ran back, shoved his left leg inside and slammed his foot on the brake.

Unfortunately he hit the accelerator. The looks-like-new seven-year-old Volvo took off at 80 kilometres an hour, with Rex's foot trapped inside hard against the accelerator, his large mayoral body hanging outside the car with his head dribbling like a basketball along the ground. I watched as the car rocketed over the gutter, over the road, over the opposite gutter, and into a park. The beautiful clean Volvo then came to a sudden stop. It had slammed into a coconut tree.

Shit, I've just killed the Mayor of Rockhampton! I ran to the car, still angrily revving against the tree, leant in, turned off the ignition and looked down at the unconscious mayor. Newspaper headlines whizzed through my mind, '*60 Minutes* Crew Kills Mayor', 'He survived being shot by a lover but not by a camera', or 'City of Rockhampton Sues Cameraman'.

As I stared in shock at him, wondering what to do next, he started to move. He opened his eyes and looked at me.

'Now what did you want me to do?' he said. 'Walk up the stairs. Is that right?'

•

Being away so often meant it was always a pleasant surprise to score a job in Sydney. It was like being back in the old news days. I found myself shooting a routine story on a notorious criminal. I'd just scored some sneaky footage of him in a cafe with other undesirables. Being the brave bloke I am I decided to forgo my cover and get some shots of him walking along the footpath—all very long lens of course. I'm not that brave, but I recall thinking that I was safe because I was on the footpath surrounded by the general public. As he got closer I turned away, pretending to be shooting something else. But he knew what I was doing. I felt him grab me. On the long end of the lens he looked like a big man, but now he was upon me he bore a remarkable resemblance to a fridge. And he was very, very angry. Suddenly, in a giant bear hug he lifted me off the ground. I wrapped my arms tightly around the camera to protect it and put my head down to protect my disbelieving face. Holding me high in the air he said, 'Give me the tape or someone will get hurt.' I figured it wasn't going to be him. I was hoping it was going to be the bloke watching from the other side of the street, but it was obvious who it was going to be. I felt like asking him for the literal interpretation of 'hurt', but with my head still buried in my arms and camera, I said rather foolishly, 'You're not getting the tape.'

'Then someone is going to get hurt.'

He slammed me against a brick wall and tried wrestling the camera from my arms. My head hit the wall and the camera slammed into my face. With my head spinning I told him to fuck off. Not smart. The fridge turned purple and everything else turned into slow motion. Once again he spat out the words 'Give me the tape!'

I heard a loud crack and thought there goes my neck. Remarkably little pain considering, but then I realised the noise was the viewfinder being ripped off the camera. His next lunge at the camera was even more ferocious. I was a dead man, but I had nothing to lose so I told him to fuck off again. I wasn't really keen to open my eyes to witness my final punishment, but I did and saw a huge hairy hand coming my way and resting on the fridge's shoulder.

'Wayne, let it go,' a voice said. 'He's not worth it.'

And with that, my saviour and Wayne the fridge, still clutching my shattered viewfinder, wandered off down the street.

Get me out of Sydney.

●

Now this story probably shouldn't be in the shit happens chapter but it *did happen*.

In the mid–1980s the world, and specifically the US, was having a small financial crisis, and no one was too sure if 'Reaganomics' was to blame or if US President Reagan and his treasury would be the saviour. Part of our story was to interview a top-ranking financial advisor to the US government who lived in a very expensive and very beautiful part of Boston. When we reached the top step to his massive front door, it opened and we were met with the perfect caricature of a nerdy accountant. Short, balding, pasty—and wearing a cardigan. It was all we could do not to laugh. In his high-pitched voice he invited us in and after a bit of small talk he asked if we'd like a cup of tea. We felt sorry for the poor little man and thought it would be the highlight of his day, so we accepted, to make him feel good. Then I looked round the room for a suitable place to shoot the interview, and suddenly, before my very eyes, appeared the two largest breasts I'd ever seen.

'This is my wife,' said the very proud finance guru. Again laughter was held in the back of the throat but struggling hard against the gravitational pull of the two large planets before us.

I know it was the 80s, but her hair was the size of a haystack, probably to give some vertical compensation for her poor load-bearing shoulders. She was overly made up, wearing a minuscule skirt and a blouse that looked four sizes too small, and every ounce of her body was crying out, 'Look at these.' Trying desperately hard not to look at those, we all said something like 'Nice to meet you', but it was inaudible. It's hard to speak with your mouth wide open.

As we drank our tea, I set up lights around two chairs diagonally across the room with a hallway leading away to my left. The reporter Jennifer Byrne and the economic guru sat in the chairs, nattering away with small talk until I was ready, then Jennifer went into heavy-duty questioning about fiscal policy, accrual accounting, active markets and anticipatory hedging, all of which went right over my head.

All good cameramen with their right eye to the lens learn to keep their left eye open to check out what's going on around them. There could be a better shot, or some danger. The image in the right eye through the lens might be an extra close-up of someone's face, or zoomed into an image hundreds of metres away, while the left eye is taking in its normal wide vision. After years of experience you can actually switch your brain to see only the image in one eye, even though both eyes are open. It doesn't sound too difficult, but some cameramen never acquire the skill.

As my left eye roamed the room, I saw some movement in the hallway. My brain switched from the right-eye image of the round-faced guru to the image in my left eye and all I could see were those breasts. And above them a big smile. Then a wink.

With my left eye totally in control of my brain, I watched as two hands slowly and seductively unbuttoned the blouse. I'd been having trouble understanding any of the fiscal chat but now I was having trouble hearing it due to the sound of my pulse thumping in my head. Slowly but surely all the buttons were undone and there they were, braless and enormous. Appearing to defy gravity they hovered for a few seconds before being shaken wildly from side to side. Meanwhile, hubby was rambling on about the principle of supply-side economics and the trickledown theory to stir growth. I stared at the jiggling breasts then up to her face. Another wink, another smile. She then did up her buttons, turned and sauntered back down the hall.

After the interview we all said our thankyous and goodbyes, including my breast friend who knew full well I wouldn't mention it. After all, who would believe me?

14

I Ain't Got No Quarrels

I was told I was off to war, and the bearer of the bad news, noticing my horrified look, told me to stop panicking. War is a hillbilly town in West Virginia and the whole town is unemployed. That's the story. Phew, what a relief. Obviously I'd hate to be unemployed, but I'd have hated going to war even more.

I was lucky not to be drafted in September 1969. I still recall how my sweaty hands had trouble opening the Australian Army's insidious yellow envelope telling me whether or not I'd been called up for two years National Service. Some blokes are naturally tough. Some of us are not. I knew I'd curl up into the foetal position if I was drafted. I was a scaredy cat and I had a huge problem with getting out of bed before eight. Plus, I'm with Cassius Clay, who famously said, 'I ain't got no quarrel with them Vietcong.'

I gingerly opened the envelope and pulled out a small white card that said, 'You have been indefinitely deferred.' And from then on, war was totally off the agenda, and I thoroughly enjoyed what was left of the 1960s and 70s. But then I got a job—and war was back on the agenda. Except, I wasn't shooting bullets, I was shooting film.

•

My first foray into anything like a real war was a trip to Rhodesia, now Zimbabwe. I figured we'd get a couple of shots of black men with guns, interview the prime minister Ian Smith, debate the worthiness of democracy, then get out of there. Simple.

I first realised it wouldn't be so simple when we were about to land in Salisbury (now Harare). The pilot said all lights had to be turned off, including his landing lights. We circled in the night sky as high as we could for ten minutes, aimed at the runway and rocketed in at full speed. This was to stop nationalist guerrillas from blowing us out of the sky, just as they had done to a passenger plane a week earlier when they scored a bullseye with a rocket launcher and the plane plummeted to earth. I had that swollen tongue feeling. All I could think was, 'I ain't got no quarrel with them Rhodesian freedom fighters.'

After our safe landing, we checked into the whiter than white colonial-style Meikles Hotel and headed for the bar. Above the entrance was a brightly painted sign declaring 'ALL GUNS MUST BE CHECKED IN BEFORE ENTERING'. A sign I saw regularly on episodes of *Bonanza* in the 1960s.

Over at the hat and coat check-in, there were at least a dozen machine guns, a few rifles and some pistols. The bar was full of loudmouthed young men, all white of course, comparing notes on warfare and massacres and complaining about having to leave their weapons at the door.

Next day we went for a wander round town. There were traffic jams of battered old cars. People, blacks and whites, ran between the traffic, while small black kids pushed wonderful wire sculptures in the shapes of cars, bikes and animals along the footpath. All of these handmade works were for sale for near nothing. I bought three and the smiles that came with each sale were so endearing I paid double and still got a bargain. War, what war?

We were rapidly brought back to earth when we were told we should go nowhere without a gun and were given an Uzi machine gun to share. It was a shark-coloured grey with a stubby barrel, everything about it looked evil. None of us wanted to touch it. I could hardly bear to look at it. We explained that we were journalists, and we couldn't take the gun.

'Die then!' was the answer. I pretended not to hear. They pointed at our station wagon and we were told, 'And you don't think you're getting around in that, do you? You need a mine-proof vehicle.'

We eventually found the recommended vehicle, at vast expense. War is expensive! Our mine-proof vehicle was a bit like a small tank with a strange conical shape underneath, making it look like a spinning top on wheels. There was a reason for the strange shape: if we hit a mine, most of the force would be deflected from the centre of the vehicle, and we'd have less chance of being killed.

But, we were gleefully told, 'You'll probably lose your balls and most certainly be deaf.'

'Imagine never being able to hear another Beethoven sonata,' said our dilettante soundman. We did wonder about his priorities.

This war had been on and off for years, but had hotted up in the last six months and all white males up to the age of 60 were on standby for periodic call-up. The Rhodesian army was extremely well equipped with all sorts of assault rifles, AK47s and rocket-propelled grenade launchers. Unfortunately the guerrillas, at least 12,500 of them, were almost as well equipped with mortars and rocket launchers. Most of the fighting was in the rural areas where many white farmers had been slaughtered.

In Salisbury, though, impeccably dressed matrons continued to have high tea in the elaborate sunroom of Meikles Hotel, seemingly oblivious to what was happening outside the capital, though most of the men in town were wearing army uniforms and carrying a weapon.

We attached ourselves to a small army convoy and went bush. We figured we'd go out with the Rhodesian army, get them shooting at some freedom fighters, interview some army major about what was wrong with black rule and be back in Meikles in time for a sunset gin and tonic on the verandah.

Well, that didn't happen. I found myself running along trenches next to young soldiers, black and white. The army recruits looked almost as young as the children I'd bought my wire sculptures from. And they all had frightened looks on their faces, probably no more frightened than mine, though luckily for me mine was hidden behind a camera. Still in our trench we were told the rebels were all around. We weren't sure if it was the truth or we were just being wound up. Suddenly we heard, then saw, we weren't being wound up. The rebels, seeing us and realising they were hopelessly outnumbered, started running. We took off after them using trees for cover until we reached another trench and jumped in, keeping low and quiet. I was hoping the guerrillas had got away and we could all go home. It was getting close to gin and tonic time.

I heard the major next to me order a skinny, slightly effeminate black private to throw a grenade to scare the enemy. I'd figured the sound of my heartbeat would already have frightened the shit out of them, but knowing it would be a great shot I stood up in the trench to get the action. With the camera rolling I expected to see the explosion any second, but instead felt a sudden whack on my back and fell face forward onto the camera with the major on top of me. Before I could turn round and berate the clumsy bastard, there was a loud explosion, sounding like it was inside my head, and dirt rained down on us.

Before I could decide if I was dead or alive, or if everyone else was dead or alive, I thought, why me? I aint got no quarrel with them Rhodesian guerrillas. Then the major managed to pick himself up and dust himself off. He turned to the skinny little guy and let him have it.

What had happened was the young private hadn't managed to reach the top of the trench with his throw, and the grenade had rolled back down into our trench, landing just a few metres from us. The major had noticed its trajectory and figured he could ill afford the publicity of causing the death of a cameraman, so he shoved me to the ground and jumped on top of me.

I stared at the slightly bent lens hood and camera covered in dirt, and figured it was better than having a slightly bent body covered in blood and far better than a very dead body, though I suspect the limp-wristed private was wishing he was dead.

I couldn't stop thinking about Neil Davis. An Aussie and a cameraman, just like me, but the similarities stop there. Neil spent years in Vietnam covering the war, and was the only cameraman to get those amazing shots of the communist tank No. 843 pushing over the wrought iron gates of the Independence Palace in Saigon. Those images made him very famous, particularly in the photographic world. He was renowned for his skill and luck, even though he was severely wounded on several occasions. I couldn't help but wonder what made guys like him want to do it. His was a very exclusive club and I had no intention of joining. I was over war. I'd had my war experience and wasn't planning on ever having another. As Bertrand Russell said, 'War does not determine who is right—only who is left.'

•

But a few months later I found myself in Israel filming a story on the latest skirmish between Israel and Lebanon. It was not Neil Davis stuff, but it was enough for more stirrings in my tongue-that-swells-from-fear. We were getting some great footage of Israeli tanks firing relentlessly into Lebanon in the areas that were now home to many members of the Palestine Liberation Organization, or PLO. Thankfully nothing was coming our way, and all I could think was, 'I ain't got no quarrel with them PLO.'

That night we had dinner in a kibbutz right on the border. Everyone sitting at our table was carrying some sort of a gun and talking as if an attack was imminent. From the kibbutz we could see across the Hula Valley into Lebanon, but could not make out the towns and villages we'd seen clearly during the day. They seemed to be no longer there, not due to relentless shelling but because they were in complete darkness. A wise move, I thought, and just maybe we should be doing the same thing. The way I saw it we must have been standing out like dog's balls. I mentioned this to our minder, Rafi Horowitz, who had been a member of the Israeli Special Forces. It triggered off a story he felt he just had to tell. During one of the many wars he'd been involved in, he had a few friends captured by the Arabs, and when his mates were found they'd had their dicks and balls cut off, shoved into their mouths and their lips sewn together. That really put me off my dinner.

Back at our motel Rafi asked us if we knew what to do if there was a rocket attack.

I replied, 'Sure do, Rafi, I hide my genitalia in a safe place then start reciting the Koran.'

Not surprisingly, he ignored me and explained that we must grab a pillow and run to the nearest bunker. We looked at each other and agreed it sounded pretty good. I asked him what were the chances of there being an attack tonight.

'Odds on,' he said.

We figured we needed a few more grogs to help us sleep, but I was worried if I had too many I might not hear the incoming fire, and would wake up in the morning with more than a swollen tongue in my mouth. The woman behind the bar, who also owned the motel, nonchalantly asked if we knew what to do if there was a rocket attack.

'Sure do,' I said. 'Grab a pillow and run for the nearest bunker.'

'No, no, no, do *not* leave your room. You get under your bed. It will protect you. You don't want to be caught running outside.' That sounded pretty good to me.

Ten minutes later her husband came over for a chat, and told us there was an electric fence between the motel and Lebanon, that it was completely useless and the PLO regularly came through and people were quietly murdered in the middle of the night. My mind was working overtime, trying to think of a good hiding place for my private parts, when he asked if we knew what to do if there was a rocket attack.

'Get under the bed,' we said in unison.

'No, no, no, grab your bedclothes and get into the bath. The bathroom is reinforced.' That sounded pretty good to me, too.

I went to bed thinking, 'Well, I have no bloody idea what to do if there's an attack, so I'll probably be dead in the morning.' But the grog took over and I was out cold immediately, and in the morning I was still in bed, alive with genitals intact.

I met up with the others for breakfast, and we all had different stories of how we hadn't slept all night, fearing the worst and hoping if the invaders did appear they might have become bored with severing penises and moved on to severing useless appendages like hands. I wasn't game to say I'd slept like a baby, so agreed with them all.

We headed out to film the damage from the last few days shelling and came across a primary school that had obviously been hit regularly. The building was sandbagged and the kids' playground was now a row of shelters. Just as I started getting shots of what was once a basketball court, we heard sounds of rocket fire and other war-type noises. Buggered if I knew what, but it was loud and it was close. We dived for shelter.

'I'll do a piece to camera now,' said Ray. 'Let's go, let's go!'

'Rolling! I yelled.

'Speed!' yelled Peter the sound recordist, letting us know his tape recorder had reached the required speed.

Ray Martin, no notes, no rehearsal, stared down the barrel of the lens, shouted of the devastation and fear around us, all straight off the top of his head thanks to his million years of experience. He was on a roll when I heard, 'Cut! The bombs are too loud!'

'*What*!' said Ray.

'The bombs are too loud,' yelled Peter, who was used to being in the studio where the sound was always under perfect control.

'The bombs are too fucking *loud*?! That's the whole fucking *reason* we're doing the piece to camera!' Ray screamed back.

His shouting continued for some time, as did the bombing, then, unfortunately for the shell-shocked soundman, the bombing stopped. Unfortunate, because Ray's yelling got louder and louder, much louder than the bombs had been. An unforgettable rare piece of reportage ruined. Ray was very, very angry. There was fear in Peter's eyes. A new war was brewing and I was way too close. I thought, 'I ain't got no quarrel with them reporters.'

•

Then, of course, a few months later I found myself on the other side—in Lebanon doing a story on Palestinian refugees. Three and four generations of Palestinians had lived nowhere but refugee camps in makeshift tin shelters. They were regularly told by whoever was in charge at the time that they were not to move throughout the huge camp, they must stay in and around their own 'house'. But underneath all those tin shelters was a beautiful free-way of tunnels, secretly dug to allow the refugees to move unimpeded throughout the camp.

The refugees were all charming and extremely hospit-able. Food was difficult to come by, yet every family we spoke to insisted on feeding us and making cup after cup of very powerful, sweet Arab coffee. It was rude to refuse anything on offer, and after 400 coffees I began to think it was some sort of trick to get us drugged. Could I really trust them with their sneaky hospitality, especially after having heard all those horror stories from the Israelis? Then an old bloke told me that sometimes at night the Israelis sneak across the border into the villages, and during one such raid some of his friends were captured, and . . . guess what? They had their dicks and balls cut off and sewn into their mouths.

Oh, now I get it. That's how war works. Thanks to Aeschylus we all know about the first casualty of war, but just in case the old boy was telling the truth, I was wondering how I could somehow get it out to the other side that, 'I ain't got no quarrel with them Israelis.'

•

Six months later I was back in Lebanon, in Beirut for a story on the civil war. Poor Beirut, once described as the Paris of the Middle East, now looked like the bowels of the Middle East. Though there were still parts that gave hints of how the place must have once been. We'd all seen earlier television ads for Beirut. Beautiful bikini-clad girls frolicking in the Mediterranean Sea with speed boats and waterskiers in the background, followed by images of flashing neon lights advertising nightclubs chockers with beautiful people all spending up big. Not anymore. All that was left of this once grand capital city were bombed-out buildings and dilapidated hospitals full of kids suffering from horrendous shrapnel wounds and scores of young men either dead or badly wounded by the enemy.

Which enemy? The Phalangist Maronite Christians supported by the Israelis or the Syrians, or Palestinian members of the PLO or the PLA, or other Christians such as the Greek Orthodox or the Greek Catholics, or other Muslims, from the Shia or Sunni or Druze clans, or the Lebanese National Movement or the Lebanese Front . . . We had no idea what was going on, who was killing who, and it looked like neither did they. Yet somehow they all knew who to target and kill. I just hoped it wasn't going to be me—'I ain't got no quarrel with all of the above.'

We were staying in the Commodore Hotel in West Beirut and it was full, not of fun-seeking holidaymakers, but journalists. Some brave, some cowards, some mad and some beautifully performing 'Hotel Room Journalism', a term created by English press reporter Robert Fiske many years later about journalists reporting on the Iraq War without ever leaving their hotel rooms. Fiske, the Middle East correspondent for the *Independent*, was based in Beirut and I doubt there had been a war in the last 40 years that he hadn't covered.

Hotel Room Journalism sounded good to me. I'd have embraced it wholeheartedly if I hadn't been a cameraman and part of a team that actually needed to be out there and amongst it. And then like a sign from above I just happened to bump into one of the bravest of the brave in the foyer of the Commodore, none other than Neil Davis. *Wow! Neil Davis. This must be a real war,* I thought. *So why am I here?*

Neil was tall with a long face and cheeky eyes, and he oozed confidence. Recognising our Aussie accents, he immediately came over for a chat. A really good bloke, not a big noter, he looked and sounded like he had been there, done that, and he certainly had. He asked what shots we were hoping to get, and I said we were going out to get footage of the Green Line, the border between the mainly Muslim faction in West Beirut and the Christian Lebanese Front in East Beirut.

Just like Tony Joyce in Kampala who had warned us not to trifle with the curfew, Neil Davis probably saved our lives. He told us it was extremely dangerous at the border and that inside two of the buildings above the intersection where we had planned on filming were two snipers who only yesterday had shot and killed a woman as she was pushing her pram across the street. Her baby was also killed. Neil took me to a window and pointed out the two buildings and the exact windows where the snipers were shooting from.

After thanking him profusely for his warning, we took his advice and went to an area he recommended to get all the footage we needed. With those shots in the can, we headed straight to the attempt at a nightclub attached to the Commodore. The club was full of journos buying each other drinks and socialising with the locals. Everyone looked very relaxed. Not us, though, we were too busy discussing how maybe we should become the 1980s equivalent of Hotel Room Journalism, and never, ever, leave the hotel again.

Sadly, the man who saved us from our stupidity, Neil Davis, just like Tony Joyce, was later killed in a war. Worse, it wasn't even a war worthy of the name.

In September 1985, a couple of years after our meeting in Beirut, while covering a pissweak little coup in Thailand, Neil and his soundman Bill Latch found themselves needing to take cover behind a small telephone junction box. Beside them were their friends Gary Burns and Daeng Kariah, filming for a different organisation. With no warning a tank fired in their direction. Neil and Bill were both hit. Neil's camera fell to the ground, still rolling, capturing his last moments. His final shot was of his own body being dragged away by his great mate Gary Burns.

Tony Joyce and Neil Davis, two great Australian newsmen who had saved our lives, both lost their own lives doing stories nowhere near as dangerous as many they had covered before.

•

Meanwhile, back in Beirut, after a few days covering the west side, we took the long way round to East Beirut. We could have done it in five minutes but that would have meant driving past the snipers who murder women and babies. So we took the agonisingly long but safe route. Long because of the distance but also because every few kilometres we had to stop at sandbagged checkpoints to show our IDs.

What a mess. It looked like these guys in the east were well and truly losing the battle, but then again I had no idea what was going on, and frankly wasn't interested. War is absurd, but civil war is fucking insane, and everyone we interviewed, from Phalangist Christians to the Syrian Socialist National Party (who were actually Lebanese), to Palestinians (who were actually Palestinians), all to a man, told us that with God's help they would win. I wonder about a god who picks sides, because someone's got to lose. Men have prayed for victory as long as there have been wars. Someone once said there are no atheists in foxholes. It may well be true, but someone else said it isn't an argument against atheism, it's an argument against foxholes.

Young men have always been the pawns in the game. There's a great scene in the movie *All Quiet on the Western Front* when Katezinsky, a born leader who despised war but who still fought his heart out, tells his mates: 'I'll tell you how it should all be done. Whenever there's a big war comin' on, you should rope off a big field and sell tickets. Yeah, and on the big day, you should take all the kings and their cabinets and their generals, put them in the centre dressed in their underpants and let 'em fight it out with clubs. The best country wins.'

I couldn't agree more, and probably every soldier who ever fought someone else's battle thought the same.

The novel *All Quiet on the Western Front* reduced me to tears. The author Erich Maria Remarque did spend time at the front. So if a book about the horrors of war can reduce you to tears, why not the real thing? I knew they were all tougher than me, but why weren't all these blokes sobbing their hearts out all day? Bashir Gemayel, Commander in Chief of the Lebanese Phalangists, a charming man with degrees in law and political science, told us he lost his daughter in a car bomb explosion and said with dry eyes, 'I don't have any hate more or less than what I had before.'

Where did all this hate come from? Bring on the generals in their underpants, I say, and speaking of underpants I needed new ones myself, after dashing with Bashir Gemayel down an alleyway full of snipers.

He looked up the alley and ran for cover. He then waved us on, one by one. I couldn't help thinking, 'How does he know we're not going to be shot? This is stupid.' But come my turn I put my head down, my arse up, and ran. I felt like I should just keep running all the way to Syria and beyond, but when I got to Bashir I stopped and stood as close to him as I could. I should have filmed as

I was running, Neil Davis would have, and it would have been a great shot, but in times like that, I think of my arse and never the story. A few months after my run with my now good mate Bashir, he was elected president. A month later he was assassinated.

At the end of our first day in East Beirut, and still in shock at our mad sniper run with Bashir Gemayel, we still had nowhere to stay. And with shit happening all around us, driving round looking for accommodation was no fun. Not like the laugh a minute day we'd just had.

We eventually found a hotel, but had trouble hearing the receptionist through all the shelling outside. We think he said, 'Do you know what to do if the hotel is hit?' Depends who's asking, I thought. 'You take the stairs and head for the dining room which is on the lower ground floor.' Sounded good to us.

The shelling and gunfire was relentless through the night. Sleep was impossible, and as I showered and brushed my teeth in the morning, the shelling seemed to be getting closer. But I was reluctant to run to the lower ground floor, thinking I must be brave, everyone else is, and after all, this must happen round these parts every day. The shelling got louder and more violent then . . . *Bang!* The wall of my room was hit with a huge explosion. My toothbrush nearly went through my gum. *Shit, I'd call that a war wound.* So with a mouth full of blood I took off. The corridors were eerily quiet with not a soul in sight. Maybe I'd overreacted. Maybe it was nothing. Maybe I should just go back to my room. What would Neil Davis, Tony Joyce and Robert Fiske have done? They'd all be outside getting a story. Not me, I'm wounded.

I raced into the dining room and there was not a spare inch of space. The place was overflowing with people, some even cowering under furniture, including my courageous colleagues who looked out from under their tables and said, 'Where the fuck have you been?!'

It appeared that I was the last person in Beirut, maybe even the whole of Lebanon, to go diving for cover. How brave was I. And I had a war wound to boot. I wished Neil and Robert were here to see this. Maybe I could even join their brave persons' club.

•

If somehow there was a clone of me in a parallel universe and I was to find myself in an army, in a trouble spot, give me the horrors and atrocities from the great Belizian–Guatemalan conflict. Belize had absolutely nothing going for it but beautiful timber, and there'd been arguments and wars over logging rights for hundreds of years. The great English writer Aldous Huxley once said of Belize, 'If the world had ends this would be one of them.'

On 21 September 1981 the Poms pulled out of the last British outpost of the Central American mainland and handed over independence to the Belizeans, making it official at exactly midnight. At Government House, for a select few hundred, the Union Jack was lowered as the new flag of Belize was meant to pass it on the way up the flagpole. They met in the middle and got beautifully stuck, neither of them going anywhere.

The problem might have been lack of rehearsal but I suspect it was the huge tropical storm that hit at five minutes to midnight. I'd set up my lights to shoot the symbolic flag changeover, but when that storm hit, all my lights blew. Well, exploded really, along with everything else, and we were all left in complete darkness. I shot as much as I could, not seeing a thing through the viewfinder and knowing the film I was using was nowhere near fast enough, but I also knew there wasn't film yet invented that could've helped. But still I lived in hope that I might fluke something. Perhaps the supercharged, highly dangerous lightning bolts coming at us from every angle might just illuminate the flags long enough for one perfectly exposed frame. My camera was full of water, as was the entire Gordon Highland kilt-wearing band trying to play 'These Are a Few of My Favourite Things'. It was a complete disaster, but luckily for the politicians, dignitaries, bedraggled band and us, there was to be a second bite of the cherry the next day. For the masses.

Mad dogs and Englishmen. The official ceremony was bewilderingly planned for the middle of the day in 38-degree Celsius heat.

Having scraped the bottom of the royal gene pool, the numero uno Pom which the British came up with as their official representative was the hapless Duke of Kent, wearing thick red velvet pants held up by a belt supporting a large gold-handled sword that hung stupidly down his left side. Above his red pants he wore a white long-sleeve jacket dripping in medals and sweat, white gloves and a red velvet cap with gold braid.

Presumably the higher-up royals had much more important things to do, like cleaning their shoes, and we could tell the bored duke was wishing he had better things to do as well, like sticking pins in his eyes. But he performed his royal duty and on behalf of Her Majesty formally recognised Belize as an independent nation.

The Guatemalans had trouble recognising Belize as anything, so continued to have a 15,000-strong army along the disputed borders, but the British also kept a small number of troops on the border, backed by helicopters, missiles and Harrier jets, just in case. Maybe they found it too hard to let go. This was their fourth-last colony, with only Gibraltar, the Falklands and Hong Kong left.

After all the pomp and ceremony, we had enough shots to make it look like we were at the official turnover so we headed up to the mountains in a British helicopter to get much-needed images of the border conflict.

It looked like a war to me. Snipers in watchtowers covered in camouflage netting, trenches with machine guns positioned hundreds of metres along the border, and troops searching through the forests for any Guatemalans who may have crossed into Belize. It was all great footage for us, but it was really just a peace-keeping exercise.

With heaps of 'war' footage in the can, we headed back to our chopper for the short trip back to Belize City. Just as we climbed into the helicopter, the pilot told us he had a problem and it'd take some time to fix. All the other choppers were out, so we'd have to stay the night. I was happy with that, better to find out there was a problem with the chopper on the ground than at 2000 feet. But again I was wondering how I could make it known across the border that, 'I ain't got no quarrel with them Guatemalans.'

We were standing around, wondering what to do next, when the commanding officer asked if we'd mind bunking in with the troops for the night, and also invited us to the officers' mess for dinner at seven.

A young recruit showed us our bunks then took us to the bar for a few beers and a game of darts. Great war so far. Most of the troops had tattoos and missing teeth but all looked as tough as nails and had difficult-to-understand accents, from Irish to Cockney to Yorkshire, and were very funny. They were comfortable in their surroundings, as if it was a training exercise, which I think it was. They were being tested in the heat and jungles in preparation for the real thing some time in the future. After our darts game they asked us to join them for dinner. When we told them we'd scored an invitation from the top banana officer, they laughed and slapped us on the backs. One of them said, 'Fuck off then, you'll be so fucking bored you'll be back here in no time.'

The officers' mess was a huge tent any circus would be proud of. And if I hadn't been out all day shooting what looked like a war, I would have thought we were part of a circus, or maybe a Monty Python sketch. As soon as we entered we were approached by a dark-skinned local guy dressed in a white shirt and black bow tie, offering us the choice of gin or cold beer.

I grabbed a beer and checked out the scene. It was extraordinary. We were surrounded by a bunch of upper-class twits, wandering around in either a dinner suit or some over-the-top formal army uniform, presumably the one kept for a meeting with a bottom-of-the-ladder duke. But he'd already left town. Most had neatly trimmed moustaches and accents just as neatly trimmed. The British class system was alive and well in the alien mountains of Belize.

The hors d'oeuvres had arrived along with my first freezing cold beer. Ten minutes later we all sat down at a huge dining table with a white linen tablecloth and an array of knives and forks that hinted we were in for a bloody long meal. The soup was superb, not too hot, not too cold, Goldilocks would have approved. An army of waiters kept the red and white wine flowing, and as the night wore on I witnessed the spectacle of the waiters being treated appallingly. After the entrée we dined on a main course of succulent beef and vegetables, washed down with copious amounts of expensive wine. The general conversation was unbelievably self-indulgent, continuing through the dessert and on to the cheese and biscuits where it became no less boring but much louder through the coffee and gallons of port. I suspected the only things killed by British officers around here were brain cells.

As Hitler once said, 'The victor will never be asked if he told the truth,' so I knew those poncy officers would go home with tall stories of the horrors of war. Much taller than mine.

•

Reporting on wars has been around as long as wars. Thousands of years ago some lucky foot soldier was sent home to report on the success or failure of the battle, but the general populace were never let in on the secret. I don't know what came first, the people's need to know, or nosey correspondents who figured living on an expense account was like Christmas every day. One of the first journalists to go to war was Crabb Robinson, covering

Napoleon's battles for the *Times of London*, but the first picture man was the Dutch painter Willem van de Velde, who in 1653 went out in a boat to observe and sketch naval battles between the Dutch and the English. Talk about a death wish. Brave or mad, I don't know, but I suspect the latter.

Today war news is instantaneous and TV reporters are instantly famous. Some television reporters love to be in wars, they are seen to be really, really brave . . . and they can get all dressed up. The latest fashion accessory for the modern 'war correspondent' is the flak jacket. The TV reporters who love to wear them are the ones that don't need them. They go nowhere dangerous but insist on wearing their bulletproof vest for every appearance on camera.

There have been some genuinely brave reporters and some very unlucky ones. According to the managing editor of the *World Press Freedom Review* an awful sea-change has happened. Conflicts in countries such as Iraq, Afghanistan, Somalia and Pakistan are seeing 'the deliberate targeting of journalists'. Now Syria can be added to the mix. From 1992 to 2015, 1140 journalists have been killed in conflict areas.

Smart journalists don't take risks, but can still be caught out. Fiske's Hotel Room Journalists hardly leave their expensive suites, and if they're on TV the viewers at home are led to believe their every move is fraught with danger due to the ubiquitous flak jacket worn over the 'look at me, I'm in a war zone' suit. The type of suit that has been de rigueur for the phoney journo since Vietnam, and so beautifully described by Michael Herr in his amazing book

Dispatches: 'He was in his late thirties and he was dressed in one of those jungle-hell leisure suits with enough flaps and slots and cargo pockets to carry supply for a squad.'

And though Herr's suited journalist appeared 45 years ago, I saw a lookalike in the West Bank after the Israelis had bombed the shit out of the place, leaving it awash with rubble and wailing women. The young reporter from one of the British commercial channels donned his flak jacket over his jungle-hell leisure suit, leant right in, using the camera lens as a mirror, then spent the next ten minutes adjusting the collar of his jacket as if it was the latest Armani suit. He tried it fully extended, then totally flat, then settled on the halfway look. Another ten minutes on his hair and he was ready to 'report'. The poor cameraman struggled desperately to find a clean shot. One that didn't capture any of the other nearby members of the media who were looking on wearing jeans, T-shirts and grins.

•

The biggies of the last ten years, Iraq and Afghanistan, I deftly avoided. Simply by saying I wouldn't go. A huge risk, after all it was my job, but I had a wife and two kids. Why would I risk that for a TV show? Mind you, there were times when I was called a coward and threatened with a job in the studio, but luckily for me there were always other people keen to go.

People such as Jon Steele, the American-born camera-man working for the UK Channel ITN. This bloke has to be mad. His book *War Junkie* is absolutely extraordinary.

For *twelve years*, he covered every war and shithole that existed, and revelled in it. The subtitle of his book is, '*One Man's Addiction to the Worst Places on Earth*'. We need people like him so that people like me can keep the world balanced. My addiction is to the best places on earth. But Steele did finally crack. He had some sort of breakdown and was diagnosed with post-traumatic stress. And why wouldn't he? How he managed to last as long as he did shows just how tough and a little bit mad he really was.

15

Kings and Wannabes

Gliding effortlessly over the hills like a serpent on a summer's day they came at me, a wave of them swaying to a mesmerising beat. Beautiful bouncing breasts, thousands of them. Now, I've seen a thing or two in my career but this was astonishing. Breasts of all sizes and shapes, and all belonging to virgins, the prerequisite for appearing in this show, the coronation of the new King of Swaziland.

To cover the coronation seemed like a very romantic National Geo thing to do. Swaziland, a small landlocked monarchy in southern Africa, was a stable country with ancient traditions. How could I lose? Then I saw the media contingent; hundreds of crews from around the world. How to get something different from the rest of them was going to be a real challenge, though just getting to Swaziland had been a challenge for us.

The only way of getting to Swaziland was through South Africa, and Australian journalists were not welcome in South Africa in 1986. The Australian government, in condemning the repressive policies of the apartheid system, was very much on the nose to the South Africans, so we were banned. But the South Africans knew there were very few routes into anywhere in Africa from Australia and they weren't about to miss out on the lucrative flight path. So they were nicely prepared. They built a hotel on the arrival side of customs. We could land and take off to other destinations in Africa without setting foot on South African soil.

When we arrived at dusk in Mbabane, the Swazi capital, we saw a wonderful sight. Half a dozen men, thoroughly enjoying themselves, walking along the road wearing full traditional gear, feathers, animal skin, spear and shield. It looked fantastic. I couldn't wait to get stuck into the pictures.

The next morning, fully prepared for my National Geo award-winners, we went in search of traditionally dressed Swazis like we'd seen the night before, but all we could find were people in Western-style suits, jeans and T-shirts. We'd been duped. The men we saw in tribal clobber were probably on their way to a fancy dress party. And to top it off, Mbabane was a dump and it was pissing down rain.

I knew these people deserved to be part of the 20th century as much as we did, but I needed exotic pictures, and nothing looked exotic. Before Swaziland gained independence in 1968, it had been a British protectorate, so we blamed the Poms for the modern clothes and soulless look of the capital. If it wasn't for all the black faces, Mbabane, with its unattractive architecture and copious gum trees, could have been any small town in Australia. There was no hint of traditional architecture or culture.

But it was hard to feel depressed with everyone wearing such gigantic smiles, just a shame they weren't wearing animal skins and feathers as well. Everyone appeared happy, full of energy, confident and proud, completely different to the poor, downtrodden black people of Zimbabwe or South Africa. All those smiles were great to see, but we needed more. We needed those exotic images that unfortunately only existed inside the head of our executive producer. Shots similar to the ones he'd seen in Tarzan movies 50 years ago.

We eventually found one such image. It was straight out of Tarzan. A traditional healer in a loincloth, with a bone through his nose. That's more like it. We asked if we could film him going about his medical duties, and in his extremely articulate English he told us he'd be delighted. Well, at least it was a start. I filmed him from every conceivable angle. Tight shots of his big black eyes, pulling focus from the bone through his nose to his long-fingered hands administering eye of newt or wart hog gizzards or whatever he had in his bag of tricks. To keep the executive producer's dream alive, I tried to keep the Pfizer skin creams and the antibiotics out of shot.

So, there was 30 seconds done, now for the next fifteen minutes. Each *60 Minutes* story is somewhere between thirteen and sixteen minutes, but to get those minutes takes four or five days of shooting. This coronation had better be bloody good, because our search for Swazi 'culture' had come to nothing. It just didn't seem to exist. And it was still pissing down rain.

We headed out to the hills to do a piece to camera on the death of the old king. The rain made everything dull and flat, the pictures were far from National Geo, and I was far from happy.

That night we went to a disco to ease our sorrows and we found a culture of sorts. A room full of hypocritical white South Africans, drooling over the near-naked Swazi girls dancing in amongst many TV monitors showing soft porn. The men were teasing and fondling the obviously not happy local women. Back in South Africa these men treated the locals like shit, used them as slaves. But the Rand was so powerful and the Swazi economy needed the boost. I guess the Swazis had grown accustomed to these hypocrites.

The rain, the lack of colour and the lack of Swazi identity had squashed my National Geo hopes but suddenly all that changed. The sun came out and led us to small villages with their distinctive 'beehive huts' made of mud and straw. We scored great shots of children bathing in rivers, and women, young and old, walking to or from markets with bundles the size of small cars on their heads. I'd seen the same thing throughout Africa, Asia, the Middle East and New Guinea, and it was always the same. Women loaded up to buggery, doing all the work. Often they'd have a bloke walking alongside carrying nothing but a cigarette. It was all great footage, though, and at last we were getting somewhere.

The big day. Coronation time. The whole extravaganza was totally disorganised and the media were getting pissed off. Finally we were all herded like children into the royal kraal, a collection of huts covering many acres and fenced off to the world. This was where the royals lived. And there were shitloads of them.

It's said the old king, Sobhuza II, had more than 60 wives and 300 children. Talk about fecund, that's a busy king. Nobody really knew the *exact* number of wives or children. It was a royal secret. But the bigger secret was how he managed, with all that action and distraction, to rule for 61 years.

Inside the kraal I went looking for the best spot for my camera. I found out where all the official stuff was about to take place and claimed the premier spot by spreading out the legs of the tripod and surrounding it with the rest of the gear. I now had ownership of a good square metre. It was mine and I was not moving under any circumstances. *How good am I?* I hadn't been doing this job for a zillion years for nothing. Being a seasoned campaigner made all the difference. The other cameramen and photographers could watch and weep.

Twenty minutes later the weeping was all mine. Everyone was kicked out of the royal kraal, gear and all, and told by disorganised organisers to wait outside. We never found out why, but finally the word to go back in was given, unfortunately at the same time as it was given to the thousands of locals who had also been invited to the big day.

There was one entrance and it was 2 metres wide. Not quite wide enough for thousands of people I would have thought, but there was no time to think. It was on, and it was dangerous. Desperately trying to protect the camera, being pushed and shoved (hopefully in the direction of the gate), I was having real trouble breathing, squeezed in by sweaty, half-naked Swazis pushing violently to get inside to catch a glimpse of their new king. It was like being caught in a washing machine. I kept my head down and pushed with them, then saw my lens hood fall to the ground. Luckily for me, my very important 85 filter was attached to the lens and not the hood. Without the filter, the king and all his countrymen would be blue, and I didn't think blue shots of Africa existed in the executive producer's head. It was too risky to try to get the lens hood back so I left it to be trampled by the mob.

I looked across at Micky trying desperately to protect his Nagra tape recorder and his microphones. He, too, had his head down and was struggling to breath. I had no idea where George Negus or Andrew Haughton the producer were, but one of them had my tripod. If they were smart they'd be using it as a weapon to get themselves some breathing space.

We made it inside, alive and bruised but also aghast that all the best spots had been taken by other media contingents and we were way up the back. How did they do that? These cameramen had obviously been working for *two* zillion years. To make matters worse, the biggest handicap for a cameraman is to be a short-arse. Like me. So now, not only was I a long way from the action, but I, and therefore my camera, couldn't see a thing.

The media were locked inside the 'press pen' and given strict instructions not to move outside, never. We were also told it was forbidden to take shots of the 'sacred' area over to our left. The sacred area consisted of a few modern buildings in amongst stacks of traditional beehive huts, which housed most of the royal wives. If either of those rules were broken, we would be dragged out in handcuffs. This time I believed them. As easy-going as this place appeared, you clearly didn't mess with royalty.

Somehow amongst the chaos the Swazis got themselves together and it was spectacular. There were already thousands of Swazis dressed in their traditional gear, all carrying shields and long sticks, blunt at both ends. They all appeared to be very proud of their sticks, which they swung from side to side in time with their slow melodious chanting. It was mesmerising. And still they kept coming, more shields and sticks squeezing into and totally filling every spare inch of the kraal. The size of the adoring crowd made it impossible for we sardines squeezed inside our media pen to have any chance of getting shots of the king or the event.

Micky and I needed to think fast. The previous night we had dinner with George Dlamini, News Director of Swazi TV, so we called over an official and told him we were the designated documentary crew for the coronation, that we were friends of George from Swazi TV and the king would be very angry if he did not appear in any of the shots of his coronation due to our position at the back of the pen. After more than half an hour involving many chiefs, it was decided it might be wise to release us from the pen and let us roam.

And we did, much to the chagrin of the rest of the media pack.

Did I say chagrin, I meant hatred, with death stares so frightening I kept my face glued to the camera, shit-scared to make eye contact with any of them. I wasn't game to gloat. But I did have a deep sense of satisfaction having suddenly remembered I'd been doing this for *three* zillion years.

Then the man himself appeared. Well, boy, really. Eighteen-year-old Prince Makhosetive, about to become King Mswati the Third, also known as The Lion, The Bull, The Guardian of the Sacred Shield, The Great Mountain and The Inexplicable.

Dressed in what looked like a brown and white spotted lap-lap with an animal skin wrapped around his waist, and carrying shield and stick, the frightened-looking adolescent joined the thousands of chanting warriors. Very slowly the warriors lifted their right foot then the left, swaying backwards and forwards as one, at the same time lifting then lowering their shields and sticks, all totally in sync with each other. Most of the warriors had one or two feathers in their hair. The Inexplicable wore what looked like a crown of twenty bright red feathers backed up by three monster white feathers.

It was truly National Geo stuff and I was getting the lot. They stamped their feet in unison, causing billows of dust and creating a soft hazy effect like an impressionist painting. I went for an impressive impressionist shot by running the camera along the ground to get close-ups of the bare feet stomping in the dust. I kept rolling past hundreds of huge black feet all wearing some kind of ankle bracelet. And then smack-bang in the middle of my long tracking shot of those exotic feet, I came across a brand new pair of white running shoes kicking up more dirt than a four-wheel drive. It wasn't the king, probably just some young guy who didn't like to get his feet dirty. Somehow it made the shot.

As I stood up for another wide shot, three or four warriors suddenly broke away from the mob, ran towards the king and slammed their shields to the ground in front of him, followed by another group, and another. And I was getting the lot. Fantastic wide-angle stuff, close-ups of beautiful black faces filled with adoration, all wanting to impress their king with their flamboyance. It was too good to be true, and I had the whole scene to myself. I ran in with the warriors and then back. I grabbed a shot from behind the king with the warriors heading straight at me. I got extreme close-ups of the king's eyes. Then, with the camera on the ground, I got the shields slamming down inches from the lens. I was beaming. *Oh my golly gosh, what to do next?*

The look on my face finally must have been too much for the penned-in, angry and envious media mob. With their faces oozing rage they broke free. There was no stopping them. They raced through the no-go sacred area. It was terrible to watch as they tripped over the assembled queens and assorted spectators. A few cameramen managed to emulate a couple of my shots, then suddenly it was all over. Bit of bad luck, I say, but I could truly feel the full effect of their anger as they struggled desperately to get something, anything, out of the day.

If the media thought they were missing out, the assembled foreign dignitaries might as well have stayed at home. Except for sticks waving through the air, they wouldn't have seen much at all. They were a good hundred metres from the action, though I did wonder if they were dignitaries or tokens. There was P.W. Botha from South Africa, an assortment of tribal leaders, Ronald Reagan's daughter, and a string of black African presidents (many of them would later be assassinated, imprisoned for corruption, or living in exile with billions of dollars). And right there was our old friend the Duke of Kent, wearing exactly the same red velvet and gold bedecked outfit he'd worn in Belize. Hopefully he'd had it cleaned. He wouldn't want to be a bit whoofy around the new king who was probably wearing the latest Chanel deodorant and aftershave along with his dead animal skin. After all, only one month ago the Boy King was at boarding school in England. No wonder the poor kid was looking bewildered. He was probably wondering if he'd have time to get his homework done before he had to kill a lion with his bare hands and choose a few virgins to marry, because it was decreed he had to do both. It was also decreed that he must be both potent and a virgin. Talk about inexplicable.

The following day, inside a giant football stadium, all the ordinary citizens of Swaziland got to celebrate. The melee I was caught up in at the royal kraal was only for royalty and the aristocracy. I was amazed there was anyone left to participate. But there were tens of thousands of people waiting breathlessly to catch a glimpse of their new king. The most excited were the thousands of nubile topless women entering the stadium, the same ones I had seen coming over the hills, chanting and seductively swaying their breasts. All of them beautiful and all of them wanting to do more than catch a glimpse of their new king, they wanted to catch him. It was from this bevy of beauties he got to choose a bride or twelve. And, if they were lucky enough to be chosen, they'd live in the lap of luxury for the rest of their lives. Unless of course they were found to be unfaithful, upon which they would be banished from the royal kraal without their kids.

The stadium celebration was, well, eclectic. Half-naked men and women alongside traditional and modern choirs, brass bands and marching girls. A bit of old, a bit of modern, a bit of bad taste. How's that for democracy in an autocracy.

This time the king arrived in an open jeep wearing a headdress almost as big as himself, made of huge magnificent black feathers, flowing halfway down his neck. I know this, because his neck was about all I could see during the nervous young royal's speech. Somehow after the debacle of the day before, the organisers had managed to get organised. The media were all squeezed into a tiny enclosure miles away from the action, and to make sure there was no repeat of yesterday's fence-jumping we were surrounded by cops.

My shot of the king's speech consisted of the royal neck, a super-abundance of microphones and the back of a cop. Every now and then if The Inexplicable cocked his head to the left, I could catch a glimpse of his left eye. Luckily it was only the speech, not riveting television anyway, and Tarzan wasn't famous for speeches, so I figured I was safe from our executive producer. But I did need to get some colour and it wasn't going to happen from where I was.

It wasn't three zillion years of experience that managed to get me out of that enclosure. For once, being a short-arse paid off. I deftly squeezed myself to the back of the enclosure while eager bodies were only too keen to fill up the area I moved from. The cops, way too busy trying to keep an eye on all the unhappy journalists *and* watch the king deliver his speech, didn't notice me slip under the rope at the rear of our enclosure and move into the huge crowd. I pushed to the middle of the football ground, past all the men, then hid in amongst the thousands of nubile women. Well, not really hidden. I stood out like dog's balls. A white man with an Arriflex camera on his shoulder in a sea of black women waving knives, shields, spears and breasts.

The new king finished his speech and the crowd went wild. It was fantastic. I was surrounded by semi-naked women, some in skirts and others in such tiny bikini bottoms I wondered why they bothered. All of them brandishing long blade knives and swaying from side to side, a brave move considering they were all bare-breasted. They began chanting, then, still swaying, they moved from one end of the field to the other, all beautifully lit by the late afternoon sun. A sublime spectacle.

The king came down to join them. The women as one moved slowly and seductively towards him, then gently away from him. They kept it up for at least half an hour, while the men ran past them to slam their shields on the ground inches from the royal feet. The whole time the king had a huge smile on his face, probably due to the knowledge that any, or many, of these bare breasted-beauties would very soon be his homework. Sure beats boarding school.

He looked so innocent standing in front of his very happy and healthy subjects, all of them looking forward to a happy trouble-free future in their paradise with their beloved young king.

•

Twenty years later I was back in Swaziland. The king had gained a dozen wives and a few dozen kilos but had lost a stack of hair along with the innocence, happiness, and hope of a trouble-free future for his subjects.

The now older, wiser, larger king had some major ruling to do. Swaziland had the highest HIV prevalence in the world. One in four Swazis was HIV positive. Men, women and children, no one was spared.

The first case was reported in 1986 and the virus had spread at an alarming rate. It particularly affected women in the fifteen to 49 age group, and 31 per cent of women had HIV compared to 20 per cent for men. In 2007, 10,000 people died from AIDS and life expectancy had dropped to 32.

The king had declared AIDS a national disaster. He had made sure there was a good supply of condoms, but they were controversial and unpopular. Religious and traditional leaders had described condoms as un-Swazi, and the blame game was alive and well. No high-profile Swazi ever admitted to acquiring HIV until Chief Madelezi Masilela outed himself, saying he had acquired HIV through the practice of widow inheritance, where a man must marry his deceased brother's wife. That evil woman.

In 2001 the king reinstated a custom that banned all girls under the age of eighteen from sexual activity for five years and any man who had sex with a virgin had to pay a cow to the girl's family. Nice try. But the king was soon accused of ignoring his own policy by getting engaged to a seventeen-year-old. At least the cow dowry wouldn't have been a problem for him.

We met the king in one of his many palaces. A large, modern building with acres of carpet, the classy royal type you see in every cinema complex and casino around the world. All the furniture, and there was plenty of it, was painted a shiny gold. Couches and chairs were covered in a bright yellow or red silk to give that regal look. The walls were covered in photos or really badly painted portraits of previous kings.

An hour before the big meeting we were allowed into the royal greeting room to check for light and seating. Satisfied with the room, I had half an hour to kill so I thought I'd take a rest. Maybe I am a royal, but I naturally went to sit on the chair that can only be used by you-know-who. It wasn't covered in jewels or anything, in fact it looked pretty ordinary to me, as ordinary as a gold chair covered in yellow silk can look. But apparently I was about to soil The Inexplicable's favourite, and before my commoner bum hit the royal cushion, our very nervous but charming young Swazi minder, Sihle Damini, hurled himself forward to stop my already off-balance non-royal arse from committing a huge faux pas. He grabbed me and swung me away from the chair, absolute horror in his eyes. Who knows what would have happened if I'd landed. Probably not a lot to me, but poor Sihle was so shaken I suspect there would be no more palace visits for him.

We were ushered out of the room to wait for the grand entrance of His Royal Highness. A short time later, word somehow reached Sihle that the time had come, so down on his knees he went and with his eyes firmly on the floor he *crawled* into the room with us walking upright closely behind.

And there he was, the king himself, sitting in my chair wearing a bright red sari-type outfit pinned over his right shoulder, leaving his left shoulder bare, a thin moustache going down the sides of his chin à la 1974, a very expensive looking watch on his right wrist and his left hand gripping the ubiquitous stick. We were all introduced to him and as I shook his hand I couldn't help but notice his necklace. It looked like two playing cards hanging off it. Court cards, of course, both had crowns on them. I was desperate to tell him he had a damn good blackjack hand there, but decided against it.

The reporter, Tara Brown, sat in her designated chair while I frantically ran around getting shots of her making small talk with the king. Then Tara hit him with, 'It has been said you are one of the ten worst dictators in the world.'

Not thrown at all by the question, the king said, 'I was surprised when I saw that and asked myself what is a dictator in the world. I don't know if people know the definition of dictator. I don't consider myself a dictator.'

Tara: 'You've been accused of lavish excess while 70 pcr ccnt of thc population is destitute.'

'It's speculation,' he said. 'I am not a big spender.'

Mswati III, cool as a cucumber and still wearing a huge smile, was totally unfazed by any of the questions. On that note I decided to tell him that Micky and I had been there twenty years ago to film his coronation. He was amazed, and said he was a very young man then, and very nervous. I told him I was pretty young myself. He laughed and I don't think he believed me. He then told us he'd never seen any footage of his coronation.

In stepped our producer, Stephen Taylor. He told the king he'd arrange for a copy of the story to be sent over immediately. Two days later we showed the footage to the king. He was mesmerised. We interviewed him as he stared at the screen. A wonderful sequence. He couldn't believe how young he looked, and when Tara made a comment about how nervous he appeared, he told us he had been totally overwhelmed by the day, and really didn't know what was going on.

Now though, twenty years later, he sure did. He was full of confidence with a super-charming soft mellow laugh, the type of laugh that makes you think he has to be a good bloke. But he needed to be more than a good bloke if he was to tackle the HIV problem. There were now 100,000 orphans in Swaziland. Ten per cent of the population.

In one of the many overcrowded orphanages we watched scores of kids running and playing happily, it could have been any schoolyard anywhere in the world. The kids sang for us, their happy faces and thick African accents sucked us all in as they sang 'Jesus Loves the Little Children'. Great pictures for us, but they were going to need a hell of a lot more than just Jesus loving them to get them to the ripe old age of 32. Their parents, if not dead, were either slowly dying at home or in one of the unbelievably overcrowded Swazi hospitals.

Swaziland's hospitals were overflowing with HIV and AIDS sufferers. At the biggest and most sophisticated hospital, I filmed rows and rows of double bunks with yet more patients lying, dying, on the floor under the bottom bunk, and this was the best hospital in the country.

Most patients stared straight through us, not concerned or interested in what we were doing. The healthier ones could slightly move their eyes, the really sick had no movement or life in theirs. To take a sip of water, their frail skeletal bodies would move agonisingly slowly. The doctor in charge told us the fear of the stigma attached to being HIV positive stopped them seeking medical attention until it was too late, and who knows how many people they may have infected along the way.

But the traditional festivities still went on and the biggy was the annual reed festival when all the virgins got to celebrate their chastity. Certainly a smart thing to celebrate given the circumstances. Part of the tradition was the girls must cut a reed for their king then, waving the reeds and singing, walk many miles from the riverbanks to the king's kraal. Their singing was so beautiful, as if they'd been rehearsing with some amazing choirmaster for years. And the rhythm of their voices seemed to swing perfectly with the swaying of the reeds. Not to mention the breasts.

Outside the royal kraal, the reed-swaying continued, with every young virgin hoping their reed would attract the king's attention and possibly a marriage proposal.

Though not all the reed carriers had marriage in mind: the leading breasts this year belonged to the king's nineteen-year-old daughter who lived and studied in California. She looked and sounded like a native Californian surfie chick with braids down to her waist, a white-toothed smile, and all of dad's charm. She was awash with American confidence. A far cry from her dad at that age, she even sang us a rap song and told us she was trying to teach her dad to rap but he wasn't too good at it.

But he did appear to be good at being king. And he sure knew how to rule.

•

Not like the French royal family. If they were allowed to rule, they'd show the world a thing or two. Who'd have thought 50 years and a couple of revolutions after the big one when Louis XVI lost his head there'd still be a French king. When King Louis Philippe was eventually forced out in 1848, the French finally celebrated the end of the royals. But there's no stopping royal blood. Like a giant golden staph it's happy to keep breeding while it sits and waits for an opportunity to rule.

The golden staph who would be king was His Royal Highness, the Count of Paris, or the Comte de Paris, for we French speakers. For some unknown reason he was happy for us to do a story on his dysfunctional and feuding family. His Royal Highness, already in his 80s, didn't have a huge chance of becoming king. But he was still hoping.

'I don't say I will be king, it might be possible'—yeah sure, I thought, as I zoomed in for a close-up—'but that is quite sufficient for me.' He then added, 'Anything is possible if it comes from the people.'

The comte and his mob were lucky to be alive, yet they still believed they were born to rule. They just couldn't take the hint, so continued to swan around France genuinely believing the Revolution was all a big mistake and that one day all that was rightfully theirs would be restored. The comte and his would-be queen spent the first twenty years of their marriage in exile. But somehow the comte managed to persuade the government of the day to let them back into France to live as ordinary citizens.

But though they couldn't rule, having royal blood meandering through their veins meant that even today there's no shortage of sycophantic royalists or, as my schoolboy French would have it, 'des lickers de arse royalists'. Faded aristocrats with nothing but pretence in their lives. They just loved to crawl and bow to the pretenders, who lapped it up with royal aplomb.

The comte certainly had a royal air about him. He was suave, with piercing grey eyes, a neatly trimmed moustache, large teeth and a penchant for V-neck woollen jumpers. His wife, Isabella, the Countess of Paris, had spent her whole life as queen-in-waiting and would hang on to that hope till her dying breath. Her petite house was filled with portraits of all the kings of France, including the Sun King, Louis XIV. It was his extravagance and excess that started the ball rolling for the French royals to lose everything, including their heads. These descendants had nothing but their heads and hope. They should be grateful. You'd think they'd lie low and keep their mouths shut. Yet here they were airing their dirty laundry, socks, undies et al to the world.

The royal son and heir, Henri, had recently brought shame on the family by divorcing and remarrying. 'It is forbidden in the family,' said the old comte. 'I asked him not to marry. Live with her is fine.'

So it wasn't only the divorce that was the problem in this very Catholic family. Marriage outside the Catholic Church was just not on. If the marriage is not celebrated in the Catholic Church, it's not recognised by French royalists, so dad had no choice but to disinherit Henri and strip him of all his titles. This, they hoped, would scare off the new wife who everyone had labelled a gold-digger, or due to the lack of gold, a title-digger. Still, the much maligned, overly made-up woman had some class; it wasn't obvious to the naked eye, but Micaëla Anna Maria Cousiño y Quiñones de Léon sure looked classy in print. What with accents not only over her vowels but also her n's she was a shoo-in to become a royal. But the sight of all those squiggly lines still didn't impress the in-laws.

Henri d'Orléans was the dead spit of his dad, except for the teeth. If we thought dad had a mouthful, this boy looked like the entrance to Luna Park. He told us, 'I'm not a hypocrite, I chose to have a divorce because I didn't want to live like that. And now I have another wife. The only thing my father was not happy about was not that I divorced, but that I got married again. It has always been like that. It is the history of France. Before, there used to be killings as well. Now the killings are finished. When my father dies I will become the Count of Paris.'

Brave man, I thought. If he wasn't careful the killing may just start all over again. But the old comte, obviously knowing murder might make an already weird family look even loopier, seized the moment and held his own coronation ceremony, handing his son's title to his grandson Prince Jean d'Orléans. Touché!

When we met the girl with the classy n's, we wondered whether they and half a dozen of her names might have been added just to seduce the wannabe king. She looked like a faded 1940s film star with a heavy fake tan, huge confidence and an equally huge cigarette holder.

When asked if she would be happy to be the next Queen of France, she said, 'I think I would be anguished by the responsibility, but I suppose there's a grace that allows people to do what they should do.'

Boy, she's good, I thought. *If the queen thing fell through she could always run for president.*

She then told us she had been offered money to leave the family. When later we hit the old comte with that bit of info, he said it was rubbish, he had never offered anyone money. Most probably because he didn't have any.

Meanwhile, having never seen the old comte and his wife together, we found the twist in the story. *Days of Our Lives* eat your heart out. The comte had left his wife years ago. No divorce, of course, but they lived completely separate lives, each with their own set of sycophants. We met her sitting regally amongst her antiques, with a triple-strand pearl necklace harnessing all the wrinkles, and she told us she missed the comte but her life was so full she had no time to think of the past. I presumed she meant the cohabiting part. She was still desperately hanging on to becoming queen.

The more time we spent with the old comte, the more I liked him. Due to his age the highlight of his day was an afternoon siesta, which suited me just fine, after all I have Spanish blood and, if I threw a few quaint little accents over some of my consonants, I might have scored one of his daughters and a title or two.

We arranged to do a horse riding sequence with HRH after his siesta, and Micky, worried that the comte may change his clothes for the horse riding, asked if he'd mind continuing to wear the woollen jumper because it was perfect for the radio microphone. Micky needn't have worried. It was all we'd ever seen him wearing.

Later that afternoon at his stables, in front of a throng of minders, the comte said to Micky, 'See Micky, I did as you asked, I have on the same jumper.'

Micky slapped him on the back and said, 'You're my kind of king.'

There was a sudden deathly silence from the minders. A major breach of protocol had occurred. But the would-be-if-he-could-be king responded with a toothy laugh and a big pat on Micky's shoulder. Micky had a new friend, but in fact the comte had won all of us over. It was impossible to dislike him.

Wearing an impeccably tailored suit over the perfect-for-the-radio-mic jumper, he looked twenty years younger than his age. His horse was a beautiful grey with a high-stepping canter and that tortured-looking curve in its neck that only perfectly trained horses have. As I pulled back from a tight shot of his boot in the stirrup, the wannabe king youthfully swung his leg over the back of his magnificent horse, gave a small kick and they were away. The octogenarian, obviously having ridden all his life, looked like he was glued to the saddle.

He never made it to the throne. He died in 1999 and his son Henri is now the king in waiting. And waiting.

•

But who needs glue to cling to power when you've got corruption, authoritarianism, despotism, nepotism, and a

Richard Carleton cooking dinner in the deep south of the USA.

Relaxing in Swaziland with George Negus and Micky Breen. *Photo Andrew Haughton*

Producer Allan Hogan with pygmy chief and his mate holding the
very dead monkey.

Paris 1980 with Ian Leslie, Allan Hogan, Peter Fragar and, balancing the
frame beautifully, Alice Springs, wife of photographer Helmut Newton.
Photo Helmut Newton

On patrol with the Israeli army—two out of three are happy.

One of many trips to Gaza. *Photo Micky Breen*

The ever-handy portable dark room. *Photo Ray Martin*

Hollywood star Lee Marvin 'hunting' marlin. *Photo Ray Martin*

Shooting George. Close-ups were big in the 80s. *Photographer Vaughan Gentle*

In London with new reporter Bob Hawke. Behind Bob is his new best friend, Steve Edwards, our good mate and driver.

Getting an exterior of Amin's torture headquarters, the State Research Bureau.

With Ian Leslie, Peter Fragar and Isaac Sowanga, reading the secret files of Amin's tortured political prisoners.

Richard Carleton and Allan Hogan on their way to interview 'mass murderer' Radovan Karadzic. *Photo Paul Boocock*

With Ian and Peter checking out one of the wonders of the ancient world. The horror horse ride is yet to happen. *Photo Allan Hogan*

Breakfast in yet another amazing pub. *Photo Stephen Taylor*

Before breakfast in a not so amazing pub. Bruce Stannard and me sleeping on deck.
Photo Ray Martin

suspension of civil law, civil rights and *habeas corpus*, plus a wife with one pair of feet but a trillion pairs of shoes.

After declaring martial law, Ferdinand E. Marcos did and said whatever he wanted. Turned out he wanted heaps, and by the end of his term as Philippines president he had billions stashed away in Swiss bank accounts. All earned legitimately, of course, as Ferdinand did a lot of overtime and sometimes even worked weekends. This was obviously true because when I met him he looked very tired.

On our arrival in Manila we were told only white shirts were to be worn in the presence of the president. None of us owned one so we rushed out and bought the cheapest and nastiest white shirts we could find. I suspect Ferdy owned all the shirt factories, hence the dictum.

Years after his death, his wife Imelda, known as the Steel Butterfly, was still telling the world how hard he had worked to gain all that wealth, that none of it was gained illegally and the people of the Philippines (the great majority existing on two dollars a day) were entitled to none of it.

Looking like schoolboys in our brand new white shirts, we were ushered into an office for the interview. *An office!* Palaces and Swiss bank accounts abound and we had to do the main interview in an office. And it looked like shit. Smart, I guess. Marcos could now look like an ordinary politician. Billions? What billions?

We were told the president would sit behind the desk and reporter Ian Leslie would sit opposite. Ian's chair was indeed opposite the president's desk, but it was also a good metre lower. It would look really stupid, I protested, but was told that's the way it is. When you're a billionaire dictator you dictate, and we'd been dictated to. It was impossible to disguise the eye line of the dictator looking down on our reporter, but rather than give him the added satisfaction of the camera also looking up to him, I extended the tripod legs as high as they would go so the camera was at least level with his eyes.

I suspect that had Ian asked if Marcos saw himself as a megalomaniacal tyrant like the rest of the world did, he wouldn't have cared less. Dictators don't worry about a thing. He owned the army and he'd got rid of his political opponents. His main rival, leader of the opposition, Benigno Aquino, was in jail on trumped-up charges.

So when Ian asked him, 'Do you see yourself as a dictator?' it was like water off a duck's back.

'No! A forceful leader, yes. We've re-established public order, the classical purpose of martial law.'

Why this tyrannical ruler had agreed to the story was a mystery. But it meant I got to experience another interesting culture with interesting food. And the producer, Warren McStoker, and I experienced some really interesting cuisine. So interesting that for me it was a rerun of the Cairo chicken livers. Of course I hadn't eaten chicken livers again, I'm not that dumb. But whatever I ate brought the same unpleasant results.

That night we were summoned to the palace to shoot the president's 62nd birthday bash. With my most recent dash to the toilet being just 30 seconds earlier, I met the others in the foyer of the hotel to tell them of my dilemma. Then I saw Warren, who actually looked like what I had just deposited into the toilet bowl. But Warren, one of the best and most conscientious producers at *60 Minutes*, was not going to let a small thing like shit in his pants or vomit on his shirt interfere with what would probably be the best sequence of the story. He asked me if I was okay and I told him no, but if he could get on with it looking like he did, so could I. To most other producers I would have said, 'I'm sick, piss off,' but somehow with him it was different.

When we reached the palace I was desperate and walking very carefully, especially since I was carrying the camera and a 25-kilo case of lights. Warren, carrying the tripod and rolls of film, was also walking very delicately, and he was so pale. Inside the palace we deposited all the gear and took off to deposit a few more kilos of our own, something neither of us could afford.

Pale and sweaty we ventured back into the birthday room where it was all happening. I picked up the camera that had somehow put on all the weight I had lost and began to shoot the handpicked senators gushing and kissing their beloved tyrant. They put all other sycophants to shame.

Then those same senators had to do it all over again as Imelda entered the room. I hate to admit it but she did look beautiful, not overly done up and with two huge pearls hanging off each ear. After much applause, the top of her list was to be introduced to the nice film crew from Australia. Still very pale and sweaty in our white shirts that no longer looked new, we stood ramrod straight, not through defer-ence to the Steel Butterfly but as a result of deft sphincter control. She walked over with a huge welcoming smile to shake our hands and welcome us to her country. First Ian, then Warren, who gingerly reached out to greet her. But before contact he rapidly retracted his clammy hand, clutched his bum and took off. *Poor form,* I thought, *obviously no self-control. What would Madame Dictator think?*

Who cares. Just as I took her hand, I felt deep rumblings. I grimaced in panic, dropped her hand and took off in Warren's footsteps. I made it to the gents' just in time. And from the next stall through clattering teeth the shivering producer said, 'Boy, that was close. She's a very lucky woman.'

Back at the birthday bash the senators were all loudly singing 'For He's a Jolly Good Fellow' (and so say all of arselickers), terrified they might miss a word, or worse, look as if they weren't singing. At the end of it Marcos cried out 'Encore!' and the mob tipped their heads back and laughed uproariously.

Imelda then decided it was Marilyn Monroe time and sang happy birthday to the president. Flat and out of tune, she warbled on and on and on, convinced she was the hottest thing since Ella Fitzgerald. Great footage.

The next day was the official birthday celebration for the masses. Tens of thousands of peasants were bussed into a huge stadium for a 'spontaneous' show of loyalty.

The ceremony was led by the Roman Catholic Archbishop of Manila, the unfortunately named Cardinal Sin, who would often use his own pun 'Welcome to the house of sin' in church. And the mob loved it, and him. The real sin was what was going on in the government. The archbishop conducted the birthday celebration for reasons known only to him. It was well known that he was no fan of Marcos.

Years later, fed up with all the fraud and corruption, Cardinal Sin became one of the architects of the People's Power Movement that eventually removed Marcos from office. The cardinal appealed to Filipinos of all religions to follow the teachings of the gospel and use peaceful means to change the political situation. It worked beautifully. And in 2001 the cardinal even managed to do it one more time by playing a major role in the ousting of President Joseph Estrada.

•

I wasn't there for Estrada's 'ousting' but I was there for his 'inning'.

It was nine years between the Marcos and Estrada stories and I'd been to the Philippines half a dozen times for other stories. The ubiquitous Aussie fat old guys marrying beautiful educated Filipinos, a staple for *60 Minutes*, plus we did poverty, rebels and one humdinger of a story that was a real fizzer.

It was alleged that during WWII the Japanese had buried in Manila tonnes of gold said to be worth billions. Some nobody reckoned he had found it and had given us the exclusive rights to the story. We should have pulled out the moment we met him. His clothes and his demeanour didn't quite match his delusional thinking. He was convinced he was Indiana Jones, but he didn't convince us. What really gave him away was the couple of flimsy Dick Smith 50-buck metal detectors and a map that looked like it had come from a Christmas cracker. And once all this high-tech gear pinpointed the buried treasure that no one had been able to find in 45 years, he was going to retrieve his booty from under eight feet of concrete with a $10 shovel. We tried. We worked in intense heat. We hired helicopters, we spent loads of money, but . . . there was no gold, of course, thus no story and no redeeming ourselves.

I never had any problems entering or leaving the Philippines for those stories, so on arrival for the Estrada story, why would it be any different?

Impatiently we stood in line at Manila airport's immigration desk, already feeling the intense humidity, and desperate to get to our air-conditioned hotel for a really cold beer. After flashing all the relevant documentation, the other three sailed through, but not moi. The immigration officer took one look at my passport, me, the passport, me, the passport, then said, 'Come with me.'

'Bloody hell,' I thought. 'What this time? It can't be the Palestinian look, why would they care? Maybe they think I'm Japanese and I've come back to retrieve all the war gold Indiana never found.'

It was same old, same old: 'Why are you here? What are you doing?' This mob had none of the smarts of the Israelis so I let them have it. What did they think they were fucking doing, I'd been to their country a dozen times and had never been stopped. 'Why now?' I demanded to know.

They told me I'd done a story on their president that was not complimentary so I had been blacklisted. But the only story I'd done on a Philippines president was Marcos, and that was *nine* years ago. I was flabbergasted that anyone would care. 'Are you blokes kidding? You should be thanking me. He was a dictator, a liar, a cheat, a thief, possibly a murderer. And a dickhead.'

'He was our president.'

I asked why I hadn't been stopped at any other time during the last nine years.

'You were always on the blacklist, but we now have computers.'

So I'd been on the blacklist for nine years but it had obviously been in the too-hard basket to check the list during that time. They were so proud of the fact that they now had computers, I was almost going to compliment them on their ability to work one. Until they told me I couldn't spend any more time in their country, the next plane out was in fifteen minutes, it was going to Singapore, and I would be on it.

I then explained I was one of a group of four, I had eighteen pieces of luggage, and I was here to do a story on Joseph Estrada, possibly and probably their *next* president. The presidential election was in two weeks and Estrada was the firm favourite.

Joseph 'Erap' (mate) Estrada had been a B-grade film star, which was lucky for him as B-grade are the only films made in the Philippines. He had always played heroes of the downtrodden so the poor loved him and couldn't wait to vote for him. He wasn't just a B-grade actor, he'd also been a B-grade mayor for a while so he'd had some experience of politics, but most of his time as mayor was spent fighting allegations of corruption, murder and rape.

When I told the immigration officials that Estrada wouldn't be too happy when he found out we wouldn't be doing the story, they folded. They agreed to let me stay, but insisted that while I was in Manila I should try to get my name taken off the blacklist. I left the airport having no idea how and where I'd start the process.

The next day we interviewed Estrada, who was a shoo-in to be president, but Richard Carleton had decided the man was a lightweight and got stuck into him in the interview, calling him a murderer and a rapist. That didn't go down well. Richard then accused him of being a drunk and a womaniser. 'During my younger days, of course,' Estrada said proudly.

His rivals not only questioned his morality but also his intelligence, so Richard asked whether you had to be intelligent to run a country. There was a long pause as Estrada, with his thin Asian mo and shifty B-grade actor eyes, took a huge amount of time to think, then mumbled, 'Well of course you don't have to be dumb.'

'Do you know much about economics?'

'Not much.' And he wasn't acting.

Listening to that, I figured I'd better get off Marcos's blacklist fast. After Richard had ripped into Estrada, there was definitely going to be another blacklist heading our way, and I didn't want double demerits. I figured B-grade actors who become B-grade mayors who become B-grade presidents probably don't have good memories, but murderers probably do, so I wanted to be off Marcos's blacklist before 'Erap' found out I was a serial offender.

One of the interviews needed for the Estrada story was with the attorney-general who seemed like a good bloke and pretty sharp. I told him of my dilemma and asked if there was anything he could do. He immediately checked the blacklist, saw my name and said he would help, but first I had to fill out a few forms.

A few forms! When I first saw the paperwork that was needed, I thought, bugger it, I'd be quite happy to never see this place again, but the attorney-general was working back late to accommodate me and had told me it would be 'very wise' to be off that list.

I wrote my life story and answered absurd questions, then every form had to be checked, double checked, triple checked, signed and stamped by as many bureaucrats as there were forms. I spent hours wandering miles of corridors searching for the right bureaucrat and more importantly the right stamps. Finally, with every i dotted, t crossed, stamps stamped and signatures signed, I went back to the attorney-general's office.

'Good,' he said, 'now you need the signature of a JP.'

At first I thought he was joking—I was with the numero uno legal guy in the whole country and I needed a JP?—but irony's not big in the Philippines. The attorney-general gave me the address of a JP only five minutes away, and from his window pointed out the direction I should take.

I soon found myself in a very seedy bar area so I figured I'd gone the wrong way. I retraced my steps and headed off in the opposite direction. Nothing but building sites and open sewers. I headed back down the original route, thinking this had to be a huge mistake, then came to a shithole of a bar that had the correct address. It was dimly lit with not a soul to be seen. I tentatively ventured inside, calling out, 'Anybody here?' But it was eerily quiet. As I turned to go, I heard, 'Can I help you?'

Through the half light I saw a totally naked man rising from a couch and a deep sleep.

With beads of sweat running down his body, he said, 'What do you want?'

'I'm looking for a JP.'

'I'm a JP.'

'I need this signed.'

'You got a pen?'

'Ahh, no.'

'Want a drink?'

'No thanks.'

The JP wandered off in search of a pen. Having seen a hell of a lot more than I needed to, I walked over to the filthy bar to wait. Finally, still starkers but holding a pen, he returned and said, 'Where do I sign?' I pointed. He signed.

'That'll be twenty bucks,' he said, scratching. 'You can have a drink on the house.'

I handed him twenty dollars then spent the next fifteen minutes chatting with the naked man while I polished off my nice cold free beer. We chatted about the weather, the price of beer and about Estrada, but no mention of why he was naked.

On my way back to the attorney-general's office, I wasn't sure if I'd been hallucinating, but there was an illegible signature with JP next to it in the appropriate spot, and that was all I needed.

I handed the papers to the Philippine's top legal eagle, who took one quick look at naked man's signature. 'That's fine,' he said. 'You're now off the blacklist.'

Two weeks later Estrada was elected president. Richard obviously didn't upset 'Erap' too much, because I went back to the Philippines many times and wasn't on any blacklist—though corrupt, charged and convicted ex-president Joseph Estrada soon found himself on quite a few. After six years of house arrest he scored a 30-year jail term for 'plunder', but after promising *never* to run for public office again, he was pardoned by President Gloria Macapagal Arroyo. But you can't keep a good corrupt ex-president down. In 2013 Estrada got himself elected Mayor of Manila.

16

No Apology, Anthropology

Charm, cracking jokes, acting dumb and the bribe of 800 bucks still didn't help get the camera gear through customs at Nairobi airport. It got the film through, a fat lot of good that did us without a camera. There was a $3000 fee on bringing in film but the customs officer politely said that for $800 (that went straight into his pocket) he'd wipe the importation fee. So I paid, foolishly thinking it would cover all the gear.

I didn't know if I should blame Sydney Pollack for actually shooting his movie *Out of Africa* 'on location', but we were well and truly done over by the Kenyan customs officers. Pollack's Hollywood crew had thrown money around Kenya like it was wildebeest droppings, and now it was always migration time for anyone with a camera. We were told we needed a $US50,000 bond to get the gear through customs, and it was *non-negotiable*. But we kept on trying, hinting that maybe we could come to some sort of agreement.

As my diary of 27 January 1987 says, 'A half hour later we were on our way to the hotel without, sans, having none, empty handed, gearless!'

The producer Warren McStoker and I spent the next two days organising the $50,000 and making twice-daily trips to customs, still attempting to negotiate. Micky and reporter Jennifer Byrne, went food shopping for our five days of camping in the middle of nowhere for our story on the famous paleoanthropologist Richard Leakey. We needed to buy food, but everything else, such as camping gear, beds, chairs, cars, drivers, cooking utensils and cooks, was taken care of by a local Kenyan camping organisation. They had vast experience of looking after film crews like us. Should be fun.

Finally with the 50 grand in our grasp, Warren and I fronted up to the Kenyan customs officials, slapped the cheque on the counter and requested the gear. Alas, the greatest legacy of English colonialism is bureaucracy. We didn't need just one stamp, we needed ten, and each Kenyan customs officer dressed in his fancy uniform had his own stamp locked away in a beautifully carved wooden box. Once outside its ornate box and before it was soiled by our irritating papers, each stamp was presented to us, sommelier-like, as if it was a bottle of Chateau Mouton Rothschild 1945.

After nine stamps had done their duty we started to relax a bit, but it appeared the only people to relax in Kenya were locals. The last stamper, the one and only who could actually release the gear, had gone home and he didn't have a phone. Another day wasted.

Next morning as Warren stayed in the hotel to placate Leakey's minders who were getting restless, I went to meet the tenth customs officer to get his stamp of approval, grab the gear and get speedily out of there.

Wrong. After presenting his Mouton Rothschild, he insisted on checking all the serial numbers. When I pointed out to him there was nothing to check them against, it fell on deaf ears. So we went through a final charade. With every bit of gear he could find with a serial number, he'd call it out. I'd then answer, 'Yep that's mine!'

It was hard not to laugh but I took solace in the fact that stupidity is its own reward. Though possibly the stupidity was all mine. The time-wasting was obviously to elicit a bit of cash. Towards the end of this agonising process another guy whispered in my ear that a hundred dollars might help. But by now I'd had enough, I told them what they could do with their stamps and their attempts at extortion. I then grabbed the gear that was all on a trolley and stormed out. Not a word was said and nobody followed. I wondered why I hadn't done it days ago.

So finally, after three days, $50,000, endless stampings of fists, feet and bureaucratic ink, we loaded the gear and ourselves onto an eight-seater plane and headed to the town of Ludwa, the bowels of the earth.

In fact, there didn't seem to be a Ludwa. There was an airport (well, a dirt runway), a funny little bar, a few lopsided houses, and waiting for us in this metropolis were our three drivers in our three four-wheel drives, each chockers with the goodies Micky and Jennifer had bought in Nairobi. Our drivers had huge welcoming smiles. They escorted us to the vehicles, and even opened our doors for us. We were already looking forward to our bit of luxury camping after a long, hot day's filming.

Fifty rough kilometres later we arrived at Leakey's camp. He had gone out fossicking. His flunky told us we couldn't camp with them. 'Perhaps you'd like to pitch your tents over there,' he said, pointing to 11,000 square kilometres of Kenya. Over there suited us just fine. We didn't like to be with the 'talent' 24 hours a day and obviously the feeling was mutual.

Over there was flat, ugly and hot. There was nothing between us and the horizon but a few dead trees. Somehow, halfway between Leakey's camp and over there, the drivers got not just one vehicle but all three bogged, and they had no idea what to do. First they tried reversing, then full throttle forward, but the rapidly spinning wheels sunk deeper and deeper into the sand. Micky asked if they were in four-wheel drive. He might as well have asked the theory of general relativity. Pushing past the blank faces, Micky jumped into the first car, flicked it into four-wheel drive and took off. He then did the same with the other two. My knowledge of cars wasn't a hell of a lot better than the Kenyan drivers' so I couldn't really have a go at them, but I did wonder how they'd managed the long journey from Nairobi. But no matter, they'd come into their own come tent-pitching time, and more importantly, dinnertime.

We pointed to a nice flat spot (not difficult, the whole place was pancake-like) where we'd like our tents erected, please. It was as if we'd asked for the Taj Mahal and the Sydney Opera House to bookend the Champs-Elysées.

Their continued blank expressions led me to believe they'd never pitched a tent in their lives and weren't planning on learning how.

We needed shelter, so sweating profusely in the intense afternoon heat, Warren and I took tent-erecting instructions from Micky who once again saved the day. Guess who sat in deck chairs under what was trying desperately to pass for a tree? And from their shady spot, the three local camping experts watched calmly as we searched for the four missing tent pegs that were crucial to our construction. Finally we came to terms with the fact they didn't exist, so we created replacements by whittling tent pegs from any sticks we could find on the ground. I'd seen the movie *Out of Africa*, it must have been shot in a Kenya in a parallel universe to ours, because it was lush and tropical. It was hard to imagine Meryl Streep and Robert Redford picnicking out here.

With tents up we tensed up for our first meeting with Leakey who was renowned for being difficult. He had no academic qualifications so was sneered at by fellow diggers with thousands of letters after their names. His knowledge had all been learnt on digs with his famous palaeontologist father. But he had made many significant discoveries so the palaeo-heavies couldn't completely ignore him. He was also at odds with most of the palaeontology world over when and how we humans split from apes.

To get him on side, our first meeting was just small talk and a few quick shots of him meticulously naming and numbering fossils, some no bigger than a nail head but obviously very important. He was charming and happy to do everything we asked. With the light fading we thanked him then headed back to our camp for dinner. Our three drivers/cooks had not moved from their deck chairs and looked as though they weren't planning on doing so. Nothing had been prepared.

We set up the gas fridge. It didn't work. We set up the gas stove. It didn't work. Nor did Mo, Curly and Larry. It was clear if we wanted to eat we'd bloody well better get cooking.

Using a few of the failed tent pegs we lit a fire, and Reporter Chef and Producer Chef mixed tomatoes, onions, canned peas and carrots with pasta and when it was ready the Stooges left their seats and strolled across to dine. Micky and I then did all washing and cleaning up. Our workers were way too full to move.

Bedtime. Inside the tents it was a furnace, so it was an under the stars night. There were no ants but we made up for that with mozzies. Jennifer's bed and my bed were missing legs so we were lying on the ground. Well, not totally. We did have camp bed hessian the thickness of graphene between us and the earth, and though graphene is a full one atom thick, I still didn't get a good night's sleep. Warren, being over six feet tall, had a choice of having either his head or feet on the ground, without the added protection of graphene, but Micky's bed was just right and after what he'd pulled off that day he deserved it.

Up at 5 a.m. 'The best part of the day,' said Leakey. I tried hard to pretend it was, but obviously not hard enough. It was pitch black, my eyes were gritty, I felt grubby, and my back was killing me.

I showered under a hessian bag strung over the branch of a dead tree. Privacy did not come into it. The shower was smack–bang in the middle of nowhere and Jennifer was one of the boys. All female reporters on *60 Minutes* are tough. Camping is difficult when you also have to work, but the girls not only pitched in to help but had the added burden of having to look amazing. Not from vanity but from an expectation of bosses and viewers. The bloke reporters could get away with looking grubby with a three-day growth. They looked rugged and people loved it, but the girls had to look immaculate at all times, not easy when camping out in Africa, Afghanistan or Central Australia.

After a breakfast (made by Warren) of eggs, coffee and burnt toast, we headed off with Leakey in search of his obsession, bones that finally show where and how mankind branched off from apes. To the rest of the world, it's the missing link. Leakey refused to use that term, and told us in great detail why. He needn't have bothered, we had no idea what he was going on about, and nor would our audience.

The harsh, inhospitable landscape took on a new look at dawn. It was so beautiful. The long shadows and pink light had a Monet feel. But it didn't last long.

We followed Leakey's every move while he uncovered animal footprints a million years old and bones even older. With what looked like a child's toothbrush, Leakey and his students slowly and methodically brushed away dirt from their finds. It was so slow I figured it would take me another million years to finish shooting the scene. Where did these people get their patience and stamina? But the good thing about the intense heat—close to 50 degrees Celsius—meant bone hunters didn't work between eleven and three. Which suited me just fine.

Back in camp at the end of that first full day, I was desperately in need of a beer, but no one was keen to make the 50 kilometre trip to Ludwa. I finally coerced one of the drivers into taking me. It wasn't easy. Their bums were permanently glued to their deck chairs and none of my crew was keen to come either. I'd have driven myself but was planning on having a few. On that one-hour trip I tried desperately to engage Mo in conversation, to no avail. He did take up my invitation to come and join me in the bar, but he didn't drink. I wasn't sure if he was a Moslem or just a really conscientious designated driver.

That first beer was the best I'd ever had. The second and third were almost as good as the fourth. I then ordered ten coldies to take back for my colleagues and myself. It'd be pointless taking any more, the gas fridge had as much of an aversion to functioning as its Kenyan work-mates, and I hate warm beer. I jettisoned thoughts of a fifth beer and requested my takeaways. There, on the bar, the ten were now twenty. When I pointed out his mistake. the barman told me my mate had ordered the other ten. How, I have no idea. Sign language, I presumed. Guess who paid? Boy, these Stooges were good, and obviously not Moslems.

The next morning after our eggs, coffee and burnt toast, Leakey informed us he was going to Nairobi and he'd be back in a few days. We had about one-hundredth of a story in the can. Diplomatically, Warren and Jennifer tried to point out how far we had come and how much we had spent to get there and was there any way he could give us one more day.

'Nope,' he said and walked off.

Back in our camp, sitting under what resembled a toothpick for shade, Warren contemplated our future while Jennifer and I both brought out our diaries. To relieve the boredom we decided to read a page or two of each other's. I was a little embarrassed. She'd been a journalist since she was sixteen, had an insatiable appetite for books, and would soon have her own book show on the ABC. She had written of the charming silk-like feeling of the early morning warmth on her skin as she contemplated what it meant to her to be writing of the evolution of the human species in what was most probably the cradle of mankind. I had written, 'Got up, had eggs. Bad sleep, too hot. Stooges giving me the shits.'

In fact, most of my entries started with, 'Got up, had eggs.' Warren said that if ever I wrote my memoirs I should call it, 'Eggstracts of My Life', and in the same breath said, 'Shit, what are we doing here? Let's get back to Nairobi.'

So we did. Hot showers, room service, cold beers and, most importantly, a real dunny. The morning ritual of wandering from camp with trusty shovel and searching for privacy behind a toothpick tree was no fun at all, not that I think a flush dunny is fun, but it certainly made life easier, as did the absence of Mo, Curly and Larry. They weren't too happy at having to stay behind to mind the camp. It meant they had to learn to cook pretty fast or starve to death.

In Nairobi we did more than just eat and drink and use a nice dunny, we got shots in the local museum, skeletons, fossils, etc., most of which were Leakey finds. We even interviewed Leakey's mum, a charming pukka Pom who looked and sounded every bit the colonial and who would not have been out of place in Karen Blixen's book *Out of Africa.*

At the end of each day we settled into the best restaurant in Nairobi. I made the most of the food and grog, knowing for the next three days I'd be eating boiled vegies and rice in sand and heat. But at least when it was all over there'd be a quick trip to Belfast then *home*!

As if. On our last night in Nairobi, after yet another fine meal with expensive wine, Warren told us he'd just been informed that after Belfast we were off to Iran. A little bit of bad news I wasn't expecting. Iran was in the middle of an unbelievably uncivilised war with Iraq. Suddenly Ludwa, the Kenyan bush and the Stooges seemed nice and civilised.

Curly met us at Ludwa airport with a big smile, and when we got back to camp the other two were just as pleased to see us. I could understand why. They all looked kilos lighter and our tents, though not totally destroyed thanks to Micky and his whittling prowess, had been badly ripped by the wind. The kero lamps were completely empty, which suggested the Stooges had sat in the dark for at least two days.

The more I thought about a trip to Iran, the more I enjoyed our tinned spaghetti, tinned meat, tinned peas, expensive wine, and cheap plonk stolen from our hotel rooms. Even the shovel-shitting took on a whole new meaning.

Meanwhile, the Stooges were amazed at how once again we had light.

Next dawn, no missing link, but we did find a rhino head that was 16 million years old. The anthropologists, archaeologists, students, helpers and Leakey were delirious. I was unmoved. Maybe I'm the missing link, but I couldn't bring myself to be caught up in their enthusiasm. I know 16 million years is amazing, but they were looking at a tiny square inch of something that may or may not have been part of a skull, and were slowly dusting away dirt with tiny child's toothbrushes and dentist's picks, if ants had dentists. It was amazing to watch, but it didn't make for good television. We could smell it and see it up close, so we sort of got the picture, but the audience at home wouldn't. A special kind of determination and stamina drives these people. They dust away hour after hour, day after day, year after year.

After a few more days and a few more tiny 'finds', the Stooges drove us to the airport. Anticipating more bureaucratic stonewalling, we arrived in plenty of time to get our $50,000 deposit back. It was all going according to plan until the officious top banana with three stripes came over and asked for our receipt for the importation of the film. The $3000 fee we thought we'd cleverly avoided by buying off the customs bloke for 800 bucks. We told him we'd lost it, but that didn't help. He said we weren't leaving the country until he saw it, so what were we going to do about it? Angrily I said, 'Absolutely nothing, mate.' Not smart. But he was annoyingly bombastic. Warren stepped in front of me to placate the little man, and apologise for my behaviour. He was right, of course, there was $50,000 riding on this. Guess who then decided for a small fee he might be able to see a way around our problem? Now I was really mad. There were signs all over the airport saying 'Please No Tipping', so the poor porters who actually did some work missed out (but not from us), while these uniform-wearing upstarts got away with daylight robbery. Warren, with his superb negotiating skills, somehow got him down to $70 and the deal was done. Let's hope he never got to hear about his colleague's $800. Then again, let's hope he did.

•

The new look Belfast appeared to have calmed down a lot since the Bobby Sands story, and the Europa Hotel no longer had barbed wire around it.

Appearances can be so deceiving. I thought this'd be a simple story with a bit of R & R before the craziness of Iran, but nothing had changed in 400 years, so why was I thinking otherwise? The Protestants still hated the Catholics and vice versa. Northern Ireland wasn't too keen on the Republic of Ireland. The local cops hated the British cops and British army. There were feuding factions within the IRA and amongst the Protestants. Conservatives hated Labour and everyone hated Thatcher. The Anglo-Irish Agreement had just been signed and nobody was happy. The whole thing was as popular as gonorrhoea. The agreement between the UK and the Republic of Ireland was aimed at ending the 'Troubles'. Fat chance.

The Republic now had an advisory role in Northern Ireland and Ian Paisley, the leader of the Democratic Unionist Party (DUP), had proclaimed, 'Where do the terrorists come from? The Irish Republic! Where do the terrorists return for sanctuary? The Irish republic!

And yet Mrs Thatcher tells us that the republic must have some say in our province. We say, *"Never, Never, Never!"'*

And smarty-pants us were going to explain all that in fourteen minutes.

Meanwhile, I filmed it all and left the cerebral stuff to the others. I couldn't fully figure out what was going on, but every day I'd read the paper to try to comprehend some of it, and now I wished I hadn't. On the day before we left for Iran, Irish news was pushed aside and the big news for the day was 'Iraqis bomb Tehran for three days'. No one could understand how. Up until a week ago, they didn't have the capacity to get anywhere *near* Tehran. I was not happy.

After a quick British Airways flight with bad food and bad service to Frankfurt, we dashed to Lufthansa check-in to find our flight had been cancelled due to 'political problems' (German for 'too many bombs in Tehran'). *Now* I was happy.

Conscientious producer Warren disappeared for twenty minutes then returned.

'You want the bad news, the *badder* news, the *baddest* news, or the *really mean* news?' he said.

A really bad set of options. I tried not to panic, knowing Warren had in the past been known to play games, though come to think of it, not all that often.

'Hit me with the bad news,' I said.

'The bad news is . . . we're still going to Iran.'

'Bugger.'

'The *badder* news is we're flying Iran Air.'

'Shit.'

'*The baddest news* is . . . we're flying economy.'

'Are you *fucking* kidding?'

'The *really mean news* is . . . the plane doesn't leave till 8 p.m.'

It was ten in the morning. I was speechless with all that bad news. Before Kenya we'd done a couple of stories in the US, and this was our 21st airport for the trip. I was about to die in an Iraqi bombing raid and my final memories would be nothing but airports.

Typically there is nothing to do in airports but drink, so we did. Which was a good thing because the flight was like a bad dream. And to think I knocked British Airways.

Seeing is not believing. How they managed to squeeze so many seats into our plane, I have no idea. I doubt Iran Air was a member of any international air safety organisation, but if they were they hadn't read the manual. The plane looked like it was stuck together with used Band-Aids. How and why we defied gravity was a mystery and I suspected the pilots were equally perplexed. The seats were made of spider web, the food was made of shit, there was no alcohol and . . . there wouldn't be for the next ten days.

•

Day one in Tehran, Jennifer stayed in the hotel to do research while Micky, Warren and I headed to the press office for local media passes. We handed over all the relevant paperwork and Polaroid headshots and were told to wait. And wait we did. Laminating was obviously a new science to the Iranians. Five hours and hundreds of dollars later, we were handed our very important, very shiny plastic laminated press passes, and the three of us busted a gut laughing. Jennifer was now wearing a hijab painted not so deftly with black texta. She looked like something between a WWI fighter pilot and a Japanese Kabuki performer.

That picture was the happiest she was going to look for the next ten days. When she got her media pass, she hit the roof, assuming we'd decided to have a little fun at her expense. Everything for the next ten days was at her expense.

Iran was a dumb place to bring a female reporter. It was not Jennifer's fault, of course, she was a mega-bright journo, but there was no way she was going to be able to prove that here. But I guess that's why she was on the story. The disconnect would help make great television.

Our first morning in Tehran, Jennifer and I were heading for breakfast and were stopped by a hairy man who told Jennifer to go back to her room and dress properly. Scarf, long sleeves, legs covered, including ankles. Jennifer was quite prepared to comply with dress regulations out in the street, to do otherwise could mean a severe reprimanding, or worse, she could be beaten up by fundamentalist Moslem men. But we were staying in a hotel that accepted only American dollars from the only Western guests, so she started berating the clothes cop. Her protests fell on deaf ears. I don't speak Farsi, but I think she got told, 'Stiff shit.' For the rest of our trip Jennifer wore a long black coat and headscarf at all times.

We were not allowed to go anywhere or film anything without permission of the government minder assigned to us, and he said no to everything. My diary entry for Tuesday, 17 February 1987: 'We asked the minder if we could shoot the American Embassy and he said we'd have to apply for permission and that would take two weeks. Here I am in my hotel room in Tehran wondering what I did to deserve this. This is the sort of place you should go to at the beginning of a trip, not after a month on the road.'

The frustration for Warren and Jennifer was immense. We needed a story and nothing was happening. We were stymied by red tape and stubborn bureaucrats. A week after applying for an interview with a government spokesman, we got the word we might be able to interview the assistant foreign minister. 'What good is the *assistant* foreign minister?' I said to Warren. 'Better than the minister for agriculture,' he said. We were not wanted in this town.

Finally, though, we had an interview. A local woman, Mrs Katagini, was to tell us of life for women in Iran. 'And she speaks English as you requested,' boasted our government-supplied minder.

As I set up the lights, a woman arrived and sat down in front of the camera. I asked if she'd mind moving her chair a few inches. She said fine, but where would you like Mrs Katagini to sit. Surprised, I asked the woman who she was.

'The interpreter,' she replied.

Warren went off. 'I was *told* Mrs Katagini spoke *English!*'

But after half an hour there was no compromise. It was this or nothing. So we did the interview with Mrs Katagini. Sort of. Actually, we did what in TV film parlance is called a 'strawberry'. We went through the motions of an interview, we lit it, we set up mics, we even rolled the camera, but there was no film in it. And a bloody good job too, as every answer was excruciatingly boring and half an hour long.

All the men in Iran are ugly, but the women, the ones who are game enough to show their faces, are unbelievably beautiful. I'm sure there's a reason but I can't think of it. Apart from the clothes we soon realised there were other problems with having a female reporter. On one of our long monotonous drives to places we couldn't film, Jennifer looked out the window.

'What's that building over there?' she asked the driver.

Silence. Again she tried, 'Excuse me, what is that building over there?'

More silence.

'*I am speaking to you!*' Jennifer said furiously. It was as if he was alone in the cab.

So I said, 'Hey mate, what was that building we just passed?'

'Oh that's the Ministry for Information,' he said happily. This was going to be a fun week.

Setting up for an interview with a top banana mufti (Islamic scholar), I had the room lit and ready to go for an informative intelligent chat with him on the pluses (and maybe a few minuses) of the Islamic Republic. Mr Mufti made his grand entrance, welcoming Warren, Micky and me to Iran and completely ignoring Jennifer. He asked where he should sit and as I pointed to his chair Jennifer went to sit opposite him. The mufti looked up at Warren, pointed to Jennifer and said, 'Who's this?'

'That's Jennifer, the reporter. She's going to conduct the interview,' said Warren.

The mufti immediately got up from his chair, said 'I don't speak to women,' and left the room.

Warren had applied for us all to go to the battlefront (there is no God). And this was some front. Modern warfare had yet to hit this side of the world. The front had been described by some journos as no different to WWI, with large-scale trench warfare, miles of barbed wire, bayonet charges, chemical weapons (mustard gas being one of them) and haphazard communications. We'd be heading into the Western Front 1916 and 'the fog of war'.

First, though, we went to a war veterans hospital where I filmed scores of maimed young men, some with no arms and no legs, telling us that as soon as they were better they'd head straight back to the front to fight for Iran, to fight for Allah and hopefully to fight for death and become a martyr. It was too depressing to even contemplate the future for these totally brainwashed and now totally disabled young men.

We needed shots of the able, dedicated young men about to go to war to become martyrs. Something I was hoping not to do. While we waited for the go-ahead for this trip to the front, we got permission to film the new recruits. Just like their mates in the hospital, every single one of them couldn't wait to get to the battlefront to prove allegiance to and love of Allah. As did all the young men on the Iraqi side.

When we hit the new recruits' training ground, the colonel took one look at Jennifer in her long coat, practical shoes and black headscarf and pronounced, 'This will not do,' as if she was wearing nothing but a G-string. He told us if the young men saw her they might 'lose control'.

They've either got X-ray vision, or Western noses and wrists are a real turn-on. Practically foaming at the mouth himself, the colonel ordered Jennifer to find a chador. Three hours later when our ordered chador failed to arrive, the colonel reluctantly allowed us, including Jennifer, to film his brainwashed cannon fodder. I didn't see any control-losing, but I did see a hell of a lot of young, uneducated peasant boys who I felt genuinely sorry for.

That night a phone call. Surprise, surprise, we couldn't go to the front. Nothing to do with their communication fog, it was because one of us was a woman. And I had a feeling it was me. It was the happiest I'd felt in days. Maybe there is a God. Let's hope for those battle-scarred, disabled young soldiers that there is.

17

The Virgin and Buddy Holly

Months after my Iran trip, and still bewildered at some people's unquestioning dedication to a higher being, I ended up in what was then Yugoslavia, doing a religious story. This one was unbelievable. So unbelievable I needed to switch off the brain as I switched on the camera.

On Wednesday, 24 June 1981, the Blessed Virgin Mary paid a visit to six teenagers from the village of Medjugorje, where we got to meet and interview two of them, Marija and Ivan. The teens told us they were walking up a hill a short distance from the village when they suddenly saw a shining light. It was the Blessed Virgin Mary, floating a few feet off the ground, holding the infant Jesus.

On her next appearance the following day she was able to gesture to the teens to come closer because she was without the child. (Perhaps Thursday was child-care day or Joseph's flexi-day from work.) For the following week she appeared on the hill at exactly 5.40 p.m. every night, wearing a grey dress with a white veil and a crown of stars. The blue-eyed brunette virgin then delivered her message while standing in/on a cloud.

After that week she did a switcheroo and appeared to them, sans cloud, inside the local church. It turned into a real money-earner for the impoverished communist village. When word got out, pilgrims from round the world rushed to be part of it, all hoping to catch their own glimpse of 'Our Lady, the Queen of Heaven' and the 'Mother of the Church'. And if seeing her was in the too-hard basket, they at least wanted to feel her presence.

The parish priest, a Franciscan monk, looked a lot like Buddy Holly in his huge black glasses. He was besotted with all the vision stuff, completely enamoured with the teens, and highly protective of them. But his boss, the bishop, who lived in the next village, was a total sceptic of the apparitions. The bishop was in charge of the diocese and didn't want his own bit of turf creating waves with Rome. I think he was just toeing the Vatican line and protecting his own ascension up the Catholic corporate ladder. He and the Vatican wanted proof, and besides, they already had Lourdes, Fatima, Our Lady of Guadalupe, Our Lady of Laus, and my personal favourite, Our Lady of the Miraculous Medal. They didn't want the Blessed Virgin spread too thinly.

When we mentioned the bishop's non-belief to the two teenagers, Ivan pronounced, cool as the Blessed Virgin herself, 'The devil can use his influence in many ways.'

The local church in the shoebox-sized village where Our Lady appeared was a huge 2000-seat cathedral.

Talk about overkill. The place was all but empty most of the time. And this giant Church of St James had been completed decades before you-know-who appeared. Now, thanks to her nightly visits, it was filled to overflowing every night. Mike Munro, a good Catholic reporter, found it astonishing that such a huge church had been built way before the sightings. Maybe a miracle.

Maybe not. I figured it was because Medjugorje is the largest of the five villages that make up the parish, and one church is easier to build than five.

The cavernous cathedral was a monumental worry for me. I only had three lights. If the Blessed Virgin could give me some of her shining, I'd be fine. I was struggling to get an exposure on the night we were allowed to film Marija and Ivan partaking of their 5.40 appointment. It was quite a sight. In the choir stalls, high above the 2000 praying pilgrims, they both knelt, crossed themselves in unison, then went into a trance, nodding their heads and whispering, both having conversations with her as they stared at a small crucifix on the wall. They must have been riveting chats. They went on and on and on. The Blessed Virgin was clearly capable of having two interesting conversations at the same time.

The next day we accompanied a handful of Aussie true believers up to the original sighting spot, the 'Hill of the Apparition'. Six women who'd flown all the way from Perth to be part of the action. Unfortunately, the virgin didn't turn it on for the Aussies. It was pissing down rain and freezing. But the good news was it meant we couldn't stare at the 'Miracle of the Sun', and do what scores of pilgrims do every year: burn their retinas, giving them permanent eye damage. According to the believers, the sun in Medjugorje appears like a spinning disc, just like Fatima, Portugal, in 1917 when hundreds of people allegedly saw the sun change colour and rotate like a wheel. You'd think that after more than 60 years since the Blessed Virgin first performed Fatima's trick, she could have come up with a new one. But as we all stood shivering in the rain with ne'er a trick to be seen, one of the Aussie women let out a scream and told us in the short time we'd been up the hill her rosary beads had changed from silver to gold. Imagine that! I looked closely at the beads. They still looked silver to me, albeit a bit dirty from the continual rubbing with wet muddy hands.

We spent a lot of time with the Franciscan priest, a very charming man who I really liked. He was a genuine humanitarian, a much nicer bloke than his boss the bishop. At the end of our shoot, the priest gave each of us some rosary beads. First Mike Munro, the good Catholic, then Jenny the good producer, then Micky the good sound recordist. Then came the time for the good atheist. I'd shown none of my atheism to anybody except the rest of the crew, but when he turned his attention to me, the priest quietly asked, 'Are you a believer?'

For a split-second, for the sake of PR and unity, I contemplated saying, 'Of course.' But I couldn't. 'I'm sorry,' I said, 'but I'm not a believer.'

He smiled. 'Thank you for being honest,' he said. 'This is a present from me to you.' And he handed me the rosary beads.

In his autobiography Mike Munro wrote that the cameraman on the trip was a gold-plated atheist, though he respected the beliefs of the pilgrims. How could I not? Rosary beads changing colour and spinning suns are a worry, but for those who come a long, long way to be part of this and say it makes them feel better, then good luck to them. But *making* them better, or healing them, is another thing, and that was the depressing side to it all. A frightening number of people gravely ill but clutching at the hope of a miracle.

•

Years earlier I'd been to Lourdes in France to do a similar story. Lourdes was, and is, the world's most popular Christian pilgrimage site, bigger than both Rome and Jerusalem. At the time, it attracted about four million people a year, hundreds of thousands of them disabled or dying.

In 1858 in the small market town of Lourdes, our ubiquitous virgin appeared and identified herself, saying '*Que soy era Immaculada Concepciou*' (I am the Immaculate Conception), to another teenager, Bernadette Soubirous. It's always confused me. I always thought the Baby Jesus was the Immaculate Conception. But no. Some say that Mary herself was conceived without the stain of original sin. I guess it runs in the family.

The Immaculada Concepciou, this time dressed in a white veil and a flowing white robe with a blue sash, spoke to little Bernadette in the local dialect. That in itself was a miracle. The number of people in the world who spoke that dialect was less than a quarter of a million. After their tête-à-tête Bernadette's asthma was miraculously healed, which started a run on miracle cures.

These days at Lourdes the sick and dying queue for miles to get to the grotto where the meeting took place so they can drink the water said to have healing properties, and if one sip is not enough, bottles in the shape of the virgin are filled up to her halo. Those in need of a *really* big miracle fill up five-litre drums, in the shape of five-litre drums.

Queuing in the sun for hours is not a complete waste of time for the sick and dying, because apart from the opportunity to buy their virgin-shaped bottles, they get to see all the rest of the merchandise on sale. The Lourdes gravy train rakes in hundreds of millions. How could you possibly pass on a lamp with the bulb lighting up the virgin's halo, or the snow dome where just a little shake creates a flurry of soft white snowflakes that land gently on her head?

When we did our story, the Catholic church had certified 64 miracles. They were very hard to prove. For those 64 certified miracles, more than 7000 had been checked out. You can't just go round saying you've been cured. Each miracle must be sudden or almost sudden, must be perfect and definitive. And you must *stay* cured. I wasn't sure if that meant your miracle was struck off if you ever died. Each claimed miracle is checked and rechecked, attacked and pulled apart by the Lourdes Medical Bureau set up at the request of Pope Pius X. To become a miracle, a cure has to be deemed scientifically inexplicable by the bureau and the Catholic church.

It was sad watching parents hoping and praying for their desperately ill kids, clutching at what they saw as their only hope. A tired Irish mother told us she had nothing to lose by coming here. 'You never know,' she said, 'it might just happen.'

After three really depressing days at Lourdes, Ray Martin and I decided we needed a break, so we hitched a ride to the nearest town for a night out. Ten miles down the road we were in a nightclub, drinking, singing and dancing with some wonderfully eccentric Irish priests and pilgrims. They, too, had needed a break. All the other patrons, young French locals, were totally unaware of, or disinterested in, all that misery down the road. They and we partied on.

And suddenly it was 6 a.m. We had to start work at eight. I needed sleep. I left Ray, like a good friend does, and fanged back to our hotel, courtesy of an overweight French girl with an unpronounceable name and a small motor scooter. Then straight to the room I was sharing with Ray to grab a quick snooze.

At 7.45 a.m., just as I woke up feeling like shit, Ray wandered in. He looked worse than I felt. He asked me what time we were starting. I told him he had ten minutes to get ready. Five minutes later as Ray was staggering out of the shower, there was a knock on our door. It was the producer.

'Good, you blokes are up,' he said. 'Meet you downstairs at eight.'

He hadn't noticed Ray's pinhole eyes or my very pale complexion. It was obvious we needed a five-litre drum of Immaculate Conception water and a miracle to get us through the day. With the sun and our heads pounding, I contemplated a small prayer to the Blessed Virgin for some relief but figured it was pointless. There were obviously millions of prayers ahead of mine in that day's queue. Not to mention there was every chance in the world the virgin was already aware of my atheism, even though that day I was prepared to convert and swear off alcohol for life. Ray pleaded with me to use only the wide-angle lens and no close-ups. That was no problem, I was having trouble seeing Lourdes, let alone Ray. And, unfortunately, the request for an interview with the Minister for Miracles was miraculously granted.

In fact, two miracles were granted that day. The first was that the minister finished the interview without wearing the contents of our stomachs. The second was obviously issued by the multilingual Blessed Virgin. When every one of Ray's questions was answered in French, Ray who doesn't speak a word of the language, didn't even notice and simply plunged on. As an Irish priest had told us a few days earlier, 'God moves in mysterious ways.'

•

Now our world is a global village, the Blessed Virgin even makes visits to the southern hemisphere, all the way Down Under. In her typical fashion, she called on not some wealthy educated believer, but another peasant. A bank clerk, born William Kamm, who was short, balding and dressed in ill-fitting clothes from Target. Kamm said he'd been given the name 'The Little Pebble' from the Blessed Virgin and since then had received regular messages from her. In 1985 he created his 'Order of St Charbel' near Nowra on the New South Wales South Coast, and somehow in no time at all, had thousands of followers.

This guy was such a buffoon I started feeling sorry for the Blessed Virgin and all her northern hemisphere believers. When our reporter Jeff McMullen asked him, 'Have you asked the Holy Mother about having *60 Minutes* here to film you having these visions?' the clerk answered, 'Before *60 Minutes* actually came here I asked the Blessed Mother is that acceptable, and the Blessed Mother said yes, she is pleased. Also she came with the Baby Jesus today and the Baby Jesus left our Mother's arms and came over to all of you and kissed you on the forehead.' This bloke was a bloody fruitcake.

The Little Pebble then told us God had told him he would be the next and last pope, because the world was about to come to a fiery end and the only people left would be him and his (equally loopy) followers. He showed us his papal robes and a vast array of pointy hats. They also looked as if they were from Target, or worse, he'd stitched them himself.

Outside, not far from his chapel, The Pebble showed us a giant rock the size of a Mini Minor which had been carried by two angels all the way from Jerusalem, and one day (he wouldn't say when) he'd strike the rock and water with great healing powers would flow from it. It had also been revealed to him by God that he had to populate the world in his image. The Pebble's, that is, not God's. To do so he'd anoint twelve queens and 72 princesses to become his wives. One sixteen-year-old girl told us The Pebble insisted that God had given him permission to have sex with her. But many others were underage.

Kamm scored fifteen years in the clink for aggravated sexual assault and aggravated indecent assault and was released on bail in November 2014 after having served just over nine years. Frighteningly, some of his believers couldn't wait for his return so they could continue to follow, adore, believe and be saved by the convicted fruitcake.

18

You Lose Some You Win Some

Not all religious stories found me so cynical. I couldn't believe my luck when I scored a story on the restoration of Michelangelo's frescoes in the Sistine Chapel, though I guess it was more of an art story than a religious one. Religion or art, it didn't matter, I couldn't wait to do it. But it was going to be near the end of a very long trip, and that's never good for anyone's artistic juices. En route to Rome we went via the US for stories on Yothu Yindi, the Aboriginal band touring America, the famous old Hollywood star Mickey Rooney, then David Copperfield, reputedly the greatest magician since Houdini. From the States to London for half a story on a gold heist (to be completed back in Australia), then on to Italy for the Sistine Chapel and finally to Uganda for a yarn on pygmies. Talk about eclectic.

The Yothu Yindi mob were all good blokes. We filmed a few of their gigs in Los Angeles where they were a big hit. The Yanks, especially the African Americans, loved them and their wonderful combination of rock and traditional music. It was a great start to the trip. We should have stopped there and then.

·

Mickey Rooney was a bitter old man who denied everything he'd written in his autobiography. The one we were giving him publicity for. He did nothing but whinge that no one ever acknowledged how big a star he really was, and how he and Judy Garland made so much money for the studios yet they got nothing for it. I suspect that was true, but he was *so* angry. He hated the world and everything in it. He didn't have a nice thing to say about anyone except Judy Garland and, surprise, surprise, Mickey Rooney. He refused to answer most of Richard Carleton's questions, and just kept ranting.

Trying to get something of a story, we took him down to Hollywood Boulevard to check out his star on the Hollywood Walk of Fame and to get him to tell us about it. He spent most of the time telling us what no-talent bums the others were. I guess with a birth name of Ninian Joseph Yule Jnr and after spending 30 years playing a 5-foot 2-inch fourteen-year-old, the chip on your shoulder would have to wear you down.

After spending a day with him doing nothing but complain, we had nowhere near enough for a story. With luck we'd get a ten-minute story out of him by using a stack of archival footage, but Allan Hogan the producer was still doubtful. We couldn't wait to see the back of

Rooney. My diary entry of Tuesday, 16 June 1992: 'Have just met the greatest arsehole of all time.'

Still in LA we figured you win some, you lose some. The David Copperfield story should give us a chance to redeem ourselves. How could we lose? Copperfield was big time right then (not 40 years ago like Ninian Yule), beloved throughout the world, and not only could he walk through the Great Wall of China, he could fly.

Before our first little get-to-know Copperfield interview, his assistant told us we could only film him from one side. At no time could I film the left side of his face. Okay, that's cool, we had reporters who had a similar preference. This was not just a preference, though, this was laid down as *the law*, and as I usually like to abide by the law, I did the right thing.

Copperfield was charming, the complete opposite to Rooney, which made us really like him. He told us how much he was looking forward to working with Aussies, and how excited he was to be going to Australia.

The following day I shot a sequence of him in a hospital, teaching tricks to doctors and nurses to use for relaxing depressed and injured patients. It was great stuff, and he had all those medicos in awe of his skills. I went to the back of the room for a wide shot: but he was a million miles away. The shot was the backs of the medical staff with Copperfield on stage a mere speck in the distance. I headed for the corner to set up but I had literally crossed the line. In mid-trick he stopped, pointed at me and waved me over to the other side. I couldn't believe it. From back there you wouldn't even know it was him, let alone be disgusted by whatever horrendous blemish he was trying to hide from the television world. I did the right thing and moved, but ten minutes later I tried again. I thought no one could be this vain, and I've worked with some beauties. This time he sent the assistant over to say I must shoot him from the other side or leave. That must be some blemish.

That night we went to see his show, not to film it, just to see what was in store for us for the shoot in a few days' time. It was amazing. He flew, he disappeared, he turned himself into a woman and he made beautiful women disappear. The whole show was unbelievable and we couldn't wait to film it.

The next night we arrived at the venue and were met by the same assistant, all over us like a rash. She told us we had to film the crowds of people filing in and buying programs. All unbelievably boring stuff, but I did it to keep her on side. We were then ushered inside and given a spot where I could shoot the show. Then out came the rules. One, there would be no changing of camera position. Two, there would be no changing of lenses. (That was a shame. I was about to put on my how-to-expose-all-magic-tricks lens.) Three, there were two parts and two parts only of the show which I could film. And four, when we got the word to stop filming, I *must* stop immediately.

The two parts of the show we were allowed to shoot were more boring than the program purchasing. I was filming bits of the show that had none of the great tricks. It was just Copperfield striding about the stage like a demented male model. It was nowhere near enough for a sequence and certainly nowhere near enough to give away any secrets. Still, yet again, we did what we were told.

I figured I'd try for better stuff once we'd ingratiated ourselves with David and told him how amazing his show was.

After the show we shot some quick interviews with heaps of mesmerised ecstatic members of the audience, before another interview with the great man himself. I had hoped he'd fly out to meet us, but no such luck, so we were ushered into his dressing room. Again he told us how much he was looking forward to coming to Australia and again we said how happy we were he was coming and we all gushed and smiled and grovelled.

'We really loved the show,' Allan Hogan, the producer, said. 'We enjoyed it just as much tonight as we did last night.'

Copperfield went white, then crimson, and suddenly the Great Wall of China stood between us and the great magician. And he wasn't planning on walking through to our side.

He glared at his PR woman. 'They saw the show last night?' he snarled. The poor woman had no idea. We'd bought our own tickets to have a look at what would be in store for us.

The tension in the room was palpable. I don't know why he didn't just make himself disappear, or even better, make us disappear. That's what I'd have done.

When Allan asked if there was a problem, Copperfield started to rave about us being sneaky and trying to figure out his tricks. 'Blah, blah, I'm a professional, blah, blah, do you realise what you've done, blah, blah.'

Richard Carleton and Allan tried in vain to placate the mad magician and his stressed entourage, telling him we really liked him, and the show was amazing, but we didn't have enough footage for a story. There was whispering between flunkies and Copperfield, they then asked us to leave while they discussed it further. As we were ushered out of the room, Richard turned and said, 'I did Margaret Thatcher. I did Gorbachev. And they gave us better access.'

That was probably our undoing. We knew we were doomed but, surprise, five minutes later, with a big smile on her face, the PR woman came out. 'Okay, David says you can film him having dinner.' Dinner? Dinner!

Allan was furious. He made one last desperate effort. 'Frankly we'll have to drop the story,' he said. 'What we have is not nearly enough. We are professionals, as he is, and we need more.'

'All right, I'll put that to David.'

An hour later she returned. 'David says no.'

End of story.

So with Rooney only a maybe, and Copperfield non-existent, Allan said, 'What next? The pygmies will probably be fucking six feet tall.' It was up to the Sistine Chapel to save the day, the trip and our careers.

•

The Sistine Chapel was truly sublime. Years earlier, in the early 1970s, I was a tourist marvelling at Michelangelo's brilliance, wandering through the chapel with thousands of other tourists staring disbelievingly at his masterpiece, but with everyone getting a little edgy, bumping and pushing each other as they gazed up at the ceiling. The experience was not a lot of fun. The Sistine Chapel is one of the world's must-see masterpieces and I remember thinking how much better it would have been without the crowds. Now, that was about to happen.

We flew into Florence, Michelangelo's birthplace, to meet Professor James Beck, an art historian who told us the restoration of the Sistine Chapel was one of the great catastrophes of art in the 20th century. As we wandered through Florence he pointed out Michelangelo statues ruined by attempts to clean them. And if they couldn't get that right, he said, what made them think they could do justice to the chapel. It was all good stuff to feed on the controversy, but we needed to feed on the great food of Florence, which we did for a few days in between filling our story with great works of art. Then it was onto a train to Rome and the chapel to get the restorers' opinions on the restoration and on Professor Beck.

Next morning we got to Florence railway station two hours early for our one o'clock train, but had none of the usual hold-up with the gear. The departures board showed there was a train leaving for Rome in five minutes so we jumped on that. Our 1 p.m. trip had been booked by our travel agent back in Australia. What sort of really stupid travel agent books a train journey for the middle of the day, ruining lunch? We hadn't been travelling the world for a million years without knowing how to make life easy for ourselves, so we wanted to get to Rome in good time for *Insalata Caprese*, *Braciole di Maiale* and a cheeky dry white on the Via Veneto.

The carriages were a little rundown, but we figured the Italians were much more into great works of art than public transport. We left the station at snail speed, travelled what seemed like two inches down the line then stopped at a small station to deposit a few little old ladies and pick up some mail. It was the first of our 1073 mail stops. Michelangelo would have had time to complete the Sistine Chapel and be halfway through another Pieta. We got to Stazioni di Roma Termini only a few hours *after* our travel agent-booked train—and headed to our hotel, starving to death and cursing our own stupidity.

Now, not only was I back in one of the great cities of the world, I was inside the Sistine Chapel gazing at Michelangelo's masterpiece up close and *alone*. We hired the chapel for four hours. Not a soul in the place but us. I think the Catholic church really needed the money. Imagine what they could put away if they rented out the pope for fancy dress parties.

Then I saw the light, or lack of. Perhaps if you're a believer, you only need divine light, but I'm a cameraman and I need the real thing. Worse still, every now and then the light coming through the six tall windows high up on the wall would vary. The sun seemed to dance all over the place, changing my exposure *and* the look in God's eyes during his universe-creating. I felt he was staring straight at me—and he knew that I was a non-believer. And now he was going to make me pay by switching the sun on and off.

Yet the always-thinking-of-a-fast-buck Vatican guys just happened to have lights for rent for atheist camera-men. So instead of the Blessed Virgin to brighten up the place, I had Mario, a happy little Italian man with eight 2000-watt lights on heavy-duty stands and, boy, did I need every watt of 'em.

More than 465 square metres of frescoes with more than 300 figures. Where to start? The masterpiece on the ceiling is 40 metres long, 13 metres wide and a staggering 20 metres above the floor, so I had to throw a hell of a lot of light up there to get an exposure. But mine was not the only exposure problem. It's said that before the masterpiece was finished, the Papal Master of Ceremonies, Biagio da Cesena, complained to the pope about all the nudity. 'It was most disgraceful that in so sacred a place to have painted so many naked figures immodestly revealing their shameful parts. It was not a work for a papal chapel but for a bathhouse or house of ill-fame,' he said.

But the nudity didn't seem to offend Pope Paul III or his successor Julius III, so it stayed, and Michelangelo got his revenge on Biagio and his shameful parts. In his depiction of the *Last Judgement* on the back wall, Michelangelo painted Biagio as Minos, the judge of the underworld, with a great serpent around his legs and donkey ears.

Years later, just a month before Michelangelo died, Biagio, who had mounted a 'fig leaf campaign' along with his wowser compagnos, got his way, and the decision was made to 'amend' the frescoes by painting cloth around those shameful parts.

But now with this latest restoration, half of the 'fig leaves' were removed and it was discovered that Biagio was actually being bitten on the genitalia by the snake. Go Michelangelo! And not only did he put Biagio into the work, he painted himself into his masterpiece not once but twice. Anticipating Alfred Hitchcock by 400 years.

I went searching for those great bits of art history for our story, but unfortunately the restoration was not complete and the whole of the *Last Judgement* on the back wall was completely covered by grubby old grey canvas with a bad copy of the *Last Judgement* tacked onto it. So it was nearly all ceiling in our story and after four hours my neck was killing me. Michelangelo painted the ceiling for up to twelve hours a day for four years, tough gig I know, but he didn't have to guess the exposure from 20 metres away or have Richard Carleton in the fore-ground. When Richard did his pieces to camera, I was struggling with the depth of field focus, plus it was not a flattering shot looking straight up Richard's nose. But when all the 'reporter' stuff was done, Richard, Allan, Micky and Mario left the chapel, and I was alone with my camera to do a Michelangelo and create.

It was fantastic. With a long lens I could see amazing detail. I could see right into God's eyes as he created the universe, a starkers Adam and Eve awash with innocence and about to be lost to original sin, and just when I was feeling that maybe I should have paid more attention in Sunday School, I zoomed in to the drunkenness of Noah. He was soaking wet and exhausted after his family were the only people on the planet to survive a gigantic flood, so he decided to take off all his clothes, hit the piss, then flaked. But his sons, with Biagio-type hang-ups, snuck up and covered his offending parts. I suspect those parts were in no condition to offend anybody, because Noah was 500 years old. Leave the poor bloke alone, I say, and I reckon Michelangelo would have had similar thoughts to mine.

Work over, still totally alone in the Sistine Chapel, I abandoned the camera and lay flat on my back on the beautiful, ornately tiled floor, itself a work of art, and stared in total disbelief at the size and beauty of it all, and my good fortune at actually being paid to do this. I lay there completely enveloped in what some say is the greatest work of art ever to have existed and I wondered what Michelangelo's thoughts would have been on the restoration. We knew Professor Beck's. He told us the restorers had ruined the masterpiece. I must admit I wasn't convinced it was ruined, but it certainly looked different to when I saw it back in 1974.

With grime and smoke from 400 years of candle burning and tourists and priests' heavy breathing removed, the chapel now looked bright and vivid, with amazingly over-the-top greens, pinks and yellows. It looked, how do I say this . . . so *Italian*.

These bright colours 'were not the way Michelangelo painted them', Professor Beck told us. 'If you like Walt Disney you would prefer this version, but if you have a real view to the past you won't.'

Which made me wonder who did he think actually painted those garish colours? Certainly not the restorers. All they did was remove paint.

I was so impressed by the Sistine Chapel story that I read everything I could about Michaelangelo, his art and his genius. My job was fun *and* educational.

•

With my head still swirling with Michelangelo images, which can't be a bad thing, we hopped on a plane to London and did something on a gold heist about which I remember nothing. Some stories just aren't worth remembering. Then it was off to Uganda for a National Geo-type story on the pygmies of the Rwenzori Mountains. This should be a ripper, as long as they weren't fucking six feet tall.

As a kid I read every Phantom comic there was and was fascinated by his friendship with the pygmies. He owed them big time. Not only did they find him on the beach and nurse him back to health, they also found him his skull cave and I always hoped if ever I bumped into a few pygmies they might find me one. The only real pygmies I'd ever seen were in a country show in the late 1950s, when I was about ten. For one shilling you not only got to see pygmies but a woman with three legs. I didn't know which was weirder. I had seen dwarfs before but never four feet tall men in perfect proportion. They looked as tough as nails with their loincloth and spears, but nowhere near as joyful as in the Phantom comics, in fact they looked more miserable than their friend the three-legged woman. My ten-year-old mind couldn't figure out why that would be. At least they could go to the toilet. I was totally perplexed as to how any three-legged woman could go to the loo without major problems.

Entebbe airport hadn't changed one bit since I was there for the Amin atrocities story twelve years earlier, except now all the officials were no longer suspicious of everyone and everything. Customs was a breeze. No bribes. Just big smiles and 'Welcome to our country'. Kampala hadn't changed much, but the people sure had. They were happy.

A local minder met us at the airport and on the way into town he asked what we were shooting. Before anyone could answer, he said, 'I hope you don't want to film pygmies. That's all anybody wants to film these days. But you can never find them!'

I wasn't game to look at Allan, so I stared out the window, wondering if six feet pygmies would be better than no pygmies at all.

After a night in Kampala we headed for the Rwenzori Mountains. It was an agonisingly slow drive up a very long, winding dirt road full of giant potholes, not as easy to avoid as the fallen trees. After a good seven-hour drive that took us almost to the border with Zaire, we met up with the group who were to look after us with food and tents, something Micky and I were not looking forward to after our comedy routine in Kenya with the three stooges. On first sighting, though, these guys did look a little more organised. They even asked us what time we'd like to eat.

We left most of our gear with our eager-to-please hosts and headed off for pygmy country up in the tropical jungle of the mountains. Even though we'd climbed a thousand metres, we were only a few kilometres north of the equator and it was stinking hot.

The hunt for our pygmies was unsuccessful and uneventful, and we were covered in bugs and sweat. On our way back to camp we were met by one of our local minders who told us our camp had moved and he would take us there. This sounded ominous as memories of Kenya and the stooges came flooding back.

After a five-minute walk back into jungle, we hit a clearing. And there in front of us was Shangri-la. It was incredible. A gigantic tent surrounded by half a dozen four-man tents, a remarkably quiet generator and scores of locals with big smiles, digging holes, lighting fires and setting up beds. We were told we had a tent each, a spare for all the gear, a generator already up and running for the charging of our batteries, a toilet almost ready to operate, fresh water in a canvas sink outside every tent for washing our faces and hands, and the shower with hot water would be available any time after six in the morning. And for now, would we like a white wine, a cold beer or a gin and tonic before dinner, which would be ready at 7.30 p.m.

Inside my tent I saw a beautifully comfortable bed, made up as if it belonged in the Louis XIV suite in the Hôtel de Crillon. Beside the bed was a small table with a large lamp, a small but very powerful torch, mozzie repellent and a bottle of water, all that was missing was a chocolate on my pillow and thick wall-to-wall carpet, though in the middle of the floor was a small grass mat.

After washing up in my own personal hessian sink full of warm water, I wandered over to the barman for my first G and T for the day. Sitting in the middle of our 'lounge area', we watched with amazement at the amount of activity around us. There must have been at least ten staff, all knowing exactly what to do and with a minimum of fuss. Then it was dinnertime. Mo, Curly and Larry would have loved it. Inside the large tent, four locals dressed in dinner suits shook our hands and pulled out our chairs for us. If we thought that was embarrassing, the rest of the night was more so. The service was impeccable. I began to feel like one of those poncy army officers in Guatemala, though we were much nicer to the staff. They were all great blokes and nothing was too much trouble.

The only too much was what we ate and drank. The amazing hors d'oeuvres were surpassed by the mild curry soup, which did not compromise our tastebuds for the perfectly barbecued steaks that came with every type of mustard and condiment that ever existed. The decision to serve ice cream with any number of toppings here in the Ugandan jungle was a masterstroke and a complete surprise, as was the huge choice of wine on offer. The port served with the cheese and biscuits was smooth as silk, though I do prefer my brie to be not quite so runny.

We waddled outside our dining tent and one of the immaculately dressed locals came up and asked what time in the morning we'd like our hot showers. This *was* as good as the Crillon. We decided on our shower times, then settled into our comfy chairs by the campfire. We were well and truly awash with port, so a palate-cleansing ale was a much-needed nightcap. Over our beers we discussed the plan of attack for the next day, which was how we'd bloody well better find pygmies or we'd be finding new jobs. The light Yothu Yindi story and the Sistine Chapel were all we had from this huge trip.

At 6.30 a.m. there was a knock on the flap of my tent. I was told there was fresh hot water in my sink and my shower would be ready in fifteen minutes. I wandered over to the loo, sans shovel and paper, and locked myself in the privacy of the drop toilet with the neatly arranged toilet seat and paper holder. My shower was the perfect temperature. Someone had heated a 44-gallon drum of water over a fire then gently poured it into another drum with a shower rose, just for my convenience. After an amazing breakfast of eggs benedict, we went pygmy hunting.

We finally we found them after a few hours of scouting the jungle. Thankfully, they weren't six feet tall, but there was not a loincloth or spear in sight. In fact every one of the little people, from kids to dads, was wearing a grubby T-shirt. One read 'New York Sux', others, obviously freebies, had Coke or Nike all over them. They sure didn't look like the protectors of The Ghost Who Walks.

But they looked very happy, and pretty soon we found out why. The number one bit of fun for this tribe was dope-smoking, and obviously it had been going on for generations. I don't think the Phantom would have approved, in fact I'm positive he wouldn't have. I figured now was not the time to ask if the pygmies could find me a skull cave, I'd wait till their heads were clearer and I knew them a bit better.

The chief pygmy, sporting a permanent smile, seemed like a really good bloke. He was alert and responded to our questions. Our interpreter told him we wanted to film a typical three or four days inside a pygmy village. Hunting, cooking, dancing, etc., and discuss his fear of losing his habitat to loggers. No probs, we were told, the chief and his tribe were ready to do anything for us. We figured hunting would be a great way to start the story so we asked the chief and a few of his mates what they hunted. There was a long dope-induced pause while they tried to figure out what they hunted. Then one of them cried out, 'Monkey!'

The hunt would be a big part of the story, the part we didn't want the facts to get in the way of, so we delicately asked if at least some of the hunters could maybe remove their Coke T-shirts and maybe replace the jeans with something a little more 'comfortable' (by which we meant primitive). Shorts, or even a loincloth like the one we had seen on an old man lying spaced out of his head under a tree. Again, no problems.

So monkey-hunting it was to be. But the pygmies had no weapons to hunt with. So our first sequence became the making of bows and poison arrows, which suggested it had been a long time since anyone had actually been hunting. They sure looked the part, each hunter choosing a good branch from a tree to create his own bow. I was worried their dope-addled brains might mean a few fingers could go missing during the arrow-creating, especially the dangerous pointy end, but all went well and they now had their armoury, and we had a great sequence.

So with a few half-naked pygmies, some (I kept out of shot) still in their T-shirts, we ventured into the jungle for the great monkey hunt. It was no Ernest Hemingway fearless adventurer after big game trophies. The poor little buggers had no idea. They tripped over each other, dropped their killing machines and giggled like schoolgirls. When we did see a monkey, the intrepid hunters pointed at it, screamed and yelled, then pointed at us, and before they could get an arrow anywhere near the string of their bow, the monkey was well and truly gone.

After a couple of hours we gave up. The hunters were exhausted. This working for a living was no fun. But I needed more footage, so I did the usual close-ups of feet walking through the jungle, eyes peering into trees, arrows being loaded into the bow, the firing off of arrows, whispering and pointing. All paragraph-one page-one of how to film a hunt. The pygmies loved every minute of it. Luckily I'd scored a few shots of monkeys off in the distance, which would at least show they were hunting something. It all looked great, made even better by the fact that our reporter, Richard Carleton, standing at

6 feet 3 inches, towered over our tiny hunters, so they looked even smaller.

Back in pygmy central, knowing full well their men would be returning empty-handed, the women were cooking yams and other unrecognisable stuff. The men couldn't wait to get stuck into the dope. Just what you need after a hard day at the office. We were figuring out what to shoot next when I noticed a really, really, small pygmy heading towards the campfire. He was struggling to walk, and the reason he was struggling was that he'd probably only known how to for a few months. He couldn't have been any more than eighteen months old, and in his tiny hand was a huge joint. He walked right up to the fire, put the joint into his mouth, leant into the flames and sucked hard. Then, still teetering dangerously close to the flames, like a true pro he withdrew the joint from his mouth, turned it round to check it was burning properly and, satisfied all was good, took a few more puffs and wandered back to sit beside mum. I should have been onto the local child protection agency in a flash, but I didn't know their number so I filmed the kid instead.

Though we didn't have a monkey kill, we decided we had a pretty good sequence and the makings of a good story. We thanked the pygmies for the day and headed back to Shangri-la and another amazing meal. After dinner, while enjoying our palate-cleansing coldies, we talked about what good people the pygmies were and how hilarious the monkey hunt had been.

Just as we were figuring out what to shoot the next day, we heard voices, and saw the chief pygmy and four of his mates emerging from the jungle. Boy, were they excited. Their smiles were more than just dope-induced. Frantically waving something in the air, the chief walked up to Richard and proudly presented him with a dead monkey. It was as if they'd found the missing link that had eluded Richard Leakey all these decades.

Then, totally amazed, they noticed our salubrious surroundings (which had also eluded Leakey for decades). Their interest in the monkey quickly disappeared when they set eyes on our beers, so we handed them one each. They, too, were into sharing, so out came the dope. The more we drank and smoked, the funnier the night became and the more keen we were to handle a dead monkey.

On closer inspection we noticed it was stiff as a board and had obviously been dead for days, maybe weeks. I'm not sure if the monkey presentation was to prove to us they could hunt, wiping out the embarrassment of the day's lack of success, or if they thought all we really needed was a dead monkey. I suspect the latter because the animal looked as if he'd died of natural causes. We thanked them profusely, praised their hunting skills and they left our camp feeling very pleased with themselves. If their skill was hunting, ours was film-making. We already had great footage of a hunt, and now we had the (very dead) hunted.

Next morning we explained to the chief and his fellow hunters that we wanted to re-enact their hunting of the monkey to show how and what they do after they find and kill one. Blank stares all round. They obviously thought they should never have given us any of their dope. It was as if we were trying to explain the connection between black holes and anti-matter, but they agreed to give it a go, whatever *it* was. They couldn't understand why, if we already *had* the monkey, must they pretend to be hunting it. We talked the youngest and fittest hunter into climbing a tree to place the corpse on a branch. Our dead monkey was about half the size of the ones I'd managed to film during the previous day's hunt, but film-making is not an exact science and sometimes your eyes can deceive you.

We told the hunters we'd film a few of them firing off arrows into the tree. The tree would then be shaken and when the monkey landed they should all run in and do whatever they normally do once a monkey hits the ground. The hunters started laughing uncontrollably at our instructions, as if it was all a bit of crazy fun before they got back to what they did best: smoking dope.

I focused on the dead monkey, the tree was shaken and I followed the monkey as it fell to the ground. Not too tight a shot, we didn't want to reveal the rigor mortis. A swarm of pygmies that Cecil B. DeMille would have been proud of, raced in and relentlessly beat the poor bloody corpse to death with their bows, yelling and screaming as if they had just felled a buffalo. Once again they were very proud of themselves. And why not? No one asked for hair and makeup, or what their motivation was. They just did what we asked, even though they obviously thought we were crazy.

They took the corpse back to their village and the women whipped up a monkey stew. Luckily they boiled the shit out of it, so any killer bugs couldn't have survived. And after their monkey meal, they put on a dance for us. It was magic. With fresh jungle leaves around their heads, necks and waists, they sang, chanted and danced round in circles for hours. Around they went, from the oldest to the youngest, the whole tribe loving every minute of it. They were all so happy and content.

I'll work with pygmies any day. They're wonderful people, but maybe not for long, because our world is moving in on them. I decided not to ask them to find me my own skull cave, my dream of 50 years ago. Their dream is for survival. Their habitat is rapidly disappearing for timber and agriculture. They have started to contract more and more diseases as 'civilisation' (and the odd film crew) enters their domain.

The reason for their height and size is still an anthropological debate. It may be from not getting enough protein, it may be that being small makes it easier to run through the dense jungle, or maybe in the tropical heat with less skin surface, heat stress is avoided. But we know they've been around a bloody long time. Hieroglyphic records show that five thousand years ago an Egyptian pharaoh captured a few of them for the entertainment of his court.

It would be a tragedy to see these people disappear altogether, though I don't like their chances.

19

To Cull or Not to Kill

Bang! Down he goes. I could feel the ground shake. Cheers all round and shouts of 'Great shot!'

Great shot? Are you kidding? How could he miss? His target was as big as an elephant. That's because it *was* an elephant. Up go the arms of the proud killer.

'Aim carefully . . . Here he comes. Squeeze . . .' *Bang!* 'Terrific shot!'

Now the ex-proud, ex-ferocious, toothless lion is dead. Up go the arms of hero number two. These big game hunters here in Africa are so tough.

All in the name of conservation, we are told. These men pay a massive amount of money to shoot something the size of a bus or something that's struggling to walk. How hard can it be? Yet these big game hunters genuinely believe they are Hemingway or Huston as they proudly pose next to their kill.

I know it's a form of culling, but this is not animal 'hunting', it's animal murder. The elephant was an old bull, and the lion had had his day. I don't get it—where is the skill in that? You can also murder rhinos, hippos, leopards, whatever tickles your fancy, and if you miss out on the great photo showing how skilful you are, there are specials. 'No kill, no bill.' How humane is that?

The lion and elephant kill was a tough shoot for me (shame the word 'shooting' covers what both hunters and cameramen love to do, because the results couldn't be more different). I love wildlife shoots, but not the wild life of bored, angry, violent, pissed youths in London, Los Angeles or Melbourne. Any story on drug and alcohol-fuelled violence was always far more dangerous than Africa. I've had fists, glasses, rocks and insults thrown at me, not to mention dinner thrown up all over me. That's the wild life I'd like to cull.

•

Apart from the big game murders, all my other wildlife film shoots, from anacondas in the marshes of Venezuela, to zebras in Kenya, were a privilege to be part of. One of the great privileges, considered one of the ten natural wonders of the world, is the annual migration of wildebeest from the Serengeti in Tanzania to the Masai Mara National Reserve in Kenya, or, as the locals say, 'The Mara'.

Our five-star camp was only a few hundred metres from where the wildebeest cross the Mara River, and looking after our every whim were half a dozen tall, lean and very happy Masai tribesmen. They carried our equipment, kept our beers cold, cooked for us, organised dunnies and showers, and laughed at our concerns about wild animals. At night they guarded our individual tents against regular nocturnal visits from lions, rhinos, hippos and cheetahs.

Our first few days produced not a hint of wildebeest so we went looking for shots of anything and everything that lived in that vast wilderness. We couldn't lose. Got the lot. Elephants, lions, hippos, rhinos, cheetahs, giraffes, antelopes, hyenas and zebras. It was fantastic . . . and it was my birthday.

Suddenly our fearless Masai warriors turned into Jamie Olivers, and somehow, with none of your 'bake at 180 degrees for 45 minutes' rubbish, they made me an incredibly moist, fluffy, chocolate birthday cake, which they cooked in a metal ammo box on an open fire. They then sang me 'Happy Birthday' and we partied through the night.

Of course, the tens of thousands of reasons why we were there turned up the next day. Because I had a hangover. We raced to the riverbank and in the distance saw an enormous mob of wildebeest cantering towards the opposite bank. The ease and effortlessness of the gently meandering mob reminded me of the tens of thousands of breasts heading my way in Swaziland, but, unlike the breasts, these creatures got uglier the closer they came.

Wildebeests look like what they really are—gnus. It's a strange look, as if designed by a Mother Nature with a killer sense of humour or one who failed miserably at design school. Gnu heads are huge, their bums tiny, they have a strange wispy beard, a mane like a horse, and their back legs are shorter than their front legs (just like the table I made in high school woodwork). But these creations can balance. Not only balance but run, and run, and run. They are born to run. Constantly on the move to find greener pastures, one and a half million of them run from Tanzania to Kenya and back again annually. That is their life, year after year.

And every year to access those greener pastures, the migrators must cross a river chockers with hungry crocodiles. The experienced wildebeest and crocs have seen it all before. They eyeball each other. 'An animal's eyes have the power to speak a great language,' the philosopher Martin Buber once said. But if I was a gnu I'd be saying, 'No, no, not again, do we have to? We did this last year.'

I already had the camera rolling as scores of wildebeest shuffled to the water's edge. Some ventured a few centimetres into the water as if testing the temperature, then retreated. Only metres from the front line, a half dozen crocs floated motionless but obvious. No gnu was willing to take the plunge. But the shoving from behind got harder to resist. In the end it was all too much, and some poor sucker took the leap. Without hesitating, thousands followed. Mayhem and water went everywhere. Our guide and wildebeest expert told us that the animals were all well aware of the danger but the urge was too great.

The river was now filled with panicky gnus scrambling all over the place. In that first mad dash, those on the outside, feeling terribly exposed, tried desperately to make their way into the middle. But those positions were already deftly taken by opportunistic zebras hoping not to be noticed.

As if. The crocs' favourite meal is zebra. They might as well have had a sign painted on them saying, 'Free lunch'.

The crocodiles move in and start spreading the gnus. We're eating today. It was a smorgasbord.

Now there was panic, fear, helplessness and bewilderment, and that was just in our eyes. The poor zebras, still trying to look gnu-like, had their eyes closed, but I think it was just pain, and fear. The crocs had amusement and determination in their eyes. With jaws wide open they thrashed their way to a stripy meal. Down went a couple of zebras. It was cruel, but it was culling, and lunch for the hungry crocs. The crocs ripped at the fur then hoed into their much-anticipated meal. In the resultant melee the chewing crocs scored some nasty kicks in the head from struggling, anxious wildebeests. The crocs, too busy attacking to care, didn't even look up, but the gnus were now even more terrified and looking almost apologetic, as if to say, 'Sorry, sorry, Mr Crocodile, I didn't mean to kick you, it won't happen again.' And it certainly wouldn't, as Mr Crocodile let go of his mangled zebra and pounced onto Mr Apology.

It really was hard to film. There was now total chaos. In the thrashing water, all we could see were legs, teeth, blood and shredded guts.

Meanwhile, the lucky ones somehow snuck past the carnage. A hundred or so wildebeest made it to the other side, but with relief came amazing stupidity: they just stood there, so the next wave had nowhere to go. The soaking wet, steep riverbank may as well have been Teflon coated and the gnus started slipping backwards down the bank into the open jaws of more patient crocs, the smarter older ones that knew how to avoid kicks in the head. And on the feast went.

After a while the crocs were so full they could hardly move, but there was still dessert to come. Half-eaten zebras floated past us as the crocs moved in for something a little sweeter, like a baby wildebeest who had no chance as mum was some metres away. Down he went. And right behind was another baby, and another croc, but this croc got a stab in the face from the horns of an ever-watchful mum. *Go, Mum!* They both made it to the other side. But there were still hundreds of wildebeest in the river, struggling through body parts and blood.

Then suddenly the killer crocs, with an almost docile look, slid backwards into the deeper water and disappeared. So although Mother Nature didn't do such a great job of designing each gnu, she knew there was safety in numbers. Most made it across the river and a few looked back at the carnage as if to say, 'Phew, that was close.'

I filmed the thousands of dripping wet, exhausted, relieved wildebeest dispersing into the vast Serengeti, the land of milk and honey. For all those that didn't make it, Mother Nature would make amends, and there would be 350,000 new wildebeest born that year.

•

If it was Mother Nature's failure in design school that created gnus, she must have studied extra hard the next year, because she also created the most beautiful living creature I have ever seen—the quintessential design, aerodynamically perfect, beautiful to watch, *Istiompax indica* or black marlin. Any plane or yacht designer needn't look anywhere else. I wouldn't be surprised if Ben Lexcen checked them out for his winged keel on *Australia II*. Maybe the face of the black marlin isn't too pretty but everything else is a work of art. A long spear-like bill, a large slightly rounded retractable dorsal fin, small strategically placed fins seemingly everywhere and two keels either side. The beautiful tail looking sharp as a scythe. These super-sleek fish can grow to well over 700 kilos, yet marlin are harmless and very happy minding their own business. The top half is black, the bottom silver, perfect camouflage from predators above or below. But it does them no good. The black marlin's only predators are the scores of very wealthy, overindulged, egomaniacs who hunt and kill them.

One such killer was Lee Marvin, the great Hollywood actor. I was a real fan. I loved his movies *The Dirty Dozen* and *Cat Ballou* for which he won an Academy Award. He loved marlin fishing. He was rich enough and had a tough guy image. Admittedly he fought in WWII and was wounded, but the tough guy image came from Hollywood. Just another act.

So there we were, doing a story on black marlin fishing on the outer side of the Great Barrier Reef with Lee Marvin. He wasn't over-friendly but I must admit he had a great voice, deep and gravelly, probably due to the fag that was never out of his mouth. He had a perfectly trimmed white beard, a white broad-brim hat and solid sunbaked forearms. A Hemingway character if ever there was one. And, surprise, surprise, just in case we missed the obvious, as soon as we met him he started quoting Hemingway, straight out of *The Old Man and The Sea*.

We were 40 kilometres offshore and the mega-expensive boat crew set up the hook, bait and line for the actor. The hook was horrendously massive. The bait, a tuna, was four times bigger than any fish I'd ever caught (and thrown back). As Marvin watched his crew setting up, Ray Martin asked him why he fishes for marlin.

'I like the threat,' he said.

Quick as a flash Ray said, 'What's the threat?'

'The threat is, that one day he's going to get you.'

So the poor innocent, minding his own business, can't survive out of water fish is going to climb up the line and throttle him? And for once the actor wasn't acting.

In goes the line. A typical day's fishing. Not a thing. Marvin gets to survive another day from those nasty threatening fish. But they'll be lurking tomorrow.

Back inside the reef, in much calmer waters and hundreds of metres from Marvin's boat, we had our own *60 Minutes* boat, with a wonderfully attentive husband and wife team looking after us. It was Shangri-la on the water. Before accepting our pre-dinner drinks, we went snorkelling. It was paradise, perfect temperature in the air and sea. Witnessing the reef and all its beauty, it was hard to believe people would want to come and disturb it.

At dawn, having slept peacefully on deck, we rolled out of bed into the water for more snorkelling in one of the world's greatest natural wonders. After a perfect breakfast, of eggs benedict and freshly brewed coffee it was back to Marvin's boat to watch some killer fish threaten the Hollywood star.

By midday he'd caught three small marlins, tagged them and let them go. He only wanted the big boys. The world record was 708 kilograms. Marvin's best was 590 kilos, and he was here to break the world record, or at least his own. At 4 p.m., with boredom setting in, and very close to gin and tonic time, he got a strike. Marvin was as surprised as us. With his line rocketing away from the reel at lightning speed, the minders quickly strapped him into his chair. He leaned back as far as he could and using his whole body pulled hard on the rod, then he leant forward, rapidly winding the reel and gaining half a metre of line. Then he repeated the process. And on it went . . . bit by bit. The fish must have been a monster. Fag still in place, more Hemingway quotes were thrown at us. No one had yet seen the fish, he was too smart, struggling for survival by diving to an immense depth. The hook must have been killing his mouth or, worse, his stomach. Often they really do swallow the lot: bait, hook, line and sinker.

It had now been two hours. The quotes were slowing down and so was the old man. I moved in for ultra close-ups of muscles and veins in his neck and arms. His hands struggled to wind the reel fast enough before the huge fish could swim away yet again. I was warned thoroughly by Marvin not to get too close, if I touched any part of him with my camera, clothes or body, his record catch would be null and void, invalid, of no consequence, and I'd be worse off than the fish.

Luckily, for no particular reason, I went for a shot of the ocean and just at that moment this magnificent marlin leapt high into the air. He was waiting for me. He was well out of the water, and heading for Mars. On his way up he shook his body violently from side to side, his back a regal purple, and as he twisted and somersaulted, his silver gut reflected the late afternoon sunlight like a mirror. It was a great shot. He slammed back onto the surface of the ocean, and disappeared. It was five hours before we saw him again.

It was now dark and I was struggling to even see Marvin. The sunset shots of the fish and the fisherman straining every fibre of their body really were *The Old Man and the Sea*. But now the sun had gone completely. Who'd have thought we'd still be fishing at 9 p.m.

The boat had a powerful spotlight on the upper deck so I asked the captain to swing it around onto Marvin. Our old man was suddenly overlit and everything around him was pitch black. It wasn't pretty but I had an exposure. Marvin continued to struggle with the line as the boat crew continued to flatter him, throwing encouragement his way. From that one and only sighting hours ago, the captain told Marvin it could be a record.

Finally the utterly exhausted fish was dragged to the side of the boat. Mind you, the fisherman with cramps in his arms and back wasn't looking too crash hot, either, but he'd had food, drinks, fags, minders and the help of a very powerful motorboat to get him to this point. We swung the light as far to the side of the boat as we could to try and get a shot of the dying marlin. The mighty fish, in one final heroic attempt to free itself, shook frantically from side to side, slamming into the boat. Then he gave up. I leant over for a close-up. He was still magnificent. Then, with those eyes gazing directly into my lens, I heard *whack, whack, whack!* He was beaten to death with a club.

That night on the deck under the stars I couldn't sleep.

In the dawn light we carted the carcass to a weighing station. It was not a world record, not even an actor's record. The experienced captain would have already known that. Ray asked Marvin how he felt and right until the end, the actor performed.

Roll camera, cue thespian. 'Mythology tells us the hero must die. In this case, it's which one is the hero, the fish or me, so I said, this hero doesn't want to die yet, so I made the other hero die.' Cue seasickness.

•

It took me years to get the image of that battered marlin from my head. And following the unbelievable hero statement, I happily filled my head with images of a battered Marvin. But over the years I moved on to more enjoyable and satisfying animal stories. White lions, baby elephants, giant anacondas, seeing-eye dogs, orphaned hippos and polar bears. All of them inspiring, all a joy to film, and all nothing to do with culling. Though the polar bear shoot went close. So close it was almost me that was culled.

Day one of the shoot, and even now I find it hard to believe I did it, but it's hard to break the habit of half a lifetime. You'd think the beanie, balaclava and gloves might have alerted me, but they didn't. I blame the kids. When they were little I'd unlock the car, and holding the car key in my teeth, I'd place the kids in their car seats. The girls now drive their own cars but I still haven't kicked the habit . . . So there I was, in Churchill, Northern Canada, and as I placed the camera gear onto the back seat of the car, the key went straight into my mouth. But it was minus 10 degrees Celsius. The frozen key was now super-glued to my lip. I looked like Jaws from the Bond movies.

Well, here goes . . . I tore the metal from my lip, saw half a lip attached to the key and tasted blood. And believe it or not, I had done this very thing before, a few years ago in freezing Minnesota. Francis Bacon once said, 'Assuetude of things hurtful doth make them lose their force to hurt.' Well, I dithagree. It dothn't. Thith time the pain wath worthe.

My lip and I were in Churchill, on the edge of Hudson Bay, to shoot a story on the diminishing habitat of polar bears. Churchill had a population of 900 people, and 1000 bears. Thanks to global warming the polar icecap is melting, and with it goes the bears' hunting ground. In the previous twenty years, 20 per cent of the Arctic ice had gone. It was well into winter now, and Hudson Bay should have been frozen but wasn't, so the starving bears went looking for food wherever they could. Churchill, with its garbage bins, dogs and people, was a town under siege. 'Never roam the streets alone, especially at night,' we were told. The bears saw humans as a meal. I couldn't blame them. We'd buggered their environment. If I was a bear I'd eat us for revenge as well as dinner.

At sunrise (8 a.m.) we headed out with the head ranger in search of polar bears. Immediately we saw a monster wandering across the snow, heading into town. He walked with a slow loping gait, a swagger that looked as if he was listening to swing music on his iPod. He was magnificent, far bigger than I ever imagined, and he was on a mission. I was hoping my balaclava would stop him from catching the scent of my wounded lip. Our ranger, carrying a rifle for protection, radioed the bear's position to a helicopter. A short time later, hovering over the bear, the chopper door opened and a ranger with a dart gun took aim. He fired, the bear went down, got up then fell again, struggled for a minute, then was still. The drug in the dart had already taken effect. I raced in to get shots of the unconscious bear and was shocked to see his eyes still open, but he was spaced out of his head.

The ranger, three of his mates and our reporter Tara Brown, lifted the unconscious bear onto a blanket and onto the back of a ute. It was a struggle even for five people. This bear weighed nearly 400 kilos. He was tagged then taken to polar bear jail where he would spend the next 28 days with no food, only water. The hope was the food deprivation would stop him from coming back into town. But it didn't work. There were many repeat offenders. And I'm on their side. I'd definitely come back to eat the bloke who shot me, gave me a huge headache and didn't feed me for 28 days.

It was time to release a repeat offender. Well, three, really. Mum and her two cubs. They'd done their time. Mum and the kids were drugged and dragged outside. The cubs were bundled into the back of the helicopter and mum was rolled into a net attached to the chopper by a 25-metre rope. I couldn't figure why the rope needed to be so long. It wasn't as if mum was capable of anything except maybe being motion sick as she swung precariously below the chopper 300 metres above the vast ultra-white landscape. We climbed into a second chopper with the door removed so I could get clear shots of her being flown back to the wilderness. The footage of the giant bear swinging in great arcs below the helicopter was fantastic, but without the door I was slowly freezing to death. I was wearing the best winter gear that *60 Minutes*' money could buy. Why hadn't Armani discovered the secret of polar bear fur? The perfect protection from cold. The Eskimos had used it to stay warm for thousands of years.

The bear's landing was a little less gentle than it should have been. Mum was still out cold, but the cubs were coming to, and as they were lifted out of the chopper, one tried to take a bite out of the ranger's arm. But the cub really didn't have a clue where he was or what was going on.

The three bears were placed close together in the snow. We were in the middle of nowhere, white as far as we could see, which wasn't far. The freezing wind made you want to close your eyes. Not a smart move. We were inches from a very hungover, very hungry, very protective mother bear. We shivered and waited. We waited until the starving bears blinked and looked around. If we'd left any earlier, other bears could have attacked all three. Since the loss of the ice and food, bears had taken to eating each other, something that was unheard of five years before.

We now had the makings of a great story, so when we hit town we jumped from the helicopter into our flimsy two-wheel drive van, hoping to grab more footage of bears before dark. Five minutes out of town, way off in the distance, we saw a lonely bear wandering in the snow. We headed towards him to get better shots. We were off the beaten track, but at least it was a track. We pulled up, and right there was the shot of the story. A hunting bear along the water's edge. I jumped out of the van, set up the tripod and started filming. It was a fantastic shot. It told the whole story. He should have been out there stuffing his face, but couldn't because the ice had melted.

Instead he was forlorn and hungry, walking along the shore, gazing out across the bay. Suddenly he stopped, turned, and stared straight at us. *Shit, he's smelt my injured lip!* These animals can sniff out prey a kilometre away. He was now heading in our direction. I got a few shots of him coming our way, said a little prayer to my very own god—the inventor of the zoom lens—and jumped back into the van.

Let's get out of here! But we couldn't. The wheels were spinning and we were going nowhere. The bear was closing in on us and our driving wheels were now buried deep in the snow. We locked the doors and waited. I changed lenses just in time. He was outside the van. My window, the front passenger side, was open half an inch. He loomed up, shoved his big black nose in and started sniffing. I was now filming a giant angry, hungry head, six inches from mine. He left my window, loped to the front of the car and tried to eat the right side mirror. He had both paws round it and bent it at right angles. Not happy with the taste but watching us the whole time, he headed across the front of the car and attacked the left mirror. Still not happy he went for the windscreen wipers, tearing them both off. He turned and stared straight at me through the windscreen and his eyes said, 'I want you!'

I knew he could smell the blood on my lip, but I was the smallest there, the others were all much meatier. Micky was at least 15 kilos heavier than me, younger *and* more tender. *Eat him.*

The giant bear came back to my side of the car, moved right up to Tara's back window, and gently placed his paw against the glass. Tara put her hand up against his. Cute.

It was an amazing shot. Suddenly he dropped his paw and stood totally erect. All 3 metres of him leant back, lunged forward, and he slammed both paws against the window. Tara was inches from the window with nowhere to go. If that glass had broken, she was lunch. *Bang*, he lunged again. *Bang! Bang! Bang!* It was terrifying. We knew polar bears had been seen smashing through a *metre* of ice to get to their prey. *Kabang*, even harder this time, *kabang, kabang, kabang*. He was very angry and if he got to us, we were very dead. I was shooting it all and wondered how he'd react if I jammed a 10-kilo camera down his throat when his head came through the window. It'd be a great shot, shame no one would be around to retrieve it. Stephen, the producer, was in the back of the van, filming with a small camera. Hopefully his footage might survive. Micky was continuously tooting the horn, the bear was oblivious to it and, unfortunately, so was the rest of the world.

Then, miraculously, our killer bear gave one last sniff, dropped to the ground and wandered away.

Hours later we were rescued. Well . . . shoved from behind by a giant bulldozer driven by a not-too-happy driver. We made it back into town for a medicinal, stress-relieving grog, served by a not-too-happy barman. We were then summoned to the not-too-happy ranger's office. All that unhappiness was weird. Up to then we'd been popular in town with our friendliness and huge tipping. The ranger told us we'd been seen feeding the bears from our van and berated us for our stupidity.

Where that story came from, we had no idea. We told him we might not look too bright but we weren't *that* stupid. We told him the van was bogged, the bear was heading our way so we'd locked the doors and waited. He burst out laughing. That bear, he said, could easily have ripped off any of the doors, locked or unlocked.

We remained unpopular in that town. I suspect they all wished we'd been killed and eaten, or at least culled. But we weren't, and once again I had some amazing footage.

20

There's no Business Like . . .

Show business is all show. Unfortunately we can't show it. Even today, the third and final story in a *60 Minutes* program is nearly always a celebrity interview with a film or rock star, writer or artist (though these days everyone's an artist). And they only agree to appear on *60 Minutes* to promote their latest book, film or CD. It's written into their contract they must do X number of interviews to push the product and to justify their grossly obscene pay. Often they're dragged kicking and screaming to the interview under threat of being sued by their promoters. Then it's tough for everyone. They complain about the lighting. They complain about the background. They then dismiss the questions with monosyllabic answers.

The whole idea is meant to be, we scratch your back, you scratch ours. You get great publicity from our high-rating program, we get a story. But often it was you scratch our back, we stab yours.

By the time I got to the story, most of the haggling, fighting and arguing had already been done. Our poor *60 minutes* producers had to grovel and get treated like shit just to get the interview. Which was in fact fifteen minutes of free publicity for the whingeing artist, and promoters.

For their ten million bucks per film, some stars do up to 40 interviews a day. Considering some of the unbelievably stupid questions they're asked by showbiz reporters, they probably figure ten million bucks is nowhere near enough. In the majority of those cattle-call interviews, the lighting, the camera set-up, the cameraman and the star are permanent fixtures. Reporters from all around the world having queued for hours are permitted one at a time to enter the orbit of the relevant star for their interview. Which consists of a half-dozen moronic questions, always just a glowing endorsement of whatever is being pushed. After five minutes the next thing to be pushed is the hapless reporter straight out the revolving door.

In 1968 Andy Warhol announced, 'In the future, everyone will be world famous for fifteen minutes.' Ten years later he claimed, 'My prediction from the sixties finally came true. In the future everyone will be famous for fifteen minutes.' But when challenged on it he would often change it to, 'In the future fifteen people will be famous.' Or 'In fifteen minutes everybody will be famous.'

Who knows what Andy meant? Benjamin H.D. Buchloh, Professor of Modern Art at Harvard University, suggests what Andy really meant was, 'The systematic invalidation of the Hierarchies of representational functions and techniques of art fits well with the belief that the hierarchy of subjects worthy to be represented will someday be abolished: therefore "everybody" can be famous once the hierarchy dissipates "in the future". Thus: "in the future everybody will be famous", not only those worthy of fame.' I couldn't have agreed more.

I myself had my own fleeting fling with fame—so fleeting it was more like fifteen seconds. My fling came courtesy of Bob Hawke. During our trip to London with the ex-PM, Rob Penfold, the Channel 9 Europe correspondent and my good friend of 30 years, asked if he could interview me about what it was like to work with the great Bob Hawke. No probs, Rob. So at the end of a big day Rob and crew set up for the interview with probably the most compliant talent Rob had had in years. I was cool, calm and collected. No nerves. I'd shot hundreds of interviews where people have said, 'Oh, I'm so nervous, I don't know what to say,' or 'Oh, I shouldn't have said that, can I try again?' From behind the camera I'd think, 'You idiot, it's not that hard, just answer the fucking questions and we're out of here.'

This idiot found it hard. Rob asked the first question, I didn't hear it. With a camera lens aiming straight at me, my mind went blank. I apologised to Rob and said, 'Let's start again.' He did. I didn't. When I finally got going, all I could say was, 'Uh uh um yeah, um, no, maybe, nice bloke, um, uh, smart, yes I think so. You're welcome.'

But something went to air.

A month later I was hiring a lawnmower from a bloke and he said, 'I know you, you're on TV.'

'No,' I said, 'I do work in television but you never see me. I'm behind the scenes.'

'No,' he said, 'I saw you on telly talking about what it was like to work with Bob Hawke.' *Wow, I'm famous.*

I have no idea how that bloke recognised me from one short news story, but it felt pretty cool. At the very least I was expecting to get the mower for free. I was rapidly brought down to earth when he said, 'That'll be twenty bucks.'

•

Fame is so attractive to some people they figure if they can't have their own they'll hang around with those who have it and some might just rub off. If I thought many of the stars were up themselves, I was always flabbergasted at the arrogance and rudeness of the sycophantic hanger-ons. Hairdressers, makeup artists, managers, PAs and PRs, all treating us like shit, probably the way they were treated.

Too often we found that the star's minders were pushy, rude and superior before the heavy arrived. But once they were in the presence of the famous one, they all turned to mush, desperately trying to prove their loyalty and totally shit-scared of upsetting them and jeopardising their job.

The worst I encountered was the woman who represented Arnold Schwarzenegger. He was pushing his latest movie, *Collateral Damage*. We always tried to do a little pushing ourselves, such as by asking if it was possible to get a walking shot or anything a little more than just a sit-down talking head. Every producer tries very hard for that little bit extra, so our producer, John McAvoy, asked for a very quick walking shot.

'No can do,' replied the sycophant.

'A shot of our reporter, Peter Overton, meeting Mr Schwarzenegger before the interview?'

'No can do.'

'A shot of Mr Schwarzenegger in his car?'

'No can do.'

'Mr Schwarzenegger signing a body-building book?'

'No can do.'

She also told us there could be no requests for autographs, no requests for still photographs, and no speaking to him apart from the interview. Then, when the famous one entered the room, she bowed like a Japanese geisha.

Arnie was fantastic. He shook hands with us all, asked a few questions about Australia and was chatting happily when his representative stepped in to interrupt, telling us Mr Schwarzenegger was a *very* busy man and we must not waste his time.

So Peter sat him down and started asking his questions. Then in the middle of the interview, my right eye to the lens, I opened my left eye to see her crawling across the carpet on her hands and knees, balancing a cup of coffee. A hand with a coffee cup then appeared in my shot. She whispered to Arnie, 'I thought you might like a cup of coffee.' Still on her hands and knees she then backed up across the floor. Arnie stared at her as if she was some kind of bug.

Apart from the sycophant ruining five seconds, the interview was terrific. Arnie was charming, intelligent and very funny. He told us he couldn't run for president of the

United States because he was born in Austria, so he was thinking of running for Governor of California instead.

Peter asked, 'If you can't be president of the United States, would you settle for Austria?'

'It would be better to become Governor of California, then *buy* Austria,' Arnie replied.

He obviously enjoyed the interview, so Peter pushed his luck and asked if he'd sign a body-building book. As Arnie said, 'Sure, no problem,' the hanger-on, standing behind her star, was running her finger across her neck and mouthing, *'No way!'* We ignored her.

With autograph done, John asked Arnie if we could film him and Peter 'going for a little walk'.

'Sure,' said Arnie, while his sycophant's face went white.

Back from the walk Peter, noticing that she was still hovering, turned to Arnie and said, 'Hey Arnold, how about a photo of you with all of us?'

'Sure,' said Arnie.

Peter handed his camera to the hanger-on, smiled and said, 'Take the picture, please.'

It's amazing that she could even see us in the view-finder with all the smoke coming out her ears. She pushed that shutter button as if it was the trigger of a gun. Arnie then thanked us for a wonderful time and walked off. The minder *went* off. Never, *ever*, would we get another interview from her company again, blah, blah, blah. We all looked at the unfortunate woman and laughed. That didn't help her, either.

•

But at least Arnie had only one minder. For our Geena Davis interview, there were *seven* hanger-ons. PA, personal PR, film studio PR, manager, promoter, makeup, hair designer, all dashing around as if God, Jesus, Mohammed and Buddha were about to make an entrance.

In came Miss Davis. I had always been a fan and was looking forward to meeting her, but when she entered the room I started to panic. Her thick sensuous lips were bright red but her hair was whiter than white. Her skin was whiter than white. She was in a white dress and sat down on a white lounge in front of a white wall. Cameras hate white. All the camera could 'see' was a pair of giant red lips. Luckily I was shooting film. If it'd been video, we could have all gone home. I quickly rearranged the lights to create as much contrast on her face as I could get away with.

'How does she look?' the PA asked.

'Well,' I said, 'you'll see her lips and not much else.'

That created quite a stir in the room, but no one was game to tell Ms Davis, who sat there being constantly groomed. The lips were the only way of knowing she hadn't snuck out of the white room. The hairdresser then told me, not asked me, that he would take a look through the viewfinder. But inside that camera is sacrosanct, a cinematographer's personal space. *Nobody looks through my viewfinder.*

Luckily there was a wonderful little button on my Arri camera that allowed me to close it completely. So I did. Hair artiste placed his eye on the viewfinder for a moment, then stepped back and pronounced to all, 'Yeah that's great.'

Then the makeup artiste said, 'I need to look too.'

Be my guest.

Once again we all heard, 'Yeah that's great.'

Both of them had seen nothing but black.

Ms Davis turned out to be unbelievably boring. She was allegedly a member of Mensa (maybe that's why). She didn't want to be there and had absolutely nothing to say. The lips gave the required ten minutes then left the room. We managed to scrape together a seven-minute story, including film clips. Like I said, sometimes we have to just go through the motions.

•

Dustin Hoffman was another megastar awash with minders who'd obviously read the rule book. We were told we had ten minutes and ten minutes only, we were not to go over time, and we were not to engage him in conversation. 'Mr Hoffman is a *very* busy man.' Yeah, yeah, we'd heard it all before.

Our reporter Jennifer Byrne was a great interviewer who knew when and how to turn on the charm, so she did. And Hoffman was hooked. At the end of our ten minutes, just as I was being told by a pushy minder, 'That's it, no more,' Hoffman said to Jennifer, 'That was great. Shame you don't have any more questions.'

'I've got a lot more questions,' Jennifer replied cheekily.

'Then go right ahead,' he said.

I quickly whacked on a new magazine of film. The hanger-ons tried desperately to stop me, telling me the interview was over and I must stop filming *now!* But none of them was game enough to say a thing to Hoffman, so the interview continued and I kept rolling. At the end of that ten minutes he said to Jennifer, 'Any more questions?'

'Yep,' she said. And on went the third magazine. His minders were furious. And like all minders they threatened *me* with all sorts of consequences rather than talk to our reporter, producer or Hoffman himself.

When our new best friend Dustin stood to leave, he said to his minders, 'Great interview that.' And they all wholeheartedly agreed . . . until he'd left the room.

Again we heard the usual tirade from the small-minded minders. But again, did we care? We had another great story in the can.

•

Luckily for us, our ratings were very good, so instead of being caught up in the conga line of showbiz interviews, we'd demand our own room with our own cameraman to do the lighting. But even then there were the stars' demands such as 'special lighting'—for example, no strong back lighting (shows up thin hair), no lights higher than the face (gives the impression of a double chin), no nose shadows (for those sporting a proboscis like the proboscis monkey).

And no low-angle shots, ordered Garth Brooks. It could make him look fat. We couldn't have that. Brooks, a US country singer, had managed to cross into mainstream pop, becoming one of the all-time best-selling recording artists. We scored two days with him. It was torture. He'd always tell me the angle I was to shoot from, and at no time would he take his hat off. It could mean the end of the world if anyone was to find out he was going bald.

What is it about country singers and hair? I've never met a star, male or female, as obsessed with their hair as Keith Urban. A really good bloke, but with a hairstyle that's impossible to keep in place even with the slightest wind. So when we took him out on a boat, he was beside himself. The shots downstairs were so boring I asked him if he'd come up on deck so I could get a few shots of him looking at the Sydney Harbour Bridge and the Opera House. He'd have preferred to smash his favourite guitar. Reluctantly he ventured up the stairs. The things you have to do to push your latest CD.

It could have been from vast sailing experience (I doubt it), but this boy knew his wind. He aimed his face straight into it as soon as he reached the deck. That wind kept the strangely plastered-down hair right where he wanted it. There was no way he was going to look at the landmarks. That would mean a tailwind and errant hair. I suppose I could have moved the Opera House and the Bridge, but like all artists he was in a hurry. A minute later Keith was back downstairs, delicately patting his hair as if it was a priceless work of art. It's a wonder he didn't put on gloves.

Hair is obviously very important in the world of showbiz. Twelve months after our no-show with David Copperfield, we were invited back. Surprise, surprise, he needed the publicity for his new tour of Australia. Most stars want soft delicate lighting. Copperfield wanted a bloody great 2000-watt light aiming straight at his face and a couple of huge industrial-type fans also aimed straight at him. He looked like he was about to be blown through the back wall by a cyclone. With the fans making noises like jet engines, Micky struggled with the sound, but Copperfield couldn't care less. At least he looked good.

•

Of course, doing thousands of stories on celebrities means that we came across some downright rudies. A la Christina Aguilera. Her interview was lined up for one in the afternoon and confirmed twice by our producer. But after one o'clock a minder rang on the hour, every hour, to say, 'She'll be there in twenty minutes.' Christina finally turned up a little before midnight. There were many times we wanted to tell these bad-mannered stars to 'Go to hell', but we never did.

Actually, there was one time . . . Liz Hayes was doing an interview with Robert Downey Jnr, who'd just been released from jail on drug convictions. His PR asked Liz what her questions might be. She told him they'd be the standard 'A to Z of life', much like the star had recently done on *Oprah* and other shows she'd seen. The PR was nervous about that but Liz had been told before leaving Australia that Downey Jnr would be happy to be involved in a 'well rounded conversation', otherwise she wouldn't have bothered showing up.

When Downey Jnr arrived it was clear to all that he was in some kind of altered state, or at the very least, let's say, jet-lagged. He immediately asked for porridge, then promptly spilt it down his shirt front. By the time he'd done makeup and downed a few more solids, Liz was hoping all would be fine. But from the start of the interview, Downey Jnr ignored Liz and kept staring at the freelance soundman. After a few patsy questions Liz moved on to his life and times and mentioned the word 'drugs'. Dead silence. The PR, in her thick American accent, yelled *'Lllliizzzz'*. Undeterred, Liz pressed on.

Finally, Downey Jnr looked her in the eyes and said, 'This is fucked.' He stood up and stormed off. Trouble is, instead of walking out the door, he walked into the makeup room. His PR followed him in. After a few minutes of whisperings from behind their closed door, she came back into the interview room and said, 'Robert would like to come and sit down and say goodbye.'

'Tell Robert not to bother,' said Liz. 'This *is* fucked.'

She stood up and left (through the correct door).

•

Stars of the calibre of Christina Aguilera and Robert Downey Jnr can be pains in the neck, but there are stars who shine a lot brighter than them. There's only one Bob Dylan.

Dylan kept us waiting for five hours, but as fans we were willing to forgive. The day hadn't started well. The American second cameraman, the one who'd be shooting George Negus asking the questions, turned up with his assistant and immediately started telling us how many Grammies, Emmies and Oscars he'd won. When I threw him a couple of rolls of film to load into his rented camera, the award-winner told me he didn't know how to load it. 'That's okay, get your assistant to do it.'

'I don't know either,' said the assistant. I then loaded all his mags for him, knowing only too well we were paying him per day what I earned in a week.

After having carted four tonnes of lights to the star's home in Los Angeles, we were told we could not enter Mr Dylan's house and that the interview would be outside. Fine with us, saves setting up lights. There was plenty of room in the large, leafy backyard so I set up two garden chairs for the interview and we waited, and waited, and waited. With the camera set up and ready to go, I noticed a strange-looking coloured filter on the front of the American's camera. I asked what it was and he mumbled, 'Aaaahh . . . yeah . . . umm . . . eighty-three FD?' There is no such filter. Except probably in a car engine. The filter he had would've made Dylan purple. I gave him my 85, and fitted to my camera the only other appropriate filter I had, an 85ND9 with heavy-duty neutral density, which had the effect of cutting down the light by three stops. It made it difficult to see through, but no problem, I knew there'd be plenty of light for the 1 p.m. interview.

As the sun was going down at 5.45 p.m. Dylan strolled out the back door, pointed to the chairs I'd set up and said, 'I'm not sitting there, I'll sit here,' pointing to the corner of a table in half sun and half shade. I got the feeling it was non-negotiable. I looked through my pitch-black filter and couldn't see him at all. With the sun sinking as rapidly as my heart, we started.

Dylan wearing aviator-type sunnies and brown leather jacket started rocking from side to side like an autistic child.

George's first question, 'What do the sixties mean to you Bob?' was met with, 'For me the sixties existed, but it's just a number really,' and the interview went downhill from there. I wasn't the only one with a sinking heart. But George soldiered on.

'The song and the phrase that people have attached to you most regularly probably is "The times they are a changing". Do you think that they have?'

'I don't know. I've got no idea.'

'Did you think it would at the time?'

'I had no idea of knowing.'

'If we talk about the sixties as a protest decade, and you said the seventies was a period of healing, how would you describe the eighties?'

'I have no idea.'

'I get the feeling that you see yourself quite differently from the way other people do, that other people have given Bob Dylan an importance that you don't necessarily like?'

"Well, I spend more time with myself than other people do, so what I do doesn't really thrill me that much.'

The sun had set and Bob was in complete shade. With my pitch-black filter the only way I could tell whether he was in my shot or not was his relentless swaying. He might be a great poet, but his first language is silence. George kept trying. We were here for an interview and we were bloody well going to get one.

'Why is there confusion about whether or not you're a born-again Christian, a practising Jew or what the hell you are religiously?'

Pause . . . 'Well, people are confused about everything these days, they're confused about what type of car to drive.'

'Do you think that you articulate your feelings and views about things much more musically than you would any other way?'

'Not only much better but the only way.'

And on. And on. If only we'd got him to sing. But I'm still a fan. Dylan's not a singer, or a rock star. He's a great musician and poet.

•

As opposed to Rod Stewart, who was once a rock star and is now a sell-out. Rod was pushing his *Great American Songbook* CD and I found myself alone with him in the studio while he was recording. Everyone else was in the control room. Before Rod put on his headphones I tried talking to him. I think he thought I was one of the microphones. It's a wonder he didn't start tapping me on the head, saying 'Testing, one, two'. He wasn't going to listen or talk. He couldn't give a fuck. For the sake of PR I asked him to let me know if he thought I was getting too close with the camera. I knew he wouldn't hesitate to yell if I was, but he just stared straight through me.

'Recording,' said a voice from the control room. Rod put on the headphones, closed his eyes and started to sing. It was woeful. To be fair, maybe he was having an off day. I could hear no music, only his voice annihilating some of the greatest classic songs ever written. How good are those music producers.

I don't expect to become everyone's best friend, but I'd like it to be acknowledged that the cameraman is a fellow human being. Just a handshake would be nice. I found the greater the talent, the nicer they are, and smarter. After all, it doesn't seem too bright to get the cameraman off side, he who is in charge of the whole look of the story. In fact, I always tried that little bit harder if I liked our subject. I know we all have off days, and maybe so do Sting (easy-going), Mark Knopfler (charming), David Attenborough (wonderful), Heath Ledger (great bloke), Willie Nelson (spaced out of his head), Isabella Rossellini (beautiful), Michelle Pfeiffer (even more beautiful), Steve Martin (super bright, unbelievably shy), Glenda Jackson (charming, nonstop swearing justified by, 'I have never been a prisoner of Anglo Saxon epithets'), AC/DC (all good blokes), Hugh Jackman (dinki di), Marcel Marceau (verbose), but none of these had an off day when I met them.

Then there are the *real* heavies. The ones who've absolutely nothing to prove. They are so comfortable in their own skins they couldn't care what's said about them.

Keith Richards is one of them. I was a fan, but nowhere near as big a fan as Micky who idolised Keith and knew everything about him. For years we had dreamt of meeting 'Keeff'. Micky would have given anything to meet his man.

After shooting a few stories in Australia, I was told I had a trip coming up, but I'd have to do it with a free-lance soundman because Micky had asked if he could stay home for the birth of his first child.

The day before I left, I rang Micky to wish him luck with the birth. 'I'm off on a trip to do, blah blah blah and Keith Richards.'

'Okay,' said Micky. 'Have a good trip. See you when you get back.' No mention of Keeff. It's amazing how a pregnancy can rearrange your priorities.

Richards was great. Dressed in black T-shirt, black jeans, black sports coat, an earring in his left ear and a skull ring on his left ring finger, he smoked and drank through the entire interview.

On drugs: 'It was an experiment that went on too long. It changes your sense of time. That was ten years? I thought it was a week.'

On rumours of changing his blood: 'Do you think I'd do that? I'm keeping this blood, my dad and mum gave this to me, we don't give it away lightly.'

On fame: 'We were having fun playing music, people were coming to see you, you were getting paid, chicks are going I love you. The events take over. You become more than just a band, you become symbols of things. Still am. You get used to it and you work your life around it. I wouldn't know what to do not being famous, 'cause I've got the hang of it now.'

When asked if there were times he looked in the mirror and didn't like the person looking back, 'Yeah . . . but we soon bashed him into shape.'

And at the end of the interview Richards hung around and chatted, telling us as that much as he loved fatherhood, he was hard-wired for the muso's life. 'So I sleep all day, read the kids a story before bed, then I'm out all night. Nights for me have never been for sleeping.' That was one cool dude.

When I got home I rang Micky to congratulate him on becoming a father and to tell him how cool Keith Richards was.

'Keith! Keith Richards? You did Keith Richards!?'

'Yeah, I told you before I left.'

'You bastard! I thought you said *Cliff* Richards.'

It's probably not a good thing to have a deaf soundman, but I'm sure his wife Virginia and first-born son Dominic will be forever grateful.

•

Then there was the ambassador to Czechoslovakia. Cool, elegant, funny and charming. And why is she amongst this lot? She was the hottest, most highly paid star in Hollywood for four years, earning an obscene amount of money (making Tom Cruise's salary look like he was on the dole). She was six years old and was *The Littlest Rebel*. Then she made *Bright Eyes* with her name above the title, a true sign that you have 'arrived' in Hollywood.

Shirley Temple's most famous years (making mega-bucks for the studio) were from age three to seven and her popularity had practically deserted her by the time she was nine. The world and her studio wanted her to be perpetually four. The studio pushed their luck and their star by casting her in *Wee Willie Winkie* (her favourite), directed by the great John Ford. In the movie she still looked and sounded six, but was actually nine. The renowned British writer Graham Greene, a film critic in 1938, wrote, 'She was too nubile for a nine year old, her admirers, middle-aged men and clergymen respond to her dubious coquetry, to the sight of her well-shaped and desirable little body, packed with enormous vitality, only because the safety curtain of story and dialogue drops between their intelligence and their desire.'

That probably says a lot more about Greene than middle-aged men and clergymen. These days the cops would be watching him. Shirley and the studio sued for libel and won.

Most child stars end up with major psychological problems when they become adults. Shirley, now Shirley Temple Black, ended up being US ambassador to Ghana, then Czechoslovakia, where we met her in the biggest office I'd ever seen. As we walked over acres of thick whiter-than-white carpet, she came round from behind her huge desk to meet us halfway with a good solid ambassadorial handshake. She was beautiful, with a huge welcoming smile and those shining eyes that were obviously a big part of why she was cast in *Bright Eyes*. In no time she was cracking jokes, and we knew we were onto a winner. 'How do you like my carpet?' she said. 'It only went in last week.' Before we could answer, she said, 'So you damn well better not damage it. If you do I'll send you the bill.'

I guess she knew film crews better than most. But we were professionals, so we all laughed and agreed to the terms.

She continued to charm Richard the reporter and Stewart the producer while Micky and I set up the lights. I was already captivated by her warmth and had decided to do a really nice lighting job on her. I didn't want her anywhere near her desk, I was going to make use of the acres of carpet and the quality furniture and lamps scattered all over the place. To create the best background I could, I asked if it'd be all right if we moved some of the furniture just a few inches, taking good care of the carpet, of course. She agreed. Micky and I were so gentle with the furniture-moving and the lighting set-up she would have thought we were midwives in a past life.

Satisfied with my set-up I turned on the first light. *Bang!* It exploded, and molten glass spewed out all over her new carpet. I stood there transfixed, but superhero Stewart jumped in to save the day. He ran to pick up the largest hunk of glass that was fast burning a huge hole in the pristine pile. As he picked up the offending incendiary he yelled, '*Fuck!*' and hurled the glass from his scarred hand, creating yet another burning hole in the carpet. We stared at each other, frozen in total disbelief. The carpet was a wreck, acrid smoke curling up from the blackened holes, and the smell wasn't too crash hot either. None of us was game to look at Ambassador Shirley Temple Black.

With a terrifying cold fury she got stuck right into us, demanding money. We were in *big* trouble.

Then, '*Gotcha!*' She threw her head back and burst out laughing she was well aware that these things happened.

That night we went to an ambassadorial dinner full of heavies from the US, all ingratiating themselves with the new ambassador in an attempt to get introductions to locals and lucrative contracts with the new improved Czechoslovakia. The ambassador knew exactly where I was the whole night, positioning herself perfectly in frame, playing up to the camera with winks and having little asides with Richard Carleton. What a pro. Everyone in the room was captivated by her and that huge smile. Including us. We left Prague as total fans of Ambassador Bright Eyes.

●

There came the day when I got to meet one of my own 'living legends'—Clint Eastwood. From 1959 to 1965 as a teenager, I couldn't get enough of the macho actor as Rowdy Yates in the TV show *Rawhide*. He was cool. In Sergio Leone's Spaghetti Western trilogy as 'The Man With No Name', he became even cooler. Then when I met him, he was the coolest. We had been offered more than just an interview. We got to spend a day with him on the set of *In the Line of Fire*.

I'd been on a lot of film sets round the world and there hadn't been too many great memories. It's not that we are seen as the poor cousins of the movie world, it's more like we were not remotely related. The worst are the Aussie film sets. I'd turn up with a camera on my shoulder loaded with film just like they had. But I guess the fact that I was shooting 16-mm as opposed to their 35-mm was what made them so superior and condescending. And until widescreen digital video emerged, to appear on set with a tape camera was to be treated with utmost derision. Not from the top-end creative brains, they wouldn't even acknowledge your existence, but from the gaffers, grips and makeup crew. All of them obviously having directed and shot their own highly successful feature films.

So it was with trepidation I stepped forward to introduce myself to Wolfgang Petersen, the director of *In the Line of Fire*. This boy was big time and I was a huge fan. His movie *Das Boot,* showing the boredom and terror of being in a WWII German U-boat, was a masterpiece. But to my surprise and delight, Wolfgang had a huge smile and couldn't have been friendlier. First thing he did was apologise, saying that today's shoot might be a little boring for us because there wasn't a lot of action.

He then took Micky and me over to meet Clint who was practising his lines inside a car parked at the arrivals entrance to Los Angeles airport. Clint jumped out of the car to greet us, smiling, shaking our hands. He said he was just rehearsing a scene they were about to shoot and he'd chat to us when it was over. I then introduced myself to John Bailey, the director of photography. He'd shot two films I really liked, *The Big Chill* and *Silverado*. He was also friendly and chatty.

While they prepared to shoot the scene, Micky and I walked away to film it on a long lens, making sure we kept out of everybody's way. Then Wolfgang yelled, 'You guys come in as close as you like.'

I looked at John Bailey, who nodded. Then Clint cried out, 'Come right up here, guys. You'll get a great shot.'

That's Confidence. That's Professional. That's PR. That's a Star.

We hung around for most of the day, with Jennifer Byrne chatting to Clint in between takes, and after a few chats they were nudging each other's shoulder and laughing like old friends. He was so easy-going and relaxed (which fits my 'nothing to prove' theory). As we prepared to leave, he called me over. 'Hey, what time's the interview? And where?'

'Beverly Hills Hotel, six o'clock.'

'Okay, see you then.'

We raced back to the hotel and the private bungalow we'd organised for the interview. After setting up the lights, Micky and I wandered outside to check out the sunset and a small four-wheel drive pulled up, and out got Clint Eastwood.

Alone! No manager. No PR. No makeup artist, no hair designer, no hangers-on at all. Just Clint. It was so refreshing.

As he stepped out of his car he said, 'This must be where the Aussies are.'

He was cool, smooth and relaxed and his sense of humour wasn't the only thing that was dry. We offered him a beer and he had two before the interview, chatting with all of us as if we were old friends. He told us how much he loved Queensland and that he couldn't wait to get back to Australia.

For the interview we had an American second cameraman who hadn't bothered to change out of his sweaty tennis gear. He acted cocky and confident. I just hoped his footage would reflect that confidence.

With everyone relaxed, we rolled cameras. The room suddenly echoed with a noise like a B-52. Micky said to the second cameraman, 'Mate, your camera sounds like a bloody chaff cutter.' He casually replied that it might be a bit noisy and suggested he could move back a few feet. Micky was furious and told him he couldn't record sound with that noise. We ended up gaffer-taping two pillows to the Yank's camera to try to baffle the sound. It helped a bit, but it still wasn't perfect. The tennis gear, pillows, gaffer tape and delay made us look like a bunch of amateurs in front of Clint, who sat calmly making small talk with Jennifer while we fumbled around trying to get organised. The tennis player's footage turned out to be scratched and overexposed, and once again his rate for a three-hour shoot was more than my weekly income.

When we did finally start the interview, I noticed Clint was a bit shiny so asked him whether he had any makeup. Stupid question. 'Nope,' he said. 'Don't worry about it.' But I did. So I asked Jennifer if she was carrying any makeup. She was. So as he drank his beer and chatted, I dusted Dirty Harry's forehead with Jennifer Byrne's girly powder puff. Then we rolled for the interview.

Jennifer asked Clint if he had any similarities with Harry Callahan of the *Dirty Harry* movies. 'No, I don't think so, maybe the only similarity is any frustration with some sort of bureaucratic quagmire that mankind put themselves in. That may be a similarity, other than that I don't have the inclination to take a forty-four Magnum out and blow everybody away. Oh, maybe I do occasionally . . . in traffic.' He then chuckled at his answer.

The interview was great. Unlike most stars, he genuinely did not want to talk about himself, but was happy to talk about movies, acting and directing. The *Dirty Harry* movies paid the bills while Clint experimented with directing, from thrillers to musicals, the kind of movies that might not be hugely popular but were interesting to make. Then there was *Every Which Way But Loose*, the film that really paid the bills. It was his biggest-ever commercial success. Clint played a trucker roaming the American West in search of a lost love. His co-star was an orangutan named Clyde.

'The script was so bizarre I thought there was something out there about it,' he said. 'Everybody kept saying, "Don't do this film, you're crazy, it's not you."'

Clint reckoned that Manis the orangutan who played Clyde, 'Was one of the most natural actors I have ever worked with, but you had to get him on the first take because his boredom level was very limited.'

And first takes is what makes Clint Eastwood such a sought-after director. He is famous for always working with a minimum of fuss and coming in under budget.

At the time he had never won or even been nominated for an Academy Award. When Jennifer asked if he'd like an Academy Award, he said laconically, 'Don't know. I guess I'd like one.'

A few months later his classic film *Unforgiven* came out. He starred, directed, produced, and wrote the theme music, and it was nominated for *nine* Oscars. It won four, including Best Picture and Best Director. Rowdy Yates had come a long way.

After the interview Clint hung round for another couple of beers before making his goodbyes. 'I like hanging with you guys,' he said, 'but I'm an old man now. I need my sleep and I need to be on set at six in the morning.' He was just a great bloke, all class and style.

•

Just like my all-time favourite of them all, the great Katharine Hepburn. Yet again she is living proof of my 'nothing to prove theory'. The greater the talent, the nicer and smarter they are.

Over many years every reporter and producer at *60 Minutes* had tried to get the one-on-one interview with Katharine Hepburn. Everyone who tried proudly displayed their rejection letters on the wall of their office.

Mike Munro, a hugely infatuated fan, put in a request for the big interview, and rather than a rejection he scored a maybe.

I was in Nicaragua with Mike, and after Nicaragua we had a not-too-certain story to shoot in New York. To cover our arse in the Big Apple (should the iffy story fall through), Mike made daily phone calls from Managua to Ms Hepburn in New York, pushing the maybe. He didn't get to speak to the megastar herself, only Bridget her Irish housekeeper. Mike turned on the charm and Bridget went in to bat for him. His charm, persistence and timing were perfect—Ms Hepburn just happened to have a book to push.

We were in, and the interview was lined up. Bridget must have gone overboard raving about Mike. A day before the interview Mike and I were invited to check out the layout of Ms Hepburn's house, a magnificent four-storey brownstone in a leafy street in the very upmarket east side of Manhattan. And there to greet us at the door was the star herself, wearing running shoes, bright red socks, her hair up and no makeup. She was stunning. With introductions over we followed her inside, and as we walked down the hall she said, 'Who's the cameraman?'

'I am.'

'Well, Nick, where do you think you'll put me?'

I had no idea where, but I had to say something fast, because even though we had only been in her presence for a millisecond I got the feeling she couldn't tolerate indecision.

'Do you have a favourite chair?'

'I certainly do.'

'Then that's where I'll put you.'

'Nick,' she smiled, 'that was the right answer.'

Wow. How smart was I?

Hepburn oozed charm, intelligence, class and confidence. This woman was Keeff, Shirley and Clint rolled into one. With the major decision over, she offered Mike and me orange juice and brownies she had made herself. While we were getting stuck into the brownies, she pointed to a bright shiny metal sculpture standing proudly on her desk, exactly where anyone would place their Academy Award if they'd won one—and she'd won *four*. She leant over, grabbed the sculpture and proudly showed it to us.

'See this hip joint, it's the latest titanium ball and socket type, exactly the same as the ones I've had put into my hips. Isn't it beautiful?'

Orange juice, homemade brownies and laughter with the greatest Hollywood star that ever lived—how could we ever top that?

Mike and I left the house with our heads spinning. 'I am now in love with an 80-year-old woman.'

We had lined up the interview for 11 a.m. the next day, and as we were leaving she told us not to be late or she wouldn't open the door. And I believed her. She had such a powerful presence, you could somehow tell she knew exactly what she wanted, and when and how to get it. She was famous for her intellect and no bullshit attitude, two things that would have been truly alien to the not-so-bright misogynistic bullies that ran most of the film studios in her time. During that period she'd often been accused of being arrogant, mostly by the press because she was renowned for not suffering fools gladly and never giving autographs.

On the big day, with a tonne of gear, the whole crew of six arrived nice and early so that we wouldn't upset Ms Hepburn. And guess what? Not a minder in sight. Just housekeeper Bridget.

The early arrival was to give me plenty of time to do a really nice lighting job. I wanted Hepburn to look like a million bucks, though with her beautifully angular face I could have lit her with a torch and she'd still look great. As beautiful as she was, I decided not to shoot her too tightly. She was suffering a slight Parkinson's shake, and I was hoping the looser the shot the less it'd be noticed.

After setting up the lights I was doing a bit of fine-tuning, checking for shadows etc. with our producer Jenny in the chair, when I heard Katharine Hepburn coming down the stairs. I looked at my watch and it was only 10.30. *Shit, what is she doing coming down now? I'm not ready.* She got to the entrance of the room, pointed at Jenny and said, 'Nick, who's that?'

'That's Jenny, our producer.'

'What's she doing in my chair?'

Now I started to panic. Have I committed a huge faux pas here by putting a common producer in the great woman's chair?

'I wanted to check the lighting to see how it'd look with someone in the chair,' I said feebly.

'There's no point having someone else sit there if I'm the one being filmed. Wouldn't it be better to have me in the chair?'

'It sure would,' I said with more confidence. 'But you don't want to be sitting here for half an hour while I fuss around with lights.'

'I'm sure you'll do a much better job lighting me,' she said. And plonked herself down in the chair. I spent the next twenty minutes lighting around her while she chatted happily with everyone.

And things only got better. The interview was one of the best I'd ever seen from Mike Munro. The two of them had such a rapport, and Mike had not only done his homework, but he flirted with her. She loved it, and him. Mike was as in love with her as I was.

In the middle of the interview while she was discussing the making of the *African Queen,* my lights blew a fuse, plunging the whole house into darkness. I nearly died with shame. But Hepburn was as cool as a cucumber, making easy small talk while we fixed the fuse, then smoothly picked up the interview, telling Mike what a great bloke Humphrey Bogart was.

'A charming actor, a charming man, a sweet, honest, nice, direct fella. Remarkable.'

Bogart had said some pretty cool things about her, too. He's quoted as saying, 'She's actually kind of sweet and loveable, and none of this late on the set or demanding close-ups or any of that kind of thing. She doesn't give a damn how she looks. She doesn't have to be waited on either. You never pull up a chair for Kate. You tell her, "Kate, pull me up a chair willya, and while you're at it get one for yourself." I don't think she tries to be a character. I think she *is* one.'

We'd been warned that Hepburn didn't ever talk about her 'friendship' with Spencer Tracy. For 50 years the whole world had wanted to know all the saucy details of the relationship, but though we'd been warned it was a no-go area, any journo worth his salt must at least give it a try. Morley Safer from the American *60 Minutes* had recently interviewed her. One of the great TV reporters, he'd tried to go there, but had got nowhere.

Mike gave it his best shot. He asked about the seemingly amazing chemistry she and Tracy had on screen. She saw straight through the question, held up one finger, waved it from side to side and said, 'Uh uh uh, don't go there, Mike.'

Giving it another shot, he said the world couldn't seem to get enough of seeing the two of them on screen, so 'What did you put that down to?'

'I said don't go there, Mike,' she replied with a wry smile.

'But the world embraced you as their couple, do you think?' said Mike.

'I'm not surprised. I can understand that. He was a wonderful sort of character and I was okay, and we suited each other. Don't you think? And we suited the period that we were in. I was a rather feisty type and he was able to control it and that was what was the style in that day.'

'There weren't many people that could control you, but certainly he could,' said Mike.

'Well, I don't know that I'd say that but, uh . . . . We'll let that pass.'

'Did he cut you down to size?'

'Now you are getting very personal. We'll change the topic.'

Mike knew he had more than he ever thought possible, and figured it wouldn't be wise to push his luck. Besides, why upset her? We were all still in love.

Mike then asked about *Guess Who's Coming to Dinner,* a real tear-jerker of a movie adored by the public. Not so the critics. But some critics, so enamoured with the two actors, tried desperately in their reviews to ignore the film and concentrate on Tracy and Hepburn. The *London Observer* wrote 'A load of rubbish, but with Tracy and Hepburn on the screen the most savage criticism is replaced by gratitude'. *Guess Who's Coming to Dinner* was the last movie Spencer Tracy and Katharine Hepburn made together. Tracy died in June 1967, two weeks after shooting finished.

Mike mentioned how moving he thought Tracy's final scene in the film was.

'I've never seen it,' she said. 'Never seen the picture.'

'Why?'

'Couldn't look at the picture.'

I zoomed in for a close shot, her eyes welled up for a split-second, then she was back in control.

Hepburn scored an Oscar for *Guess Who's Coming To Dinner,* making it her second. A year later she had her third for *The Lion in Winter* and thirteen years after that, her fourth Academy Award for *On Golden Pond*. Not once did she attend the ceremony to pick up her statue.

'I'm not terribly interested in honours because so many people go to contributing to that honour that for you to pick it up and take it seriously is liable to misinform yourself about how good you are.' Wow.

But then she went on, 'Now at the same time from a vanity point of view I wonder if the reason that I don't go is that I'm afraid that I'm not going to win it.' Big laugh, then 'So, there you have the human animal.'

She's human after all and I'm more in love than ever. At the end of the interview she leant across to Mike, patted him on the knee and said, 'You know you got a much better interview than Morley.'

Then she stood up. 'Right,' she said, 'lunch is on downstairs.'

Unbelievable. There were six of us. As I packed the lights I was wondering how I could ask Kate (as I now called her, as I'd decided to marry her) whether I could have an autograph, something I'd never done. I always figured it was bordering on the rude and tacky, having been in the inner sanctum, so to speak. This was the first autograph I'd ever requested. I couldn't pluck up the courage to ask her, so I asked Bridget if it was possible. 'No,' she said regretfully, 'Miss Hepburn *never* gives autographs, and besides, now she has Parkinson's her handwriting isn't the best.' I apologised and let it go.

Fifteen minutes later Kate shouted from the doorway, 'Nick, I understand you want an autograph.'

Shit, what do I say? Have I crossed the line and buggered a good day?

'Yes I did ask. I'm sorry, it's just that I've got a daughter called Kathryn.'

'How do you spell it?' she asked.

'K A T H R Y N,' I spelt out.

'It's wrong, change it!'

Not knowing what to say I mumbled, 'I guess that's the Russian in me.'

'That ain't Russian!' she said.

She then asked how many children I had. I told her I also had a daughter called Jessica. Ten minutes later I had in my hot little hand an autographed copy of a beautiful black and white portrait shot of Kate from the 1940s, and written in what looked like a child's handwriting thanks to the Parkinson's, was 'To Jessica and Kathryn from Katharine Hepburn'.

Lunch downstairs was one of the most unforgettable hours of my life. I have no idea what we ate, but I made sure I sat right next to Kate. She talked about Hollywood, women in Hollywood, Hollywood stars, feminism, Academy Awards, Huston, Bogart. It would have been great to shoot, but she knew and we knew that we had the story she'd planned on giving and we were more than happy. So we just listened, enthralled.

And once again I couldn't believe my luck. It was my job to be at that lunch and everywhere else in this book. To think I was actually paid for that story. And for all those stories, and more.

Tick tick tick tick tick . . .

Thanks

For all their help and encouragement, I'd like to thank Micky Breen, Tara Brown, Joanne Duncan, Liz Hayes, Allan Hogan, Anne Kirby, Belinda Lee, John Little, Helen Lunn, Kirsty Thomson, Ray Martin, Michael Munro, Stephen Taylor, and a special thanks to my brother Christopher for all his writing and editing tips.